Successful
Environmental
Management

First Published 1997
© **JOE SHEERIN 1997**
No part of this publication may be reproduced or transmitted in any form or by any means, including photocopying, recording, or by any information storage and retrieval system, without written permission from the publisher.

ISBN 0 9530904 0 X

Printed by Colour Books Ltd.

Publisher : Enviro Éire
'Camelot',
Strandhill Road,
Sligo.

Sponsors:-

This production has been supported by the County Sligo LEADER Partnership Company with financial assistance from the European Union LEADER II programme.

The production has also been sponsored by the following organisations:

European Pallet and Container Pools

Contents

Acknowledgements   *ix*
Introduction   *x*

Part 1   The Environment
1.1   The Environment in context   17
1.2   Europe and the Environment   18
1.3   Ireland and the Environment   21
1.4   Information on the Environment   28
1.5   Environmental Topics   30

Part 2   Environmental Management System (EMS) Framework
2.1   Considering an EMS   37
2.2   Links between an EMS and other management
      systems   39
2.3   Differences between the Eco-management and Audit
      Scheme (EMAS) Regulation and Environmental
      Standard ISO 14001   40
2.4   Preparation of the Environmental Policy   42
2.5   The Initial Steps towards an EMS   44

Part 3   Environmental Regulation
3.1   The Regulatory Situation   47
3.2   The Environmental Protection Agency (EPA)   50
3.3   Integrated Pollution Control (IPC) Licensing   54
3.4   Application for, and implementation of, an IPC Licence   56
3.5   The Waste Management Act, 1996   66

Part 4   Recent Regulatory Developments
4.1   Waste Management (Licensing & Planning)   73
      Regulations, 1997
4.2   Waste Management (Packaging) Regulations, 1997   83
4.3   Waste Management (Farm Plastic) Regulations, 1997   88
4.4   New EMAS Regulation and IPC Licensing Initiative   90

Part 5   Environmental Management System Standards
5.1   Choice of an EMS Standard or EU Regulation   93
5.2   The ISO 14000 Series   101
5.3   Responsible Care® Management Systems   114

Part 6   Environmental Risk Management
6.1   Risk Management   129
6.2   The Legal Situation   131
6.3   Standards   132
6.4   The Risk Environment   133
6.5   Loss Control Initiatives   136
6.6   Guidelines for Pollution Prevention   143

Part 7   Management Of Environmental Performance
7.1   Organisation   147
7.2   Planning   148
7.3   Water   150
7.4   Air   153
7.5   Soil   156
7.6   Noise   158
7.7   Chemicals   160
7.8   Waste   161
7.9   Energy   167
7.10   Products & Packaging   169
7.11   Occupational Health & Safety   170
7.12   External Safety   172
7.13   External Contractors   173
7.14   Environmental Impact Assessment (EIA)   173

Part 8   Preparation Of An EMS
8.1   Initial Environmental Review   177
8.2   Environmental Effects Register   178
8.3   Register Of Environmental Regulations   180
8.4   ISO 14004   183
       Environmental Management System   183
       Commitment and Policy   184
       Planning   185
       Implementation   187
       Measurement and Evaluation   191
       Review and Improvement   192
8.5   Education and Training   193
8.6   Information and Communication   197

Part 9   The Environmental Audit
9.1   Introduction   199
9.2   What is Environmental Auditing   199
9.3   The Objectives of Environmental Auditing   200
9.4   Why Undertake an Environmental Audit   201
9.5   The use of External Consultants   203
9.6   The Audit Process   205

Part 10   Company Profiles
10.1 Airport Services:
    a) Aer Rianta   I.S. 310 and ISO 14001 Experience   207
10.2 Computer Software:
    a) Symantec Ltd.,   BS 7750 and ISO 14001
                                      Experience   221
10.3 Computer Hardware:
    a) IBM PC Company   ISO 14001 Experience   233
10.4 Chemicals/Fibres:
    a) DuPont (UK) Ltd.,   Responsible Care® Experience   257
10.5 Engineering:
    a) G. Bruss GmbH   I.S. 310 and ISO 14001 Experience   273
    b) EG&G Sealol   EMAS & BS 7750 Experience   281
    c) Chep Ireland   ISO 14001 Experience   289
10.6 Pharmaceutical Sector:
    a) Smithkline Beecham   IPC Experience   299
    b) Yamanouchi Irl. Co. Ltd BS 7750 and ISO 14001
                                      Experience   309
10.7 Printing/Electronic Media:
    a) Printech International   BS 7750 and ISO 14001
                                      Experience   319
10.8 Telecommunications:
    a) Nortel   I.S. 310 and ISO 14001 Experience   331

Appendices   343
References   351
Index   353

*I would like to dedicate my efforts in this
book to my parents, Jimmy and Mai, my
wife Bríd and children Dylan and Megan.*

Biographical Notes of Contributors to the book

Dr. Pat Macken

Chapter 3 has been written by Dr. Macken, Director of the Environmental Management Services (EMS) Unit of Price Waterhouse, Dublin. Pat has had considerable practical experience of environmental management in industry. Price Waterhouse's EMS unit provides a wide range of environmental services to the manufacturing and service sectors including advising on environmental performance, management systems for certification to ISO 14001 and EMAS, and IPC and Local Authority licensing.

Mr. Sean Coleman

Chapter 6 has been written by Mr. Coleman, Loss Control Consultant with J&H Marsh McLennan Ireland Ltd. Sean has extensive experience of risk management and consulting on health, safety and environmental matters over a wide range of sectors. In addition he provides assistance to clients with EMAS and ISO 14001 Environmental Management Systems. J&H Marsh McLennan, Inc. are the largest insurance broking and risk management consultancy in the world.

Mr. Michael Brophy

Chapter 9 has been written by Mr. Brophy, a consultant with EMA International Ltd. Michael was formerly a freelance environmental journalist, and has published work for a range of organisations including the European Environmental Agency. EMA International is an environmental consultancy providing environmental audits, integrated management systems (health, safety, quality and environmental), IPC licence applications, environmental monitoring, and information support systems for business and industry.

ACKNOWLEDGEMENTS
I am neither an environmental scientist nor environmental expert. Rather, I see myself as a 'general practitioner' on the topic of environmental management who has been fortunate enough to have an all-consuming passion with learning. I am impressed by those individuals who nurture learning and those 'learning organisations' who have been profiled in this book. Those who wish to impart their knowledge and experiences to others deserve most of the credit for this book. They may have contributed directly to the book by providing subject material and/or financial support with its publication. Without the support of those individuals and organisations this book would not have been possible.

I would like to thank the following individuals for providing guidance, knowledge and enthusiasm:

- Dr. Billy Fitzgerald - Head of Environmental Science in Sligo Regional Technical College.
- Mr. John Hussey - National Accreditation Board.
- Mr. Clive Cathcart - Irish Pharmaceutical and Chemical Manufacturers Federation (IPCMF).

I am indebted to the following organisations for their generous financial support and allowing me to impose on them the merits of the project:

- The Sligo Leader Development
- Intel Ireland
- Aer Rianta
- Nortel
- Chep Ireland
- G. Bruss GmbH.

Finally, a special thank you to Theresa Milmoe for assistance with text layout and Gerry Byrne of Colour Books Ltd. for practical advice on publishing the book.

I. INTRODUCTION

This is an exciting time for those involved in environmental management whether they are working in the industrial or service sectors. They will be hard pressed to keep pace with the changes that are taking place. In the last couple of months of writing this book company registrations to the new environmental standard ISO 14001 were being approved by the various certification bodies, the Waste Management Licensing and Planning Regulations 1997 had just been published and the National Accreditation Board (NAB) and the Environmental Protection Agency(EPA) have formed a joint initiative towards increased coherence between Integrated Pollution Control (IPC) Licensing and the Eco-Management and Auditing Scheme (EMAS) Regulation. In fact, the problem which I had was deciding when to publish the book given the pace of change on the environmental scene.

A recent survey by IBEC, the Industry Business and Employers Confederation estimated a cost of £450 million to Irish companies with IPC Licensing system. This involves licensing of industries under one single integrated license. In the past this would have required different licenses granted by the local authority or council. It is estimated that 1,000 industries could be licensed by 1999. IBEC is proposing a review of the IPC system in view of the huge costs involved.

On a voluntary basis many organisations are now implementing an Environmental Management System (EMS) to prepare themselves for impending regulation via the IPC licensing system or indeed to formalise their environmental performance practices. This is one way that organisations might be able to reduce the cost of being licensed or as a way to reduce or avoid the cost of annual surveillance under the IPC system. Indeed the new initiative being taken by the NAB and the EPA would reduce costs by having a combined audit to EMAS and IPC Licensing, a common reporting format based on the EMAS Environmental Statement, and a common EMS for both IPC and EMAS.

An EMS is a management system that enables an organisation to manage the environmental impacts of its products, services and processes. The system is formalised to ensure that the environmental policy, objectives and targets and environmental programme(s) are effective. Central to an EMS is the environmental policy and the pursuit of continual improvement. An EMS is an integral part of the management activity of the company and involves employee involvement throughout the organisation. Also it is not possible to implement an EMS direct from document without some form of guidance or experience in other management systems.

Once an organisation has implemented an EMS it can become independently accredited by a certification body to an environmental standard, i.e. ISO (International Standards Organisation) 14001 or EMAS (Eco-Management and Audit Scheme) Regulation. In Ireland the most popular certification bodies are the National Standards Authority of Ireland (NSAI) and SGS Yarsley. The National Accreditation Board (NAB) is responsible for accreditation of environmental verifiers for the EMAS Regulation.

Before deciding on a particular certification body, organisations should examine their options. It is best to look at projected fees over a three to five year period and the number of surveillance visits. Organisations that already have achieved registration to the Quality Management System (QMS) might be able to have surveillance to a QMS and an EMS during a single visit of the certification body. This would lead to a reduction in the surveillance fees.

II. THE SCOPE OF THIS BOOK
We are living in a time of change. Advances in information technology are driving the pace of change in the way we do work. The marketplace is looking for quality products at lower costs. Market perceptions are changing too. Social and environmental issues are now part of the consumer's decision on which products they buy. All these changes are putting ever-increasing pressures on organisations to continuously improve their competitiveness and satisfy their customers.

There is plenty of environmental information and expertise available in third-level institutions, consultancies, research laboratories, industries, service and other agencies. However, some companies and individuals have difficulty in accessing this information and in getting good advice. This book will simplify the information gathering and learning experience.

I felt compelled to write this book for two reasons:
1) To make the information and experience gained in implementing an EMS available to others.
2) To address the gap in the market in providing a practical and concise guide to Environmental Management and an EMS.

As an Industrial Manager, I am very conscious of modern management techniques. I am reluctant to give advice or offer an opinion without first understanding the other person or organisation. This book will not provide all organisations or individuals with all the answers but will however, give others the benefit of my experience in gathering information and developing an EMS. I would have found such a book useful myself, had it been available.

I believe that it is important to fully research a project prior to starting it. Some organisations who implement Quality Management System ISO 9000 or an EMS system do not fully understand their requirements and as a result do more or less than what is required by the standard. Consequently, they end up spending too much or not enough time. Time is a very valuable resource and by having the correct information, from the start, organisations can match the magnitude of the task with the correct amount of time. This book provides the information required and by project specification, suggests allocating time as a constraint. As the book is concise, it will not take too much time to read, enabling Environmental/Project Managers to have the correct information from the start.

The book is structured into a preface, acknowledgements and is then divided into ten parts. The preface begins with a short introduction, sets out the scope of the book and the likely readership.

The Ten Parts are as follows:
1. Puts the environment in a general, European and Irish context. Some basic information is provided to familiarise the reader with sources of information available and some environmental topics are dealt with.

2. Deals with setting an environmental agenda for the organisation. It details the benefits of an EMS to the organisation and what

work will need to be done in preparing an Environmental Policy and initiating an organisational structure for an EMS.

3. Describes the regulation and legal situation, the Environmental Protection Agency (EPA), Integrated Pollution Control (IPC) licensing application and implementation, and the Waste Management Act, 1996.

4. Presents the recent Waste Management Regulations, 1997 governing licensing and planning, packaging and farm plastic.

5. Covers EMS standards, with particular emphasis given to the new EMS ISO 14001 standard. Responsible Care® systems are covered, including management system verification (MSV) and the respective roles of the different membership organisations.

6. Considers Environmental Risk Management and provides practical advice to organisations on loss control and pollution prevention.

7. Looks at an organisations environmental performance agenda. Practical information is provided on management of environmental effects.

8. Outlines the establishment of an Initial Environmental Review, Environmental Effects Register and Register of Environmental Regulations. Guidance on implementing an EMS as outlined under the 5 principles of ISO 14004 is given. Finally, a description is given of essential elements of an EMS, i.e., education & training and information & communication.

9. Covers Environmental Auditing, objectives, reasons, use of consultants and the audit process.

10. Details the experiences of twelve organisations who have successfully implemented Environmental Management or an EMS standard.

I hope this book makes the task of Environmental Management easier for individuals in organisations and gives the public an understanding of the magnitude of Environmental Protection. If it encourages even a little more balance between economics and the environment, it will have been worthwhile.

III. WHO SHOULD READ THIS BOOK?

Managers, employees, students and concerned citizens are expected to do more with less time to do it. They want to come "up to speed" with issues with limited time available to do so. They want their information to be concise, professional, realistic, reliable and useful.

This book is aimed at:

- The Senior Executive who will want to know what an Environmental Management System (EMS) entails. If the organisation already has implemented the Quality Management System (QMS) ISO 9000, then they will be aware how much company resources are consumed by the standard. Perhaps, some will view an EMS with reluctance, not knowing what is involved. This book should enable such people to understand better that an EMS does not entail huge costs or time but that many savings will result and it can be implemented using existing personnel.

- The Environmental Manager or person with responsibility for implementing Environmental Management, an EMS or setting up environmental project teams, will want a gameplan for how to achieve it. He/she may not have the time to spend in attending courses on Environmental Management or an EMS. This book should give the necessary practical tools for how to go about organising and eliciting the support of others, while at the same time having enough knowledge to lead them effectively. Explanations are given in a concise, easy to read, descriptive way of the various elements and issues involved in organising environmental management.

- Training Managers or those who must make presentations on EMS or who must train management and employees in best environmental practice techniques, will find this book of great value.

- The book will be useful to environmental groups or concerned citizens, who want an understanding of the issues and extent of organisational involvement in protecting and minimising their environmental impact. The general public nowadays, are very knowledgeable, competent and eager to understand the complexities of organisational environmental protection. This book will be good source material for them.

- The student of EMS, who is interested in a practitioner's guide to implementing Environmental Management, an EMS and understanding environmental issues.

- Those who are involved in pollution control, licensing or in regulatory authorities.

This book is designed for:
- Casual readers,
- In-depth readers.

Casual readers may choose to increase their general awareness of Environmental Management and EMS's or may wish to concentrate on a specific topic. In-depth readers may need the information and tools required for an EMS implementation. It is best to work sequentially through the book, deciding what best suits your needs and then adopt a suitable approach to implement environmental best practices or an EMS.

1 THE ENVIRONMENT

1.1 The Environment In Context

We are living in an age of increasing globalisation, where manufacturing and services can take place anywhere. World-class multinational companies will have to maintain world-class environmental standards wherever they are located, despite differences in local laws. This will eventually mean global standards for the environment. Those organisations who cut corners will be liable for the resultant environmental damage. Globalisation will force us not to have one set of standards in one part of the world and a different set of standards elsewhere.

Sustainable development is now part of the European Union's objectives, encouraging, not only the compliance with directives and regulations, but awareness among industry and the public in the trend towards a greener culture. The basis of sustained development is balancing environmental protection with human needs to achieve growth. It is to avoid conflict between economic development at the expense of the environment but to improve it continually.

In moving towards sustainability, the overall objective is to improve the quality of life by conserving our natural resources. We move forward in an economically, ecological and socially desirable way. Achieving more with less, i.e. creating more products/services with less resources, not only makes sound economic sense but is kinder to the environment too. It is virtuous to pursue good environmental management and performance. So, it is better that as concerned citizens and interested organisations that we respond to environmental improvement in a positive way. This will give us, in return, business opportunities and competitive advantage.

Today, in the global age, an increasing number of organisations are interested in sustained development and an increasing number of consumers will buy products and services which have an environmentally friendly image associated with them. These organisations will invest in environmental control and consumers in their products and services. Environmental consideration will become one of the benchmarks for a better society in this global age. People's views about the quality of their lives and surroundings are now important. This will mean adopting a more cyclical approach towards nature by recycling, re-manufacturing and reusing products. Using techniques such as Life Cycle Assessment (LCA) products will be examined for their environmental impacts during the entire product life from raw material to final disposal. There will be a greater sense of responsibility in investing in our children's inheritance. Ultimately, the future of the environment and quality of future life depends on us.

1.2   Europe and the Environment

Why organisations should be aware of European environmental developments:-
Knowledge of European environmental developments in policy, targets, directives, legislation, trends etc. is important to enable organisations improve the general quality of the environment by setting and improving their standards on environmental protection.

The European Environment Agency (EEA) is located in Copenhagen. It was established in 1990 (came into force in October 1993) and is responsible for providing Member States with:

> "objective, reliable, and comparable information enabling them to take the requisite measures to protect the environment, to assess the results of such measures, and to ensure that the public is properly informed about the state of the environment".

The role of the EEA is not to amass information in the hope that someday someone might find it useful, but to put data to work by applying information and technology to tackle real problems. The European Environmental Information and Observation Network (EIONET) is a co-operative activity between the EEA and European Union (EU) Member States in providing reliable environmental information.

The Agency is also responsible for the Corine programme (co-ordinating information on the environment). The major project areas, land cover, air emissions and biotopes are integrated into the Agency's work programme. Databases and information systems will be developed for these. Many of the reports commissioned by the EEA are available free on request.

Significant European Developments

1957: foundation of European Community with the Treaty of Rome commitment to improve living and working conditions

1972: UN Conference on Environment, followed by EU response which lead to the development of an environmental policy

1985: EC adopted a directive requiring Member States to carry out an environmental impact assessment on major projects

1987: Single European Act committed Member States to protective measures in response to deteriorating environmental conditions

1990: formation of European Environment Agency as a scientific and technical centre to combat pollution

1991: Directive for Civil Liability for Damage caused by Waste. This would enforce:
      (a) strict liability in environmental regulation
      (b) 'Polluter Pays' principle

1992: EC Fifth Environmental Action Programme (5EAP)

1993: Maastericht Treaty - to promote harmonious and balanced development of economic activities

1993: EC adopted community Eco-management and audit scheme (EMAS)

1994: Implementation of Integrated Pollution Control (IPC) licensing

1994: Oslo Symposium on Sustainable Consumption

1994: European Conference on Sustainable Cities and Towns

1995: Oslo Ministerial Roundtable Conference on Sustainable Production and Consumption

1995: EMAS open for participation by companies

1995: Review of Fifth Environmental Action Programme (see below)

1995: The European Environmental Agency publishes a pan European state of the environmental report: "The Dobris Assessment" (see below)

1996: Second European Conference on Sustainable Cities and Towns

Review of Fifth Environmental Action programme (5EAP)
The review examines progress towards the EU environmental
targets, i.e. to avoid adverse effects on human health and
ecosystems. It concluded that:

> chlorofluorocarbons (CFC's), halons, nitrogen oxides
> (NOx), volatile organic compounds (VOCs) and heavy
> metal targets for 1994/95 would be met. The EU would
> be set to meet targets for the year 2000 in relation to:
> sulphur dioxide (SO2) emissions, ozone depletion
> substances, heavy metal disposal to North Sea and
> carbon dioxide (CO2) emissions. It also assesses that the
> EU is heading in the right direction in relation to
> acidification, waste management, nitrates etc.

The 5EAP report considers EU progress towards sustainability,
environmental trends and the enlargement of the EU to include
Austria, Finland and Sweden from 1995. In addition environmental
themes are judged on a regional, European transboundary and
global scale.

Europe's Environment: The Dobris Assessment
The Dobris Report, as it is better known, was commissioned during
a conference held in Dobris Castle (in former Czechoslovakia). The
report gives an assessment of the state of the environment in 46
countries. It was written by the European Environmental Agency
(EEA) and provides an analysis of different environmental fields
and the pressures which impact on these. The EEA will provide
regular updates to the text.

The review shows that some improvements have been made in the
quality of Europe's environment but there has also been some
deterioration. While progress has been made, for example, in
reducing sulphur dioxide emissions, further improvement is
restricted by limited 'carrying capacity' of the environment. The
'carrying capacity' is the ability of the environment to sustain growth
in human and species populations without damaging the ecosystem.
Environmental deterioration is apparent in the Central and Eastern
Europe Countries due to poor efficiency of production systems.

The Dobris Report is structured into 6 parts:
      Part I   : Context
      Part II   : Assessment
      Part III   : Pressures
      Part IV   : Human Activities
      Part V   : Problems
      Part VI   : Conclusions

The Dobris Assessment identifies 12 key problems affecting Europe's environment:
1. Climate change
2. Stratospheric ozone depletion
3. Loss of biodiversity
4. Major accidents
5. Acidification
6. Tropospheric ozone and other photochemical oxidants
7. The management of freshwater resources
8. Forest degradation
9. Coastal zone threats and management
10. Waste production and management
11. Urban stress
12. Chemical risk

The Dobris Report concludes that there is no simple answer to the question of how healthy is Europe's environment. There was information provided on air pollution in European cities, for example: Paris, Budapest and Rome had the least favourable climatological conditions while Toulouse, Dresden, Hannover and Stuttgart had the most favourable climatological conditions. Information was also compiled on European countries waste production. Austria was the most wasteful per capita, generating nearly 600 kg/year/person.

1.3   Ireland and the Environment

Environmental consideration features prominently in Government policy. In its policy "A Government of Renewal" (Dec 1994) it committed itself to a National Sustainable Development Strategy. This would address all areas of Government policy that would impact on the environment by setting objectives, targets and reviewing these on a regular basis. Progress has been made with:- providing information on the environment (Environmental Protection Agency and Environmental Information Service - ENFO) and increasing public awareness, environmental legislation, environmental impact assessment, integrated pollution control licensing etc. There are problems in increases of:- waste generation, energy consumption, pollution of some waterways etc. As a growing economy Ireland must examine the ability of the environment to carry increased production and population intensity impact.

"Quality of life" and environment attractiveness are probably the best selling points for the tourist, food processing, aquaculture and natural resource based industries. Increasing numbers of tourists visit Ireland each year. To maintain our attractiveness will mean the shared responsibility of all sectors of our society in environmental management and protection. Our economy depends on a healthy tourism industry promoted by a clean environment.

Recent Irish Developments
1977 & 1990: Local Government Water Pollution Acts

1987: Air Pollution Act

1990: The Government Environment Information Service (ENFO) established

1992: Establishment of Local Agenda 21 (LA 21)

1993: Environmental Protection Agency (EPA) enacted in line with EPA Act, 1992

1993: Regulations on the Freedom of Information on the Environment

1994: Publication of Irish Environmental Management System I.S. 310 by National Standards Authority of Ireland (NSAI).

1994: The publication of the national recycling strategy Recycling for Ireland

1994: Requirement that certain established activities listed in the EPA Act, 1992 Order 1994 apply for Integrated Pollution Control (IPC) licensing

1994: Establishment of Irish Energy Centre

1995: Eco-management and audit scheme (EMAS) open for voluntary participation

1995: Waste Bill published and expected to be passed by an Act in March 1996

1995: Formation of "REPAK" scheme to co-ordinate and finance the recycling of packaging waste by IBEC.

1996: EPA Report on State of the Environment in Ireland

1996: EPA National Waste Database

1996: Waste Management Act (1995 Waste Bill) came into operation

1997: Waste Management (Planning & Licensing) Regulations

1997: Waste Management (Packaging) Regulations

1997: Waste Management (Farm Plastic) Regulations, 1997

Sustainable Developments

Two key frameworks developed to enable the implementation of sustainable development are:

- Local Agenda 21 (LA 21)
- Charter of European Cities and Towns Towards Sustainability

Local Agenda 21 was established and agreed during the Earth Summit Conference in Rio de Janeiro in June 1992. It is a programme of action to achieve a more sustainable pattern of development throughout the world for the next century. Local action plans would form the basis for implementing the European Union's Fifth Action Programme "Towards Sustainability". It is envisaged that national governments, business, industry, non-government organisations (NGO's) and members of the community would participate in forming strategies, agree objectives and implement policies based on sustainable development. Local authorities would have the role of creating partnerships, sharing information and expertise with local communities and organisations.

The Charter of European Cities and Towns Towards Sustainability otherwise known as the Aalborg Charter came about as a result of a European Conference on Sustainable Cities and Towns held in Aalborg, Denmark in May 1994. The charter was in draft form and was later amended and developed at the Second European Conference on Sustainable Cities and Towns held in Lisbon, Portugal in October 1996. Both conferences were attended by

European local authorities, national governments, NGO's, consultants, scientists and individuals. By signing the charter cities and towns committed themselves to Local Agenda 21 and the development of long-term action plans towards sustainability.

Freedom of Information on the Environment

With the introduction in May 1993 of Regulations on the Freedom of Information on the Environment, this would have considerable implications for organisations. This allows any member of the public access to information enabling their involvement in protecting the environment. It is indeed conceivable that organisations will involve members of the public in their environmental decision-making process. Progressive organisations will welcome this in that only the public can truly determine the effects of their actions.

Documents relating to ordinary license applications and applications to the Environmental Protection Agency for Integrated Pollution Control Licensing is covered under EPA (Licensing - Amendment No. 2) Regulations, 1995. Public inspection of these applications will be available to the public for a period of 3 years.

Implementation of EU Legislation

Part of the European Union's mission is to align or harmonise the standards of the member countries, which heretofore varied from country to country.

EU Regulations are first agreed by the Council of Ministers and then become law within the Member States.

EU Directives are developed in order to provide a uniform legal basis for harmonising legislation within Member States. They set out a framework for implementation and Member States are obliged to transfer the directives into national law.

Both the European Commission and the Council of Ministers are responsible for agreeing directives.

In Ireland, Directives are usually implemented through the European Communities Act, 1972. Safety and Health Regulations are also implemented under the Safety, Health and Welfare at Work Act 1989. In the absence of enabling legislation (Acts) many EU Directives were implemented.

Eco-Tourism

Ireland is ideally poised to take full competitive advantage of 'green tourism' or an environmentally sustainable tourism industry, given the unspoilt environment that exists. This would mean maintaining its booming tourism industry by adhering to standards which ensure that the environment is protected and enhanced. West of Ireland regions - West Donegal, West and North West Mayo, Connemara, Galway City and the Brandon in Kerry are participating in an EU environmental tourism project called the Eco-Label. This would resemble other schemes, such as, the 'Blue Flag' for beaches or the ISO 9000 standard.

Eco-Labelling is a three year demonstration project which will establish the criteria and methodology whereby areas that have a high quality environment will be recognised by an Eco-label. If accepted the Eco-Label could be used in the same way throughout the EU.

The Eco-Label standard involves submitting an application form for acceptance to an independent panel of assessors. The region applying must be able to demonstrate a partnership between their community group and the local authority. A self-assessment and resource inventory must have been undertaken and an improvement programme must be drawn up. The assessment will include evaluation of: air, water, land use, planning, transport, the natural and cultural environment, built environment, waste and energy.

Other tourism growth areas are activity-based holidays and agri-tourism. Ireland has a great advantage over other competitor countries in promoting outdoor holidays given its clean environment and availability of mountains, hills, lakes, rivers and seas.

However, the image of a 'green country' is a hard reputation to live up to, if indeed we can be classified as such. 'Greenness' needs to be more than an image or perception by others. It needs to be backed up by demonstration of environmentally sound production, products and services. Communities need to be involved in enhancing their environment. This will demand increased public environmental awareness in maintaining good environmental standards and substantiating our reputation of a 'green country' with tangible evidence.

Ireland needs to plan its tourism industry within the framework of sustainability. Tourism has its positive and negative effects on the environment. Revenue derived from tourism allows investment in the environment. But on the down-side mass tourism puts pressure on selected areas, such as, mountains, woods and coastal areas, by increased traffic, noise, water usage etc. There needs to be a strategy in place to protect these areas by strict enforcement of standards.

Sustainable tourism is based on respect for nature and the environment. If properly planned it can contribute to the prosperity of tourist areas and the tourist industry.

Sustainable Farming

Modern farming methods are not unlike modern production methods utilising new technologies and mechanisation to achieve maximum production at the lowest cost. This type of farming has been referred to as "factory farming". Those in favour of this intensive farming method suggest the consumer has benefited by its output - cheaper food in the marketplace. Those against highlight the adverse environmental effects of such practices including soil erosion, contamination of groundwater, increased chemical use, increased water and energy use, air pollution from dust, increased traffic, spraying etc.

Intensive farming has meant a dependence on nitrogen fertilisers, slurry and pesticide use, which although they promote crop growth lead to pollution of water and death of wildlife. "Clean-up" costs associated with pollution and more recently demonstrated by the BSE (Bovine Spongiform Encephalopathy) crisis, (brought about by intensive farming), can be great. These costs are not reflected in the market price for such produce but indirectly the costs are borne by individual taxpayers.

Sustainability is based on meeting present needs by not comprising the ability of future generations to meet their needs. Sustainable farming promotes an alternative approach to intensive farming methods by reconciling environment, economics and social considerations in using sustainable farming practices. The emphasis is placed on the farming process as an eco system by managing its local and global impacts. The responsibility lies with all those involved in farming - authorities, suppliers, farm owners, workers etc. All those who participate in farming have an important contribution in making farming more sustainable and have a role to play in preventing pollution.

In 1994 the Department of Agriculture's Rural Environmental Protection Scheme (REPS) was launched.

It's objectives are to:

- establish farming practices and controlled production methods which reflect the increasing concern with conservation, landscape protection and wider environmental problems
- protection of wildlife habitats and endangered species of fauna and flora
- produce quality food in an extensive and environmentally friendly manner

The scheme seeks to recognise and financially reward farmers in protecting their environment. To participate farmers must have a detailed five year agri-environmental plan drawn up by an approved REPS professional. This plan must detail measures to fulfil the following:

- waste and grassland management;
- watercourse and habitat protection;
- maintenance of hedgerows and stonewalls;
- protection of historical and archaeological features; *and*
- methods for following environmentally sound farming practices.

The following are some suggestions to be borne in mind in making farming a more sustainable activity:

- Protection of habitat - woods, ponds, lakes, rivers, hedges, grasslands, wetlands etc. to ensure wildlife and other species co-exist and are not destroyed
- Reduction in the need for chemical usage by substitution e.g. using predatory insects, crop rotation etc.
- Proper disposal of farming wastes e.g. preventing entry to waterways by using slurry in a controlled manner and not spreading it during heavy rainfall, constructing and locating silage pits away from and so as to avoid leakage to waterways.
- Conservation of water and energy on the farm.

A return to more organic farming methods would be advantageous to everyone in ensuring that areas are not overfarmed and that soil and water is not depleted or polluted. Public consciousness brought about by food poisoning, salmonella and BSE will require a new sustainable approach from those involved in the food chain. Organic and free-range farming produce have been found not to cost significantly more to the consumer than intensive farming produce. When the total cost of BSE, pollution etc. is taken into account it will surely be more economically viable to use sustainable farming methods. Indeed it is likely that increasingly discerning consumers will demand food produced in this way.

1.4   Information on the Environment

Apart from the practical guidance and source of environmental information which this book and others provide, there are also many other excellent information sources. These include:

- The Environmental Protection Agency (EPA). The EPA provide publications and guidance notes on various environmental topics. Integrated Pollution Control (IPC) licences can be viewed at their offices by the general public.

- ENFO: The Environmental Information Service. This information service is provided by the Department of Environment and has an extensive library and database on environmental topics.

- Chambers of Commerce of Ireland: They have access to databases of information including European information and have produced a very comprehensive Guide to Environmental Self-Auditing.

- Colleges and Universities: They have environmental expertise available and many have their own dedicated environmental units that cater for a wide range of research and consultancy services.

- Consultancies: There are now many consultancies establishing themselves in line with the business opportunities which environmental protection presents. The range of services provided by consultancies cover advice on environmental engineering, IPC licensing, emission abatement technologies, release monitoring, environmental management systems, environmental impact statements etc.

- The Internet: It is fast emerging as a very valuable medium for providing very up-to-date information including information on the environment. All that is required is a personal computer and modem. There are over 200 environmental Web Sites from which to choose. The range of information provided includes environmental research and data, database access, reports, publications and even books. It is also possible to share information and communicate with environmentalists, scientists etc.

Some of these companies also display detailed and comprehensive annual environmental reports on their activities for public perusal.

- Other services provided by the state include The State Laboratory and The Environmental Research Unit. Their work involves research, sampling analysis, monitoring and advisory services.

Two Irish periodicals with information on environmental developments, distributed free of charge are:
- "Environmental Bulletin" by the Department of Environment,
    and
- "Environmental Management Ireland" (EMI).

To keep informed or participate in environmental issues, environmental organisations, such as:
- Friends of the Earth
- Greenpeace
- Sierra Club
- Stockholm Environmental Institute
- International Institute for Sustainable Development
- SEAC Student Environmental Action Coalition (USA)

have Web Sites which can be accessed and memberships welcomed.

1.5   Environmental Topics

The purpose of this section is to introduce some environmental topics which might interface in some way with industry. To deal with environmental topics in detail would involve examining the impact environmental effects on humans, flora, fauna, air, water, soil etc. This would be beyond the scope of this book. This text will deal briefly with some topics by way of introduction.

Pollution Prevention

It sounds very simple and we all favour it, but very few take positive action to prevent pollution. Instead modern civilisation has adopted extravagant lifestyles and spend huge sums of money managing waste, rather than avoiding the creation of wastes that causes pollution. The emphasis has been on end-of-pipe waste treatment, whereas the focus should be on avoiding the problem to begin with by developing processes that do not create or recycle waste residues and design our products so that they can be recycled or composted.

The main types of polluting wastes are:

- industrial/commercial   • consumer/household   • agricultural

Each one is of equal importance in contributing to pollution. Not only must industrial policies and practices aim to prevent pollution, but so must our personal practices. We must understand that every activity from the simple act of brushing one's teeth to ordering food in a restaurant has environmental implications.

In principle, pollution regulation only makes people comply with a 'control level' and fear the consequences of non-compliance. To rely totally on regulation to prevent pollution is not enough. It is necessary to go beyond the 'acceptable level' defined by regulation in preventing pollution. Economic incentives should also be encouraged, such as:

- the principle of 'deposit' refund applied to bottles should be extended to as many items as possible in promoting reuse and recycling;
- product tax credit scheme
- "polluter pays" principle

- waste disposal taxes would persuade people to rethink before disposing of products and influence us in conserving resources;
- tax concessions for best practices and technologies employed in waste avoidance;
- reduction in liability insurance by using practices which prevent pollution.

There is also a very sound financial justification for reducing/eliminating waste throughout the product life cycle, in that it costs much less to industry and society. Most industries do not adopt this strategy in designing products, because initial costs in designing such products can be high and regulation promotes threshold limit values (TLV) based on acceptable risk.

Pollution prevention means that we do not make that which causes pollution to begin with. We therefore do not need to regulate it later. Pollution prevention promotes a cyclical approach by reuse, recycling and composting and reducing the environmental impacts of processes.

In order to prevent pollution, we must respect and understand the natural world and how we affect it. Society needs to change from promoting consumption and the consequential 'throwaway society' to a more balanced one, where we rethink the need for and how we discard our waste. Waste reduction and pollution prevention are integral to this new approach.

Acid Rain

The burning of fuels containing sulphur and sulphur dioxide, power stations and vehicle combustion engines generate nitrogen oxides and sulphur dioxide. Fertiliser plants emit nitrogen oxides and ammonia is released from livestock plants. These dissolve in water to form acids. The resultant acid rain, with a pH of 5.6, causes damage to buildings, trees, plants, insects, fish, birds, water supplies, etc.

Steps taken to reduce acid rain include: the fitting of catalytic converters to cars, using low-sulphur coal and energy conservation measures. In 1987 the Geneva Convention on Long Range Transboundary Air Pollution came into effect. Thirty-four countries, known as the '30% Club' ratified the agreement to reduce sulphur emissions by at least 30% before 1993. Ireland, England and the USA did not ratify the 30% reduction agreement.

The Ozone Layer
The ozone layer has been described as the earth's 'life support system', preventing harmful ultraviolet rays from entering the earth. These rays damage life forms such as animals, trees and plants. They can also cause skin cancer and eye cataracts. More recently scientists claim that UV can affect human and animal immune systems, phytoplankton and crop damage.

Ozone is a type of oxygen molecule but has three atoms instead of two. It is very toxic and affects breathing and the eyes. In cities, ground-level ozone is an ingredient of smog, brought about by hydrocarbons and nitrogen oxides reacting with sunlight. In the higher atmosphere it is beneficial, forming a protective ozone layer.

Global Warming
The global air temperature and the temperature of oceans has increased by about 0.5 degrees centigrade in the last ten years. Global warming is believed to be causing disturbed world weather phenomena - floods, droughts, storms etc. Global warming and ozone depletion are already at an advanced stage and are increasing as we continue to emit 'greenhouse gases' (CO_2, CH_4)into the atmosphere. These gases include CFC's (chlorofluorocarbons), halons and others containing chlorine and bromine.

Chlorofluorocarbons (CFC's) and Ozone Depletion Substances (ODS's)
CFC's have been used as refrigerants, insulating foams and as solvents in the electronic industry. HCFC's (hydrochlorofluorocarbons) have hydrogen in the parent hydrocarbon replaced by chlorine or fluorine. They have been presented as an alternative to CFC's. CFC's are inert and after many years enter the stratosphere where UV radiation breaks them up releasing chlorine. HCFC's are more reactive in the stratosphere and release chlorine much faster than CFC's but destroy less ozone. Non-CFC fluids, for example, propane-isobutane mixtures are now being used to replace both CFC's and HCFC's in air conditioners.

Another ODS is methyl bromide used as a fumigant and given off during the burning of biomass. Also halon is an ODS and is used in fire extinguishers and carbon tetrachloride (industrial chemical).

The 1987 Montreal Protocol has directed that CFC emission should be halved and that production of CFC's, CC_{14} and halons should be stopped by the year 2000. This phase-out schedule was brought forward at the 1992 Copenhagen Agreements, banning CFC production in 1995 and by four years for the others mentioned. It is expected that after the year 2000 the ozone layer will recover over a fifty year period, assuming these targets are met.

A seventh meeting of the Montreal Protocol took place in December 1995 and new adjustments were made to the Protocol for developed countries and developing countries. For developed countries, methyl bromide will be reduced by 25% by 2001, 50% by 2005 and total phase-out by 2010. Also HCFC's will have gradual reductions until phase-out in 2020. Developing countries will be subject to similar targets but with a greater timescale to eventual phase-out.

Other programmes that are being initiated world-wide to improve air quality and the ozone layer are: reducing Volatile Organic Compounds (VOC's) and Nitrous Oxide (NOx) emission from vehicles and cleaner fuels, improvement in industrial facilities and power plants etc.

Toxicology
Toxicology is the 'study of the harmful effects of chemicals on living systems'. In predicting the dangers that chemicals present to humans and their environment, the focus is on how it can affect the biological system (i.e. toxicity response, immune system effects, reproductive system effects, carcinogenicity etc.) and how it can access the body, i.e. 'routes of exposure' (inhalation, ingestion and skin absorption).

Workplace exposure to chemicals may be high relative to the levels found in the environment, but while some protection will be provided in the workplace this may not be the case in the environment e.g. air emissions. In fact many people will be exposed to chemicals without knowing it e.g. printer solvents, artists paints, degreasing agents used in general workshops and garages, dry cleaners etc.

In making comparisons between chemicals the quantity of chemical that produces toxicity known as dose is used. LD_{50} and LC_{50} are used as methods of comparing doses. LD_{50} is a direct measure of toxicity or lethal dose, while LC_{50} is a measure the airborne concentration that is acceptable and is used in the setting of Occupational Exposure Limits (OEL's).

When carrying out a toxicological evaluation on a chemical the following must be examined:

- Properties of the chemical
- Toxicity testing on animals
- Prediction of effects on humans
- All available information on the chemical

What presents a chemical as environmentally hazardous is how it is discharged or emitted.

Disposal of chemical is a significant environmental issue and needs to considered in the light of it's impact on the environment and how best to minimise this.

Workplace Chemical Threshold Limit Values (TLV's)
A TLV is a level below which there is no evidence of damage. It is determined from a workers exposure over an 8-hour day/40-hour week to average chemical concentrations. Provided there is no evidence of adverse effects at a threshold value it is deemed acceptable.

In theory, TLV's protect workers but in practice their determination is difficult. They are based on the best available information, but for many chemicals information on their exposure and environmental effects are scarce.

Arguments against the use of TLV's include:

- TLV's are based on the average worker who is young and healthy and do not consider other people's sensitivity to certain chemicals or those with certain existing ailments;
- People can be continuously exposed to chemicals and not just over an 8-hour day, pro rata which is what the assessment considers;

- TLV's are based on exposure to a single chemical and not the effect of exposure to more than one chemical. Today's environment has many chemicals present which we are exposed to. There is little information available on the synergy of chemicals and the effects of these.

'Precautionary Principle' and 'Zero Discharge'

'Precautionary Principle' or the 'Principle of Precautionary Action' says that there is no basis to presume that a chemical is dangerous in the absence of scientific proof. The argument against this is that all chemicals are deemed safe until proven harmful.

'Zero Discharge' concept means that we must strive to reduce our discharges to a minimum. 'Zero Discharge' may never become a reality but similar to 'Zero Defects' applied to quality of products, it stresses continual improvement. It gives organisations a goal of continually striving to reduce their discharges.

By setting a discharge limit, this gives us a tangible target to be achieved. However, when this target has been reached, we must then reduce the limit further, so that our objective is to reduce our discharges to the lowest possible level.

'Risk Assessment' and 'Choosing the Least Damaging Alternative'

Risk assessment determines 'safe' levels for exposure to chemicals.

'Choosing the Least Damaging Alternative' examines how to minimise the risks in examining alternatives. It is based on causing the minimum amount of harm to our environment. 'Choosing the Least Damaging Alternative' looks at all the available options. The question which is considered is: What is the least harm that can be done to the environment?.

Risk assessment is a mathematical means of establishing risks but examining alternatives is a more consultative process involving all the stakeholders in the business, in examining all available data and cost/benefit analysis. It must therefore be encouraged and included in the decision-making process.

Renewable Energy

Renewable energy sources such as solar, wind biomass and hydropower are inexhaustible and do not produce greenhouse gases. In contrast fossil fuels are non-renewable, finite and produce carbon dioxide and other greenhouse gases.

In Ireland, the current utilisation of renewable energy sources provide 6% of our electricity generating capacity. Europe has set a target to increase the renewable energy share of the market from 3.7% in 1991 to 7.8% in 2005 under its ALTENER programme. Currently Ireland is below the European average for renewable energy sources. The Irish Government introduced the Alternative Energy Requirement (AER) initiative with the intention of making renewable energy economically viable. AER1 was launched in 1993, AER2 in 1995 and AER3 in 1997 respectively. The latest of these programmes AER3 sets a target of increasing renewable energy to over 10% of the total electricity generating capacity by 1999. Within the goal of a total of 100 MW new renewable energy generating capacity individual targets are as follows:
- 90 MW Wind
- 7 MW Biomass/Waste
- 3 MW Hydropower

Prospective generators for the above must submit their applications to the Department of Transport, Energy and Communications.

Life Cycle Analysis

Life Cycle Analysis (LCA) attempts to accurately assess the burdens placed on the environment by the manufacture of a product by collecting and interpreting as much data as possible. This data would include the product's energy consumption, manufacture and use and the type of waste generated.

Used correctly LCA is a powerful tool that can help the formulation of environmental legislation, assist manufacturers to analyse their processes and improve their products, and can allow consumers to make informed choices when they purchase products. On the other hand it has been incorrectly used to prove how superior one product is over another and to exaggerate advertising claims.

2 ENVIRONMENTAL MANAGEMENT SYSTEM FRAMEWORK

2.1 Considering an Environmental Management System (EMS)

A definition of an EMS has been given in the introduction. In planning an EMS, the aim of the organisation is to improve its environmental performance and to decrease its environmental effects (impacts). The attainment of sound environmental performance can be achieved by operating a model system which can be subject to assessment. There are eight elements to an EMS.

1) Environmental performance must conform to stated policy requirements.
2) Environmental performance criteria must be specific and quantifiable (where possible)
3) Continuous improvement.
4) Top management leadership must promote commitment to environmental protection and sustainable development.
5) Voluntary implementation and certification to a recognised standard.
6) Provision of assurance on environmental objectives and minimisation of risks.
7) Compatibility with QMS (ref. ISO 9000)
8) Inclusion of key features among their structural elements, i.e. environmental policy, environmental management structures, environmental programmes, environmental awareness and training, records, communications and reporting, and internal audit and review functions.

Benefits of an EMS:
1. Market Strategy
Increasing environmental awareness will mean organisations being able to market products and services as "environmentally friendly". This will give such organisations considerable competitive advantage and may stimulate sales of their products.

2. Customer Requests

Customers are becoming more concerned about protecting the environment and consequential environmental impacts of the supply-chain. Suppliers can add value to their products by having an EMS. This may command a higher price premium for their products/services.

3. Cost Reduction

Organisations can considerably reduce energy, raw material usage and their associated costs by conservation programmes. In addition costs can be minimised by reducing losses e.g. waste.

4. Site Condition

Increased awareness of site condition should improve the overall visual impact of plant and activities. This will lead to a positive public perception of the organisations activities.

5. Legislation

The volume of government policies, pollution control licensing, regulations and their enforcement will demand stringent controls by organisations. It is better for organisations to prepare for impending legislation rather than waiting for its implementation and then reacting to its requirements.

6. Company Image

Today organisations are aware of negative influence on their corporate image. Public attitude is very important and publication of an environmental policy in addition to an accredited EMS should greatly enhance local and national attitude towards the organisation.

7. Accident/Spillage Prevention

With documented procedures, accidents and spillages will be minimised. Emergency procedures will reduce the environmental impact of these and consequential organisation liability.

8. Record Retention

A database of environmental effects (impacts) that are monitored will ensure any queries/complaints can be dealt with speedily and accurately.

9. Communication

An EMS calls for openness and dialogue with all employees and the public. This should increase motivation of employees and have a positive influence on the public.

10. Insurance

Organisations may avail of reduced insurance premiums as they are able to demonstrate that they can limit their exposure to environmental accidents of mismanagement.

11. Continuous Improvement Strategy

An EMS supports continuous improvement in an organisation.

12. Business Opportunity

Some organisations will carry out EMS activities themselves, while others will contract services externally. This will have the affect of creating additional business opportunity for the organisations concerned and outside contractors. There will be opportunities associated with making organisations competitive by reducing energy costs and minimising losses (waste etc.).

As part of the overall management activity of an organisation an EMS is of enormous benefit. Good communication with employees and the public embraces and enhances other modern management techniques in a world-class manufacturing environment. Bottom line performance of a company is improved by better energy consumption and losses reduction.

2.2 Links between EMS and other Management Systems.

An EMS should not be considered by an organisation in isolation of other management systems. Organisations may have, or may be developing systems to handle quality, safety, occupational health, security and Integrated Pollution Control (IPC) licensing. Other organisations may be registered to one of the ISO 9000 quality standards. The experience gained through the development of these systems in implementing an EMS will be invaluable. For this reason, many interested organisations will use existing personnel who have been experienced in the ISO 9000 quality standards to also implement the EMS.

Special care must be taken to avoid conflict of interest between various management systems in an organisation. This would mean, for example decisions made in setting or achieving targets in developing one system might have a controversial affect on another system.

There are many similarities and links between ISO 9000 requirements and an EMS Standard ,such as, ISO 14001 or EMAS Regulation. The Environmental Manager or person with responsibility for implementing an EMS must be aware of these.

Those organisations who already have ISO 9000 and who plan to implement an EMS must be careful to integrate the EMS into the overall management activity.

2.3   The main differences between the ECO - Management and Audit Scheme (EMAS) Regulation and Environmental Standard ISO 14001:

EMAS conforms with I.S. 310 (Irish EMS standard) BS 7750 (Former British EMS standard) core requirements, but ISO 14001 does not.

ISO 14001	EMAS Regulation
• International standard	• EU legislation
• Will be widely known beyond EU Member States.	• EU Member State recognition
• No restriction beyond EU.	• Confined to EU Member States
• May apply to only part of site	• Applies to single site but confined to manufacturing, power and waste disposal sites.
• No restriction, any activity	• Restricted to the above activities
• Optional third party verification	• Third party independent environmental verifier complying with EN 45012 requirements
• Does not specifically require an initial environmental review	• Initial environmental review advisable but not a requirement
• Unspecified minimum audit	• Audit frequency defined not

interval

- Identification of significant environmental aspects

- Improvement of environmental aspects

greater than 3 yearly.

- Register of environmental aspects

- Improvement of the EMS to reduce impacts.

A comprehensive public environmental public statement must be written in order to comply with EMAS and this has to be verified by an independent verifier. It also requires that environmental objectives and targets are available to the public. In contrast, ISO 14001 only requires the environmental policy to be publicly available.

Other differences include:

- **Documentation**
  EMAS requires records on the extent of the achievement of environmental objectives and targets. ISO 14001 does not, nor does it require a register of environmental effects.

- **Objectives**
  Unlike EMAS Regulation ISO 14001 does not require a time-frame within which to reach stated environmental objectives.

- **Contractors and Suppliers**
  ISO 14001 only requires that the environmental policy is communicated to suppliers and contractors, whereas EMAS requires the site to ensure they comply with the organisations environmental policy.

In choosing an appropriate environmental standard, an organisation will most likely consider the location of the market of its products. If that market is international then ISO 14001 may well be the choice. If the market is within the EU then EMAS may be chosen, or indeed those who have been registered to I.S. 310 or BS 7750, or otherwise, may choose subsequent registration to the EMAS Regulation knowing that it is the more stringent than ISO 14001 and represents the long-term view of increasingly stringent EU legislation and public availability of information.

Organisations would be wise to take a long-term view of environmental developments when choosing a particular standard.

An environmental standard should not be seen as a means to an end, but looked at in the context of all environmental issues affecting the organisation e.g. IPC licensing (cf. Section 3.1) etc. To satisfy only the requirements of a chosen standard is not enough. In the context of continuous improvement, the corporate culture should promote environmental improvement and protection.

2.4   Preparation of the Environmental Policy

In formulating and writing an environmental policy organisations may look at several sources of information depending on the nature and extent of their business. These may include:

1. National and International Environmental Programmes
2. Business Charter on Sustainable Development
3. European Environmental Agency information.

In the policy, the organisation outlines its commitments to the environment by managing its impact and striving for sustainable development. A typical Environmental Policy will begin by explaining that the organisation will conduct business and adopt behavioural practices which are conducive to the environment. It will then outline how this will be achieved. These may include:

- Conforming to applicable standards
- Hazard identification and risk control
- Employee participation, duties, knowledge of policy and procedures and initiation of corrective actions.
- Management commitment in ensuring managerial, technical and administration controls are maintained.
- Reviewing environmental targets and objectives at least annually.
- Reference to the applicable documented EMS Standard.
- Relationships with suppliers and third parties.
- Responding to employee and public environmental concerns.
- Consideration of environment in investment decisions and proposed changes.

Environmental policies will depend on the business activity, but all organisations need never consider environmental work to be complete and must emphasise its continual improvement.

Implementing the Environmental Policy must be undertaken in a systematic and goal setting way. Management commitment should ensure managers and employees fully understand their obligations.

Most organisations committed to protecting the environment will not just conform to applicable standards but where technically and economically feasible exceed standard and legal requirements. Some organisations will set their own standards (more than the legal requirements) and will continually strive to meet or even surpass these.

Employee involvement is essential to the success of Environmental Policy and an EMS implementation. This will be best achieved through environment project or action teams who engage in process improvement and the achievement of environmental goals and objectives. Teams will need adequate resources of personnel, equipment, procedures and training to achieve their aim. The provision and development of knowledge with respect to environmental effects of products and processes will be critical to the team's work and the decision making process.

The Environmental Policy should show how continuous improvement is to be achieved. Organisations will review environmental targets set at least annually. The EMS will be audited at appropriate intervals to verify its continued effectiveness. Published results of performance against environmental targets and the EMS audit results will form the basis of a good knowledge based system for continuous improvement.

The organisation's interaction with the public, suppliers, third parties and customers must be one of openness and dialogue. Employees, customers and the public should be provided with all the relevant information regarding environmental impacts of products and processes. Responding to public fears, queries or concerns about the effect of operations on the environment is important feedback in the corrective action loop. Suppliers, contractors and vendors should be informed and encouraged to have similar environmental standards.

Environmental management and policy sustainment is part of the organisations daily work routine. Management and employees at all levels should ensure they pursue the policy in their daily work and understand the significance of it in the importance of their tasks. All employees must have the necessary knowledge and training to this end.

Having read an organisations Environmental Policy, any interested member of the public should be able to ascertain how the organisations development of plans and programmes will be achieved in the protection and enhancement of the environment. The policy must be written in a clear and unambiguous way so that it can be easily understood by all.

2.5   The Initial Steps towards an EMS

The most favourable approach to the development of an EMS in an organisation, is by a project team. Those familiar with project management will know how to initiate such a team. The following approach is suggested:

1. **Appointing or expanding some key person in the organisation to the role of Environmental Manager/Co-ordinator.**
   This person does not have to be a trained environmental scientist but should be familiar with an EMS and the necessity to change in order to attain an EMS. This person should have positive influencing skills, as they need to get others to buy-into their mission to become an environmentally protective organisation. If there is not complete management team commitment, they should get a mandatory overview of the benefits, of an EMS. Generally, those who do not understand something will kill it. Sceptical managers or employees need to be encouraged and persuaded about the advantages for them and the company.

2. **Draw up a project specification.**
   This is very important in defining and eliciting the support of the project team., i.e. those who will do most of the work. It is also important in providing focus for the team and organisation. When it is specified and stated what work needs to be done, when and by whom, people usually commit themselves to the tasks involved. This does not have to be too formal.

The project specification might include the following details:

   • Project leader, facilitator and steering group

- Team members
- Defined Objectives
- EMS Implementation date, manpower requirement (if any), total cost and time investment
- Documented EMS completion date, training needs and training programme.

Each organisation will have its own ideas and level of detail which they will provide on a project specification.

It is also very helpful to draw up timing plans showing the timing of different events. This will also be valuable in identifying what work will be carried out internally and what will be done externally (contract).

Organisations may also consider it important to carry out a cost justification. When sceptics are provided with a costing of a project showing where money can be saved in the long-term, it usually diffuses the strength of their argument. With an EMS it is easy to offset the expenditure in implementation and cost of maintaining the standard against potential savings in energy, waste etc.

3. **Establishment of Environmental Policy.**
   The views of all management should be known and their aims on environmental issues. Complete involvement of management is crucial in gaining commitment and later integrating the policy into normal company operations.

4. **Investigation into the current environmental performance of the organisation.**
   Knowing the organisations strengths and weaknesses will enable management to know where they are now, in order to plan effectively and chart their course of action by way of targets and objectives.

   Accurate information on current environmental performance will allow realistic time-scales to be set for an EMS implementation.

5. **Development of EMS elements and Environmental Programme.**
   This should be looked at initially to determine the extent of the work involved. Some thought should go into what is the most effective way for subsequent implementation.

Organisations can also at the initial stages consider the Initial
Environmental Review. The early stages of considering an EMS is
in establishing the extent of work involved in each element/step
and knowing how much the organisation will depend on outside
expertise or how and who will conduct the work internally.

3 ENVIRONMENTAL REGULATION

3.1 The Regulatory Situation

The 1960s and 1970s were times of global awakening and developing awareness of the impact that 20th century lifestyles were having on the natural environment. The initial response at European level and in Ireland was one of command and control and the development of a large number of specific regulatory measures. In an industrial context these were primarily aimed at controlling:

- emissions to waters
- emissions to air
- the transport and disposal of waste
- noise

In the course of the 1970s and 1980s the European Commission generated a great number of Directives which had then to be implemented by Member States. In Ireland this is achieved by way of specific legislation (Acts) followed by the issue of Statutory Instruments, commonly referred to as Regulations. In some cases EU Directives have been implemented directly by way of such Irish Regulations alone. The record of the Irish Authorities has been good in this respect. A 1996 review of the extent of implementation of EU directives in Member States indicates that Ireland has implemented 127 of the total of 133. This ranks amongst the top performers in the EU.

Key Irish Legislation

Many of the legislative and regulatory instruments implemented in Ireland have been in response to EU Directives. However, in some areas the Irish Authorities have taken concepts being developed in Europe and have implemented them ahead of the rest of many Member States. For example Integrated Pollution Control (IPC) licensing has been implemented in Ireland (cf. section 2.8) since 1994 while the parent Integrated Pollution Prevention and Control (IPPC) Council Directive 96/61/EC was not finalised until 1996. The IPC Licensing legislation is very similar to the IPPC Directive.

From a regulatory viewpoint the more important Irish legislation would include:

- Local Government (Water Pollution) Acts, 1977 and 1990
- Air Pollution Act, 1987 and associated regulations
- Waste Regulations. relating to toxic and dangerous wastes, waste oils, the movement of waste within Ireland or across frontiers, amongst others
- Environmental Protection Agency Act, 1992 and associated regulations
- Waste Management Act, 1996

The major provisions of the Waste Management Act (cf. section 2.10) were brought into effect on July 1, 1996. At this time specific regulations to deal with the management of hazardous waste, oils, transport issues and so on were not issued. However, the Waste Management Act will in time repeal all existing Waste Regulations (referred to above) and replace them with regulations issued under the Waste Management Act itself.

A further important area is the issue of public access to environmental information held by public authorities. Following an EU Directive Irish regulations were issued in 1993 and revised in 1996. In essence any individual can request to view, or obtain copies of, files of information held by public authorities in relation to any environmental issues. This could relate to developments in an area, licence applications, licences issued, monitoring programs and communications between the public authorities and external individuals or organisations. The term "public authority" includes:

- a Government Ministry
- the Commissioners of Public Works
- a Local Authority
- a Harbour Authority
- a Health Board
- any board or body established by or under statute
- a company effectively owned by the State, or other bodies mentioned above.

There are provisions for withholding information and for deeming certain information held as being confidential. Such decisions are often difficult to make and it would be prudent for any individual or organisation to assume that all information submitted might be in the public domain. Some public authorities do operate special systems to ensure separate control of information agreed to be confidential and identified as such.

Environmental Control (Local Authorities)

Prior to the establishment of the Environmental Protection Agency (EPA) and its implementation of IPC licensing in 1994 all environmental issues were regulated and controlled by individual Local Authorities. For those operations which are not regulated by the EPA through IPC licensing (cf. section 2.8, 2.9) the above-mentioned legislation is, in outline, implemented as follows:

(a) **Local Government (Water Pollution) Acts,** 1977 and 1990. Most discharges of trade effluent or sewage effluent to a water body requires a license. Similarly any discharge of trade effluent to a sewer also requires a licence. Such licences may set various control conditions, require monitoring to be carried out and require reporting to the Local Authority

(b) **Air Pollution Act,** 1987: This Act defines thirty classes of industrial process to which its licensing provisions apply. In some cases the scale of operations must be above defined thresholds in order to be included.

Since February 1, 1989 any new activities in any of these defined classes require a licence from the Local Authority before commencing operations. In practice most such activities will come within the scope of IPC licensing by the EPA (cf. section 2.8, 2.9) and will not therefore be subject to Local Authority licensing. There are however a few exceptions particularly in respect of the scale of activities.

In the case of existing activities the Air Pollution Act to date has only been applied to a reduced set of activities rather than to the entire thirty classes defined in the Act. This relatively small number of activities had to apply for licences in 1989. Again, most of those established activities which potentially could be required in the future to seek licences under the Air Pollution Act fall within the scope of IPC licensing. Thus any significant extension of licensing under the terms of the Air Pollution Act appears unwarranted.

(c) Waste Regulations

Licences or permits must be obtained from Local Authorities in order to store, treat, dispose of or transport various special wastes.

Under the terms of the Waste Management Act, 1996 new (or revised) regulations may be issued to be implemented in some cases by Local Authorities.

From this brief outline of Environmental Control it can be seen that an operation may be required to obtain one or more licences from, often, different sections of its Local Authority in order to comply with all environmental legislation.

3.2   The Environmental Protection Agency (EPA)

The Environmental Protection Agency Act, 1992 is an important piece of framework legislation under which the EPA was established, its duties defined and the concept of IPC licensing was introduced.

The EPA is an independent, national body formally established in July 1993 with the purpose of protecting Ireland's natural environment. Its own Mission Statement is:

"to promote and implement the highest practicable standards of environmental protection and management which embrace the principles of sustainable and balanced development".

The EPA has a full-time executive board consisting of the Director General and four Directors. The organisation is divided into four divisions each one of which is managed by one of the above Directors. These divisions are:

- Corporate Affairs
- Licensing and Control
- Environmental Monitoring and Laboratory Services
- Environmental Management and Planning

The headquarters is in Wexford with Regional Inspectorates, Offices and Laboratories located around the country.

The EPA is assisted by an advisory committee of twelve members appointed by the Minister for the Environment following nominations from various organisations involved in environmental protection issues. This committee makes recommendations to the EPA and to the Minister in relation to the EPA's functions.

The procedures for selecting the full-time executive board and the advisory committee are defined in the EPA Act itself and reinforce the independence of the organisation.

It is the expressed intention that the EPA will take over responsibility from Local Authorities for the licensing and regulation of large, complex operations deemed to have significant polluting potential (cf. section 2.8). Operations which remain outside of the EPA's scope of activities will continue to be regulated by the Local Authority alone, as already outlined (cf. section 2.6).

Powers and Functions
In its own documentation the EPA outlines how it protects the environment through the following powers and functions:

(a) Control
  • Licensing major developments and enforcing compliance
  • Authorising certain public sector activities
  • Imposing conditions on marine developments

(b) Monitoring
  • Monitoring general environmental quality
  • Monitoring the quantity and quality of water resources
  • Monitoring specific problems

(c) Promotion
  • Issuing guidelines on environmental issues
  • Issuing codes of practice
  • Encouraging environmental audits
  • Encouraging environmentally friendly products and services

(d) Assistance
  • Co-ordination of environmental research programmes
  • Encouraging Local Authorities in environmental protection
  • Providing training in environmental protection

(e) Advice
- On policy matters
- On the need for legislative changes
- On environmental quality standards
- On emission standards
- On environmental impact statements

(f) Supervision
- Supervising environmental monitoring by other authorities
- Overseeing the environmental activities of Local Authorities

(g) Consultation
- Providing consultation for developers seeking licences
- Consulting with public authorities about their environmental functions

(h) Information Services
- Publication of monitoring results
- Provision of public access to environmental databases
- Publication of 'State of the Environment' reports
- Holding of seminars and conferences

(i) International Co-operation
- Liaising with the European Environment Agency
- Consulting with similar international bodies about environmental issues

Strengthening Management and Regulation
The agency advises on public policies and objectives, encourages sustainable development and exercises a precautionary approach. Applying the 'polluter pays' principle, the agency aims to achieve a balance between environmental and developmental needs. Overall the EPA states that it significantly strengthens the management and regulation of the environment in the following ways:

- Regulating and controlling development
- Monitoring the quality of the environment
- Encouraging environmentally sound procedures
- Advising and assisting public authorities
- Promoting environmental research
- Overseeing Local Authority environmental functions

- Providing access to environmental information
- Providing lines of contact to Europe and other international networks

Licensing and Control

From a commercial viewpoint this function may be of primary practical importance. In the case of any development, whether it be a new, green-field situation or a modification to an existing operation one must explore:

- what environmental issues are involved?
- are there any regulatory implications?
- who is the relevant regulatory authority?

The regulatory authority, if applicable, will either be the EPA or the Local Authority.

EPA

The EPA Act, 1992 defines in Schedule 1 those processes or activities to which IPC licensing will apply (cf. section 2.8). It now applies to all new, scheduled activities. It is being progressively applied to established, scheduled activities. This programme commenced in May 1994 and it is expected that 800 to 1000 operations will be licensed by perhaps 1998.

While in the case of most of the scheduled activities it is easy to determine whether they are applicable to one's operation or not, this is not always so. It is the operator's responsibility to ensure that an IPC licence application is lodged by the required date if one is needed. Thus the definitions need to be read carefully. Where any doubt exists the guidance of the EPA should be sought.

An IPC licence will regulate all environmental issues in one document.

Local Authority

If the activities are not included in Schedule 1 of the EPA Act, IPC licensing will not apply.

In this case it is necessary to review the environmental impact of the operations and determine whether any regulatory licences must be sought from the Local Authority.

- are there any emissions to water or sewer`?
- are the activities required to have a licence under the Air Pollution Act?
- are there regulatory issues arising from the nature of wastes produced?

An outline of the implementation of environmental regulation has been given in Part 3.1 of this book.

3.3   Integrated Pollution Control (IPC) Licensing

The traditional approach to environmental regulation has very much been one of command and control and of prescriptive regulation of a range of environmental issues by different groups within a Local Authority.

The IPC concept, framed in Europe some years ago, is an attempt to move away from this approach. The key word is "Integrated". In this new regulatory regime all environmental issues can be considered together. The best general solution can be developed in order that the environmental impact of a particular activity can be minimised and that pollution is not simply shifted from one medium to another.

IPC Licensing is intended to result in a move towards a more expansive approach to environmental management. Rather than simply setting limits for each and every emission the IPC concept concentrates on avoiding or minimising wastes and emissions in the first instance. The remaining wastes and emissions from an operation must then be considered in their entirety and integrated solutions sought to reduce overall environmental impact.

This IPC approach represents a culture change to one of proactive management of environmental issues with the aim of continually improving performance and continually reducing environmental impact.

The Scope of IPC Licensing

Schedule 1 of the EPA Act defines thirteen categories and a total of sixty one sub-categories to which IPC licensing applies. These classifications are essentially based on the nature of the process or operations utilised by the activity. The principal categories are as follows:

- Minerals and other materials
- Energy
- Metals
- Mineral fibres and glass
- Chemicals
- Intensive agriculture
- Food and drink
- Wood, paper, textiles and leather
- Fossil fuels
- Cement
- Waste
- Surface coatings
- Other activities

The full list is included in Appendix 1.

IPC licences must be sought for all new scheduled activities. The licensing system is being applied progressively to existing activities which fall into the scope outlined above.

The Minister for the Environment has the power to extend the scope of IPC licensing to such additional sectors as are defined in Schedule 1 of the EPA Act. This is achieved by way of issuing a Statutory Instrument (or regulation). This process commenced in May 1994 and should be completed by perhaps 1998.

It would be an offence under the EPA Act to continue operations beyond the date defined in the relevant regulations without having applied for a licence. It is an operator's responsibility to make themselves aware of such regulations and the dates for applications.

It is important to note that the EPA has no authority to deviate from the regulations as issued by the Minister. Their function is simply to carry out the requirements of the regulations.

BATNEEC
The EPA uses a reference set of procedures, techniques and standards for each sector it licences. These are referred to as "BATNEEC Guidance Notes" and such notes will be available for each scheduled sector.

BATNEEC, a European concept, is an acronym for Best Available Technology Not Entailing Excessive Cost. BATNEEC is intended to represent a set of sectoral operating techniques/procedures and emission limits for which all operators licensed by the EPA must aim:

- new activities would be expected to comply with BATNEEC from the start of operations. Thus the BATNEEC principles must be built into the design process.

- established activities will be required (through the licensing process) to comply with, or at least approach, BATNEEC standards over a period of time defined by the EPA. The timing of this is a matter for the EPA.

The EPA Act, 1992 gives the EPA the power (section 5) to define what is BATNEEC. It is intended that these processes, technologies and techniques are proven in practice, in use in the industry (perhaps in other countries), and available in terms of cost.

Under the EPA Act [83(3)(f)] the EPA must not grant a licence to an operator unless it is satisfied the BATNEEC will be used.

- to prevent or eliminate emissions
  or, *where this is not possible*
- to limit, abate or reduce emissions.

From this statement it is clear that the preferred action is to avoid and/or minimise problems and wastes at source, rather than use "end-of-pipe" technology to clean up afterwards. Thus changes in the processes or the materials used may be required. It should be noted that established activities will be expected, in principle, to achieve BATNEEC standards over a period of time. This issue may be specifically addressed in the licence issued.

3.4   Application for, and implementation of, an IPC Licence

Any one of the following reasons will make it necessary to apply to the EPA for an IPC licence. A "scheduled activity" refers to those activities included in Schedule 1 of the 1992 EPA Act (cf. Appendix 1).

(i) You plan to commence a new operation which includes one or more scheduled activities. In this case the IPC licence must be actually issued before the new operation may commence.

(ii) Your existing operation includes one or more scheduled activities. Regulations have determined a date by which an IPC licence application shall be made for one or more of these scheduled activities.

In this case operations continue beyond the lodgement date under the terms of any existing environmental licences until the IPC licence is decided upon.

(iii) You intend making changes to the nature or scale of existing scheduled activities such that emissions are likely to be materially changed, increased, or new emissions result.

Regardless of whether these existing scheduled activities are yet licensed by the EPA or not, any such changes to scheduled activities must be notified to the EPA who will decide whether a licence application or review is required.

In practice this requirement is difficult to be specific about. In many cases this issue can be most easily resolved through direct contact and discussion with EPA personnel. Indicative factors would include:

- change in the materials used
- change in the waste generated
- change in the emission (nature or load) to air
- change in the emission (nature or load) to water
- changed noise pattern

It is important to note that once an application for an IPC licence has been lodged with the EPA, they then become the sole regulatory authority for all environmental issues relating to your operations. This includes all other activities which are not scheduled in the EPA Act. The Local Authority or any other body will cease to have any primary regulatory role. The EPA will effectively operate and manage all existing licences until the IPC licence itself is issued.

Once the IPC licence is issued all existing environmental licences are also superseded.

Getting Started

Given the complexity of many industrial activities it would be prudent. at the earliest opportunity, to confirm the status of one's activities with respect to IPC licensing through direct consultation with the EPA, if necessary. This may take the form of attendance at an official pre-application briefing or an individual consultation. Such briefings are normally held for sectoral groups affected by new regulations which extend the scope of IPC licensing activities for established activities.

One can obtain from the EPA a copy of:

- the current IPC licence application form
- the current associated guidance notes
- BATNEEC notes for relevant scheduled activities

Some or all of these documents may be made available in electronic format.

Further necessary documents are:
- the EPA Act, 1992
- current Licensing Regulations
- current Application Fee Regulations
- legislation and regulations referred to in the application form itself

The EPA also publishes a "Guide to the implementation and enforcement of IPC licensing" which is a very useful, readable document. Other relevant IPC licence applications or licences (available from the EPA) may be worthwhile reviewing particularly if they are for the same sector.

Consideration must be given to the personnel needed to assemble a good application. In practice a mixture of internal and external resources will often provide the most cost effective solution.

Internal:
- technical person familiar with the detail of operations who can be seconded to co-ordinate this project. The duration of the project will be related to the complexity of the activities and to the extent of existing environmental knowledge and systems. Eight to

twelve weeks would represent a reasonable schedule for many organisations.

- secretarial support.
- facilities to prepare drawings, preferably electronically
- further assistance would depend on the scale and nature of the activities

External:
- significant benefits may be obtained by adding practical external experience and expertise to one's team. This should ensure a shorter, more cost effective application process and a resulting document which is properly scoped to meet the needs of the EPA.

Completing the Application Form

The application form is quite a complex document in itself. By the time the application is submitted to the EPA a large number of further attachments, drawings, supporting documents and reports will have been included. It must be realised that there is no such thing as a "standard" response to the completion of the form. All operations are different in terms of detail, location, environmental issues arising, existing knowledge and many other areas which impact on the IPC application document. However it is worth keeping some general points in mind.

(a) Completion of the application form should not be seen as an end in itself but rather the start of a process which will continue to be an important business activity as long as the organisation continues to operate.
Thus:
- one needs to be aware that much of the information submitted in the application form will later influence the detail of the IPC licence requirements.

- the individual who will be responsible in practical terms for the actual implementation of the licence should be a key member of the team preparing the application. Such continuity will pay dividends later.

The implementation programme that will follow the issue of an IPC licence represents a significant challenge for most organisations. It will include the need to develop a management system which will include most of the key elements of formalised Environmental Management Systems (EMS) such as EMAS or ISO 14001. To date a certified EMS is not a formal requirement of IPC licensing although the existence of such an EMS would be welcomed by the EPA.

(b) Review the entire application document briefly at the earliest opportunity in order to identify information which:

- is available
- is not available
- needs to be developed and/or studies performed

In many cases where information is unavailable then this will simply be stated in the application. However, where it is possible or necessary to obtain missing information then this work must be prioritised. Where specific external assistance, perhaps technical is required, it is important that this be advanced so as not to delay the whole application process.

If one is in the position of knowing that an IPC licence application will have to be made well into the future it would be very beneficial to complete this review process at the earliest opportunity. An outline project scope can be developed and many items can be usefully acted upon even if an application date is not yet set by regulation. This would certainly include lists, document files, and drawings noted in (d), (e) and (f) below.

(c) Decide on a structured format for naming and organising:

- the application form itself
- associated attachments containing additional, supporting information
- drawings

The various pieces of information need to be easily accessed as the total application form grows in size.

(d) All materials used, materials produced and wastes generated should be listed and characterised. Existing emissions to air and water should be treated similarly.

(e) Complete files relating to current and previous planning permissions or environmental licences are not always easily available and are items to be prioritised.

(f) Drawings for many sections can be sketched and first drafts prepared as another priority item. Plot plans of the site, various drainage drawings, and process description flowcharts would be key areas to start with. Note that a variety of National Grid References will be required. It is useful if this grid can be superimposed (as required) on all drawings produced.

(g) The EPA will generally facilitate consultation meetings while the application form is being prepared. This is very useful for the applicant and should be availed of. Draft content can be discussed with EPA officials and their opinions sought. This is an important measure in ensuring that the application form, as submitted, will best meet the needs of the EPA. In such cases subsequent delays in processing the licence should be minimised. This may be a critical point in the case of a new activity which requires the licence before commencing operations.

(h) While the application form and associated guidance documentation from the EPA are very necessary and useful in themselves, one must not lose sight of the fact that the IPC licensing process is governed by the EPA Act of 1992 and by specific licensing regulations.

Where specific requirements are set down in these cases an applicant must ensure full compliance in the application. Otherwise the EPA is precluded from processing the application and delay will result.

Lodging and Processing the Application
(a) In keeping with the policy of ensuring transparency in the IPC licensing system specific public notices must be posted by the applicant as determined by the regulations. These are:
  - newspaper notice
  - notice at the site of the operations (or planned operations)

Again care must be exercised with respect to:
- the content of such notices
- the timing in relation to the application lodgement date where placed

These matters are all specified by regulation.

(b) A signed, original IPC licence application form, accompanied by five full copies and the appropriate fee must be lodged at the EPA headquarters in Wexford.

If an Environmental Impact Statement (EIS) is required then at least fifteen copies of this EIS must accompany the IPC licence application. The question of the need for an EIS is most commonly part of the planning process but may alternatively be requested by the EPA.

(c) The EPA is allowed a two month period to issue a "proposed determination", effectively a draft IPC licence. However two particular issues commonly delay this process:

- the application form as lodged is not deemed by the EPA to be fully complete and in full accordance with the regulations. Until this situation is rectified by the applicant, the review period does not actually start. Seriously inadequate applications may be rejected and returned.

- when the EPA has completed a review of the application it may require that additional information be submitted. Such a situation will have to be addressed by the applicant to the satisfaction of the EPA.

In theory at least the two month review process only commences once the EPA is in possession of all of the above information. In practice, if the omissions are not so serious, the licence review process may proceed in parallel.

(d) The EPA will announce how it proposes to determine the particular IPC licence application and effectively publishes a draft licence which is made available to the applicant and to the general public.

Statutory time periods for objections then commence:

- up to 28 days for the applicant
- up to 21 days for any other party

Applicants may find it necessary to object for many reasons. This may be due to particularly stringent conditions being set but could equally be necessary in order to correct factual errors which have crept into the licence. The applicant may, in good faith, have supplied erroneous information in the application and has subsequently became aware of this. Data may have been misinterpreted or improperly transcribed during the licence preparation process. It may also be necessary to seek flexibility in order to be able to manage monitoring programmes in cases of staff unavailability, contractor unavailability, plant shutdowns and so on. Many such issues can often be addressed to everyone's satisfaction by small changes in language.

It must be stressed that any applicant needs to check the "proposed determination" line by line, number by number. Once transcribed into the actual IPC licence any errors or oversights may make licence implementation more difficult and tedious than it needs to be.

The conduct of the whole objection process and the subsequent resolution is all defined in the EPA Act and the Licensing Regulations. It should be noted that the EPA itself controls the appeal process.

(e) If there are no objections then the "proposed determination" effectively becomes the IPC licence after a period of one month.

This could be extended for up to four months if a comprehensive objection process has to be managed. There is provision for the use of oral hearings. At the end of this process the EPA has three choices:

- grant the licence without any changed conditions
- grant the licence with changed conditions
- refuse to grant a licence

(f) In either case once the "proposed determination" is issued by the EPA, the implementation process must immediately be given high priority. If no objections are lodged then this document will have to be implemented after one month has elapsed with consequent reporting required shortly afterwards.

This intermediate waiting period represents valuable planning time not to be wasted.

Implementing an IPC Licence

The EPA is a national body applying the same set of standards to all operations within a sector. These same standards should apply across all the scheduled sectors also. It must however be recognised that minor variations will occur particularly in response to the specific set of circumstances which each operator is subject to. The core principal would be that competing businesses within Ireland should all be treated similarly in respect of environmental regulatory requirements. No competitive disadvantage should arise as a result of the location of facilities.

IPC licence conditions are concerned not only with emission limits but also with the quality and extent of environmental management processes and procedures. The IPC licence will certainly define limits and control parameters to be complied with. It will require reporting of defined monitoring programmes, normally monthly. It will also require that an Environmental Management Programme be prepared, submitted to the EPA and thereafter reported on annually. For many operators there will be one or more once-off reports to be prepared and submitted to the EPA within a specified time period following the issuing of the licence.

It is clear that the first one or two years of implementing an IPC licence will involve a significant additional workload for many organisations. It may be that some additional resources will be required in order to properly implement the IPC licence. Such a requirement will vary greatly depending on the extent and suitability of the existing environmental management system and structure within the licensee's operations.

As a legal document the IPC licence needs to be implemented carefully and in a planned way. The development of an "in-house" or formally certified Environmental Management System is an excellent vehicle through which IPC Licensing can be managed in a controlled fashion. Assurance can be obtained that activities will take place when required and that necessary reporting will be completed. This reduces the need for management input.

The benefits of an Environmental Management System to any organisation are many and would include:

1) cost effective compliance with IPC licensing and other regulatory requirements
2) waste avoidance and aggressive waste management resulting in associated cost reductions
3) improved operational efficiencies including utilisation of resources

The principles of IPC licensing would seek and concur with these benefits.

Data acquisition, processing and reporting is a particularly important function required by the licence. Prompt, accurate reports in defined formats will be required for the EPA, for any public information programme, and for one's own management. A flexible approach is thus necessary. For many a database concept proves to be most suitable. Data is only entered once and from this the range of necessary reports may be automatically printed. Reports can be modified in future as required.

Review of an IPC Licence

An IPC licence may be reviewed for a variety of reasons. The process will effectively mirror the original application process and the appropriate fee must be paid.

Such a licence review can be initiated by either the licensee or by the EPA. It can be carried out at any time at the request, or with the consent, of the licensee. The EPA may independently initiate a review in the case of any IPC licence which has been issued for three or more years.

Any significant change in the scale or nature of operations might trigger a review. It may also be the case that important, relevant information has come to light concerning wastes or the effects of emissions on local environmental impact, for example, and that a review is considered necessary by the EPA. New national or international environmental standards of relevance might also raise the issue of a licence review.

Monitoring and Enforcement

IPC licence conditions will include the requirement for the licensee to monitor (or have monitored) its own activities and to report results to the EPA. Such information will be on the public file.

The EPA maintains its own extensive laboratory facilities at several locations. It also has mobile laboratory facilities at its disposal which will visit licensed operations in order to monitor licensed parameters. The results of these programmes would also be placed on the public file. The EPA will also conduct environmental audits of licensed operations.

Failure to comply with any licence condition is an offence and significant legal remedies are available to the EPA.

- summary conviction may result in a fine of up to £1,000 or up to twelve months in prison, or both.

- on indictment the maximum fine is £10 million and up to 10 years in prison, or both.

3.5   The Waste Management Act, 1996

This Act is an important piece of modernising legislation which sets out a comprehensive framework for the prevention, management, storage, transport and disposal of waste. It includes definitions of waste and of hazardous waste.

The Waste Management Act (WMA) emphasises the hierarchy of preferences with respect to waste management:

- avoid producing waste at source
- minimise quantities and toxicity of waste
- re-use
- recycle
- dispose of safely

It also clearly focuses on the need for a shared responsibility with respect to waste generation and management. This responsibility must be shared between private citizens, the state sector, commerce and industry if we are to seriously address what is an increasingly critical issue.

When the WMA was substantially brought into effect on July 1, 1996 the Department of the Environment identified key provisions as follows:

- there is now a general duty on all persons holding waste to do so in a manner which avoids environmental pollution

- the penalties for causing environmental pollution or for other offences under the Act can now be a fine of up to £10 million and ten years imprisonment

- vehicles and equipment used in the commission of an offence can now be forfeited

- there is an obligation on all persons involved in agricultural, commercial and industrial activities to take all reasonable steps to prevent and minimise the production of waste

- the Environmental Protection Agency is now mandated to prepare a national plan in relation to hazardous waste

- Local Authorities are required to adopt modern and systematic local waste management plans

- Local Authorities are authorised to make bye-laws controlling the presentation of waste for collection; for example, to reduce the incidence of litter and to assist the segregation of waste for recycling

- Local Authorities have strengthened powers as to the monitoring and inspection of waste activities, and the procurement of information regarding waste production and management

- Local Authorities and the Environmental Protection Agency will be able to recoup costs incurred in carrying out investigations, taking legal proceedings and preventing environmental pollution from waste

- Local Authorities can exercise wide-ranging powers to take measures, or to require others to take measures, to prevent or limit environmental pollution from waste

- important new powers are given to Local Authorities to require the making of farm nutrient management plans

The WMA will clearly result in increased costs for waste management and disposal. It also allows for such costs to be paid by the waste producer in keeping with the "polluter pays" principle. Local Authorities will have to provide and operate high quality, modern landfills and will be empowered to pass on the full economic costs. Assuming that this concept is made to work in practice it will have major implications for everyone at home, in the office, in a factory or on a building site. The focus, for cost reasons alone must then come onto waste avoidance and minimisation.

The whole regulatory situation will be upgraded and Local Authorities as well as private companies or individuals may require permits in respect of holding, collecting, moving, recovering or disposing of waste.

The Minister has wide powers to issue regulations in pursuit of the aims of the WMA. Specific areas where regulations may be issued include, amongst others:

- a direction to business to carry out waste audits and waste reduction programmes
- deposit schemes to be implemented for specified packaging to encourage returns
- separation of wastes
- charging for the use of specified packaging
- retail outlets to provide "bring-back" facilities for packaging waste
- the restriction or prohibition of the use of certain materials in a production process

Thus it should be recognised that in the years to come the WMA can and will effect the way businesses operate, if for no other reason than cost alone. The 1997 regulations in relation to Packaging and Packaging Waste are the first in a possible series of challenging measures to be put in place.

Estimates of a five-fold cost increase for solid waste disposal may well become a reality. This will encourage, if not force, all businesses to properly evaluate their contribution to this waste mountain.

Successful waste reduction programmes will produce significant financial savings.

Measures already implemented in other countries are worthwhile considering. Producers and retailers in many EU countries are required to have systems in place to facilitate the return of used packaging by the consumer. Such waste must then be managed so that recovery and recycling targets are met. In practice producers pay a levy to national organisations who provide collection facilities at suitable locations and who sort and process all waste collected. The producer foots the bill and will thus focus on the need to avoid or minimise unnecessary packaging.

- TOOTHPASTE:
  The traditional consumer package consists of a tube in an individual carton. Encouraged by laws requiring the producer/retailer to accept returned packaging many producers no longer use this carton. They simply stack the tubes on trays on the supermarket shelf - a waste minimisation approach which has already reached Ireland!

- PLASTIC BAGS:
  The use of plastic bags for rubbish disposal constitutes a big landfill problem in terms of the volume disposed of and the fact that the bags do not degrade. In Germany such bags are no longer used in supermarkets. They were simply banned. Consumers reverted to the use of their own shopping bags. This is an example of avoidance. It is interesting to note that America never moved away from using simple brown paper bags for this purpose. A case of "the old ways are the best" being true?

- METAL CANS:
  Recycling generally requires the further input of materials and/or energy and thus imposes some cost. In considering the overall environmental picture, the benefits of some recycling operations are not always clear. Denmark decided to simplify their waste position with respect to beverage containers. They decided to use glass only, implement a deposit/return system, and banned metal beverage cans entirely. A fairly radical

example of avoidance! Of course such a move would have serious implications for the beverage and other industries.

- COMPONENTS:
  The manufacturers of cars and white goods now concentrate on waste issues at the design stage. They aim to reduce the mixture of materials used and, in doing so, facilitate recycling when the product has reached the end of its useful life. The manuals being supplied with many new cars now devote some pages to detailing the mix of materials used, whether they are recycled or recyclable, and so on. These manufacturers are thus turning their waste management challenges into marketing advantages.

Everyone would endorse the concept of prevention being better than cure. In the same way, waste avoidance is certainly cheaper than waste disposal. However a world with zero waste is one without any human or industrial activity and as such remains an ideal, but practically unattainable, state. So given that we are going to have some wastes, the disposal of which will shortly become much more expensive, how can we manage most efficiently? How can we minimise the waste?

Start with a comprehensive overview of the wastes produced by the organisation - be it a factory, an office, or indeed a household.

Each waste source can then be examined in detail

- Can it be avoided altogether and thus totally remove the problem. This is a key consideration at the design stage of any product, process or package.
- What possibilities are there for minimising it and thus reducing disposal costs?
- Is re-use or recycling possible? These options will become increasingly attractive as the costs of disposal rise.

Waste "produced" includes the general waste arising from the factory, office or canteen as well as any packaging waste which one may have to take responsibility for, directly or indirectly, as a result of "bring back" systems. The important point is that no matter how the waste is actually handled the producer will have to meet the cost.

Too often organisations have no idea how much waste they currently produce, where it actually originates, and what is the full cost of disposal. When such an examination is completed the need for cost reductions will come into sharp focus. The issues that would most benefit from some innovation and give the best financial return should be clear.

A waste minimisation programme forms a central part of an Environmental Management System. The structured, ongoing examination of waste issues will ensure efficiency and cost reductions in the new waste climate.

4   RECENT REGULATORY DEVELOPMENTS

4.1   Waste Management Regulations, 1997

These were published in March 1997 and include two statutory instruments:

- Waste Management (Licensing) Regulations, 1997 (SI 133 of 1997)
- Waste Management (Planning) Regulations, 1997 (SI 137 of 1997)

Waste Management Planning

The purpose of the Waste Management Planning Regulations are to give effects the provisions of:

- Council Directive 74/442/EEC on waste, as amended by Council Directive 91/156/EEC
- Council Directive 75/439/EEC on disposal of waste oils, as amended by Council Directive 87/101/EEC
- Council Directive 91/689/EEC on hazardous waste
- European Parliament and Council Directive 94/62/EC on packaging and packaging waste.

The Regulations are divided into 6 parts outlining the requirements of the Waste Management Plan, as follows:

Part 1   Preface to the Waste Management Plan.
This will provide complete details, area (features, size, population, domestic households), nature, scale of activities (including commercial, industrial, agricultural, waste generating), transport infrastructure, groundwater usage (including vulnerability), land use (including designated areas) and a list of relevant legislation.

Part 2   Present position regarding waste management.
2.1 Waste Generation.
Specify quantities of waste arising, classifications and movements under the descriptions provided in the regulations and where appropriate hazardous component of wastes.

2.2 Waste Collection.
Specify waste collection systems (including bring facilities), capacity, segregation and separation of waste types.

2.3 Waste Prevention and Minimisation.
Describe measures of waste prevention and minimisation and give extent of information to business and industry on the impact of such activities.

2.4 Waste Recovery.
Describe waste recovery activities, specify volumes, types of waste, estimated waste recovery rates and markets/uses for recovered materials/products.

2.5 Waste Management Facilities.
Provide information on facilities for collection, handling, storage, treatment, recovery and disposal of waste under the descriptions provided in the regulations.

2.6 Other relevant matters.
Specify the cost of waste management activities, revenues accruing and indicate deficiencies in waste management infrastructure or other inhibitive matters.

Part 3   Anticipated developments over the period of the Plan.
In line with section 22(7) of the Waste Management Act provide an assessment of likely trends and developments which will impact quantities, types of waste arising, recovery/disposal facilities etc. Include in the assessment details as outlined in the regulations and description of feasible, possible alternative scenarios.

Part 4   Waste management policy.
4.1 Evaluation of policy options.
In line with section 22(7) of the Waste Management Act provide an evaluation of policy options as outlined in the regulations and assess the environmental impact and cost implications of each option.

4.2 Statement of policy.

The local authority should state its waste management policies and objectives and assign priorities to these in line with section 22(7) of the Waste Management Act.

Part 5 Implementation of the waste management policy over the relevant period.

5.1 General.

Outline proposals for monitoring implementation of the plan including waste recovery or other targets and measures to provide data and information on waste management improvements.

5.1 Roles and responsibilities.

Describe the roles of all those listed in the regulations.

5.2 Waste prevention and recovery.

Provide information on methods the local authority will use, promotion of public awareness, organisation of activities and interfaces with community and other organisations/authorities as outlined in the regulations.

5.3 Management of packaging and packaging waste.

A separate section in the plan should deal with management of packaging and packaging waste in support of the measures outlined in the European Parliament and Council Directive 94/62/EC (including measures for purposes of articles 4,5 and 13 of Directive).

5.4 Waste Collection and Disposal.

In line with section 22(7) of the Waste Management Act, provide information on rationalisation, development of waste handling and waste facilities. Include measures for co-operation with other local authorities in applying the proximity principle (i.e. disposal of waste in nearest installations). Information should be included on the "polluter pays principle" and consultation and co-ordination of measures with other local authorities.

Part 6 Matters relating to a Plan generally. The plan should include table of contents, summary, references including methodologies used and investigations/surveys undertaken, illustrations as appropriate, maps, diagrams and tables of information.

Waste Management Plan

A waste management plan must be drawn up by the local authority in accordance with section 22 of the Waste Management Act, 1996 and submitted to:

- the Minister for Arts, Culture and the Gaeltacht,
- the Minister for the Marine,
- An Taisce - The National Trust for Ireland,
- Bórd Fáilte,
- Teagasc,
- any local authority whose functional area adjoins that of the first mentioned local authority, and
- any District Council in Northern Ireland whose functional area adjoins that of the said local authority.

Waste Management Licensing

An operator of a waste management facility is now required to apply for a waste license under section 39 of the Waste Management Act, 1996. The purpose of the waste licence is to ensure that the waste management activity is operated in a manner which will not cause environmental pollution and will prevent any harm to humans, animals and plant life.

Waste licensing will be implemented in a series of phases. The first phase of applications is set down in the Waste Management (Licensing) Regulations, 1997, which outlines the nature and size of the activities which are required to be licensed by particular dates. It is expected that further regulations are to be made which will require those other waste management activities not listed in the 1997 Regulations to be subject to licensing.

The Waste Management Act - Section 40(a) states the EPA will not grant a waste license unless it is satisfied that:

- the waste management activity will be operated in compliance with all relevant;
- the activity, after it has been licensed, will not cause environmental pollution;

- the best available technology not entailing excessive costs is being used to deal with any emission from the site;
- the applicant and any other relevant person is a 'fit and proper' person to hold the licence (it should be noted that this section only applies to applicants who are <u>not</u> local authorities); *and*
- that the Agency's requirements (if any) in respect of the making of appropriate financial provisions in respect of the licence are satisfied.

Once granted, a waste licence supersedes any licences issued under the following legislation:

- Air Pollution Act, 1987;
- Local Government (Water Pollution) Acts, 1977 and (Amendment) 1990;
- Fisheries (Consolidation) Act, 1959
- Foreshore Act, 1993.

A waste licence will also supersede any permit issued by the local authorities under the following Regulations:

- The European Communities (Waste) Regulations, 1979;
- The European Communities (Toxic and Dangerous Waste) Regulations, 1982;
- The European Communities (Waste Oils) Regulations, 1982;
- The European Communities (Waste) Regulations, 1984.

Type of Licensable Facilities
(a) Established Activity
(i) This is an activity which requires a waste licence and for which planning permission had been granted before the date set in the regulations and such permission had not ceased to have effect on the set date.
or
an activity which requires a waste licence and which had been carried on during the twelve months prior to the date set in the regulations provided it is not an authorised structure or an unauthorised use within the meaning of the planning Acts.

(ii) an activity not referred to in (i) which was lawfully being carried on before the commencement of the Waste Management Act that requires the use of BATNEEC.

(b)   Certified Facility
A certified facility is a local authority facility within its own functional area the development of which was certified by the Minister for the Environment under the planning regulations having regard to an Environmental Impact Statement.

(c)   Existing Facility
An existing facility is one which is either a certified facility or one at which the disposal of waste was carried on during the twelve months ending on 1st May 1997 and such disposal was carried on in accordance with a waste permit (where required) granted by the local authority.

Significant Stages of Licensing Procedure
The significant stages in the licensing procedure are shown in Fig. 1 below.

A licence is obtained by applying to the EPA, who provide pre-application clarification/consultation facilities for the applicant. Special attention must be paid to EPA publications e.g. Landfill Manuals, BATNEEC Guidance notes. The EPA manuals Waste Licensing - Application Guidance Notes and Waste Management Licensing - Guide to implementation and enforcement in Ireland were published to aid applicants.

Application Procedure
- To alert third parties of the applicants intention to apply to the EPA for a licence the applicant must:

  ➢ publish a notice in a newspaper circulating in the area (2 weeks prior to lodging application)

  ➢ erect a notice on the site

  ➢ notify the planning authority for the area where the facility is located.

The contents required for the above notices are set out in the regulations.

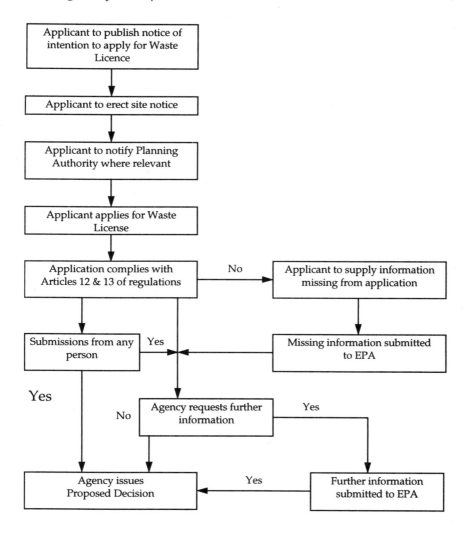

Fig. 4.1 - EPA Waste Licensing Procedures [Application to Proposed Decision]

Application Procedure (cont'd.)

- Applications should be submitted to the EPA headquarters including:

  ➢ completed application form (5 copies)
  ➢ copies of newspaper notice

> ➢ copies of plans and documents showing location of site notices, emission and sampling points
> ➢ appropriate fee.

The EPA may seek additional information necessary to make its decision on the application. Where the application is for a new facility the Environmental Impact Statement (EIS) must be submitted (15 copies).

- Any person may make a written submission to the EPA in relation to the application for the licence. Submissions must be made within one month from the date the EPA makes documentation available for public inspection. The applicant and planning authority will be notified of any submissions and decisions about these.

- The proposed decision will be:

  > ➢ available for public inspection
  > ➢ forwarded to the planning authority for public display and inspection
  > ➢ displayed in EPA offices and copies provided at a reasonable cost.

Figure 4.2, below, outlines the process of the issuing of a proposed decision on an application.

If there are no objections the EPA will issue its decision in line with its proposed decision.

Objections
- Any person or body can object to the EPA headquarters within 28 days from the period of notification date of issue of the proposed decision. Objections must be made in writing and include the appropriate fee and full details of the objection and the grounds/reasons/considerations/arguments on which it is based.

- The applicant and those who have submitted a valid objection will be issued with a copy of all other valid objections within one month from which a copy of the objection is issued. Objections will be fully considered by the EPA and it has absolute discretion in holding an oral hearing.

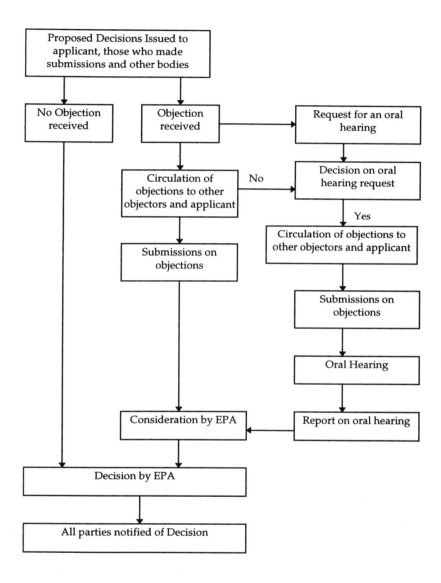

Fig. 4.2 Environmental Protection Agency Waste Licensing Procedures [Proposed Decision to Final Decision]

Objections (cont'd.)

- Requests for an oral hearing by a person making an objection must be in writing including fee and within the set period for objections. The EPA will notify the applicant for the licence and the appropriate local authority (7 days in advance) and will appoint a person to conduct the oral hearing. After the hearing the appointed person will inform the EPA of the recommendation to grant or refuse a licence.

- The EPA will then consider the application, objections, submissions, report and recommendation of the oral hearing to arrive at its decision. When a decision has been made the EPA will inform all parties and bodies who were involved in the process and those bodies specified in Article 18 of the regulations. The decision will be available for inspection at the offices of the EPA, planning authority offices and must be available for purchase.

Environmental Impact Statements (EIS)

An EIS may form part of the application for a waste licence for most new activities and for activities specified in the European Communities (Environmental Impact Assessment) Regulations 1989 to 1996 and must comply with these regulations.

Review of a Waste Licence

The EPA can review the license at any time. Licences authorising direct or indirect discharge to groundwater of certain substances listed in Council Directive 80/68/EEC of December 1979 must be reviewed at least once every four years. Requests by a licensee for a review must be made in writing including necessary documentation and required fee. When the EPA decides to review a licence the review in general follows the same procedures for application for a licence.

Changes in Activities

The EPA must be notified in writing of any cessation of an activity or proposed alternation or reconstruction of an activity that may increase emissions or lead to new emissions. The EPA may then review the licence under section 46 of the Act.

Enforcement

It is an offence not to comply with any condition of the licence and may lead to a fine or imprisonment. The EPA can also pursue the licensee where there is non-compliance with licence conditions or where environmental pollution might occur.

4.2   Waste Management (Packaging) Regulations, 1997

In 1994, the Irish Government adopted the then published strategy document "Recycling for Ireland" which set out the general approach to waste recycling for the period to 1999. The strategy established an overall objective of diverting 20% of commercial and domestic waste away from landfill to recycling. The target recycling rate in relation to packaging waste is 30%.

At the time of writing this book the Waste Management (Packaging) Regulations were in draft form. On the 18th February 1997 the draft regulations were published and the period of three months was given during which time any comments (in writing) could be made which might strengthen or improve the effectiveness of the draft Regulations. The target date for the Regulations to be brought into force was May 1997. The Regulations will be implemented under the Waste Management Act, 1996 and will give effect to articles 6 and 11 of the Council Directive on packaging and packaging waste (94/62/EC).

The purpose of the proposed Regulations is to implement the Council Directive and to follow national waste policies. There are two options open to organisations:

- become a member of an approved body
- comply independently by registering with their Local Authority

Recycling obligations are being imposed on suppliers who place packaging materials, packaging or packaged products on the Irish market. The Regulations cover all packaging waste that is used or released at industrial, commercial, office, shop, service or household level, regardless of the materials used or whether it concerns primary, secondary or tertiary packaging.

The Packaging Directive

In December 1994 the Packaging Directive was adopted by the European Union and came into operation in June 1996. A derogation has been granted to Ireland, Greece and Portugal which allows for lower recovery and recycling targets which other Member states must achieve within five years. The targets which Ireland must attain are as follows:

- by 30th June 2001, recovery of a minimum of 25% by weight of all packaging waste,
- by 31st December 2005, recovery of a minimum of 50% and maximum of 65% by weight of all packaging waste: such recovery must include:-

  ➢ recycling of 25% of packaging waste,
  ➢ recycling of a minimum of 15% of packaging waste from each individual packaging material.

Producer Responsibility

The draft Regulations describe a 'Major Producer' as a person who imports, manufactures, sells or otherwise supplies packaging material, packaging or packaged products where the aggregate weight is greater than 25 tonnes per year and has an annual turnover of more than £1,000,000.

According to article 5 and subject to article 15 of the Regulations a major producer must:

- display a conspicuous notice complying with Part 1 of the First Schedule indicating that packaging waste will be accepted

- provide adequate facilities at each premises for the acceptance, segregation and storage of packaging waste in accordance with these Regulations and whereby customers may remove and deposit packaging products or substances purchased at that premises. The facilities should be commensurate with the number of customers which normally frequent the premises concerned

- accept from any person, free of charge, at each premises any packaging waste of a type or brand supplied by that producer

- within one week of being requested to do so, arrange for collection of packaging waste from a producer

- ensure that packaging waste accepted or collected is recovered by or on behalf of the producer by a recovery operator

- comply with any request from a recovery operator for segregation of any component of waste made available for recovery by the recovery operator

- ensure that in any calendar month, the aggregate weight of packaging waste which is accepted or collected by the producer is not less than 40% of the aggregate weight of packaging supplied by that producer in the preceding calendar month (this target will only apply to suppliers who package products for supply or who import packaged products)

- export packaging and packaging destined for reuse will not taken into account for the purpose of aggregate weights

- a major producer who supplies packaging material or packaged products otherwise than from a premises in each county and county borough in which the producer carries on business, for the purpose of complying with the above requirements

- a major producer must register with their local authority on annual basis and pay a fee on the basis of £5 per tonne for any packaging that is handled (minimum £200 and maximum £1,000 payable)

- maintain records and information as set out in Part 3 of the Second Schedule and provide the local authority with monthly summary information on the amount of packaging which they place on the market. This information must be retained for a period of three years and be available to the public free of charge

- take steps as practicable to ensure that packaging waste arising from the producer's premises, (including secondary and tertiary) is either:

  ➢ taken back by the supplier

> ➢ recovered by or on behalf of the producer
> ➢ offered and made available for recovery.

- it is prohibited to import, manufacture or use packaging material and packaging after specified dates unless the aggregate concentration of lead, cadmium, mercury and hexavalent chromium does to exceed levels as outlined below:

Date	Concentration of metals - Aggregate
30th June 1998	- 600 parts per million by weight
30th June 1999	- 250 parts per million by weight
30th June 2001	- 100 parts per million by weight

Packaging composed of lead crystal glass is exempt.

A major producer who proposes not to accept packaging waste at a premises should:

- apply to the relevant local authority for authorisation to cease to accept such waste at the premises concerned unless so authorised in writing by the local authority

- not less than one day before ceasing to accept such waste, display a conspicuous notice complying with Part 2 of the First Schedule and must state the following from the Waste Management Act, 1996:

> "The acceptance of packaging waste on these premises for the purpose of recovery, will be temporarily suspended from [Date] and will resume on the 1st of [month] "

- the local authority will give a decision on an application for authorisation to cease within two working days.

Approved Bodies

Major producers who are members of an approved body such as Repak (an industry, IBEC scheme) are exempt from many requirements of the Regulations but not all its obligations. They avoid the need to accept the recovery of packaging and packaging waste on their own premises but must be granted a certificate by the approved body. They must display a notice to the effect that they are complying with Part 5 of the First Schedule and that they are participating in such a scheme.

In applying to the Minister for Environment for approval as an approved body, an organisation or association must provide details including financial plan, targets etc. as outlined in Article 15 of the Regulations. Approval is subject to the following conditions:

- measures to be undertaken for the recovery of packaging waste
- targets to be achieved for the recovery of packaging waste
- determination and verification of the effects of the above measure
- dissemination of information for the public regarding packaging and packaging waste
- submission of information (including financial accounts) to the Minister of Environment

The Minister of Environment may vary by notice in writing any condition attached to an approval under this article and may revoke an approval if an approved body is not complying with the above conditions.

An approved body must notify the local authority of any producer situate within the functional area when a certificate has been granted or revoked.

Enforcement
Each local authority will be responsible for the enforcement of the Regulations within their functional areas and will have a wide range of powers and penalties at their disposal as provided in the Waste Management Act, 1996.

Non-compliance with the Regulations is an offence and may result in:

- on summary conviction, a £1,500 fine and/or 12 months imprisonment, and
- on conviction on indictment, a fine of up to £10,000,000 and/or imprisonment for a term of up to 10 years

Under the Waste Management Act, 1996 an offence attributable to the neglect of an officer of the approved body, that person as well as the body will be liable to the proceedings and penalties accordingly.

4.3   Waste Management (Farm Plastic) Regulations, 1997

On the 29th January, 1997 the draft Regulations on farm plastic were published by the Minister for Environment. Farm plastic means polyethylene sheeting, wrap or bags for use in agriculture, horticulture, aquaculture or peat extraction. The purpose of the Regulations is to promote recycling of farm plastic in line with the Government's recycling objectives and to improve the amenity of the countryside. The Regulations came into operation in March 1997.

Producer Responsibility
The Regulations describe a 'Producer' as a person who imports, manufactures, sells or otherwise supplies farm plastic. "Offer and make available for recovery" means doing the following:

- segregating farm plastic waste into relevant categories (i.e. sheeting, bale, wrap and bags)
- notifying waste recovery operators about availability, nature, amount and location of waste
- providing farm plastic waste, free of charge
- storing that waste for not less than four weeks after notification or until collected by a recovery operator.

According to the Regulations a producer must:

- operate a deposit and refund scheme in relation to sales of farm plastic except where it is being supplied outside the State

- collect or arrange for collection of farm plastic waste and give the customer the deposit amount (equivalent to £200 per tonne supplied)

- obtain written statements for the amount of waste collected and retain these for a period not less than two years

- ensure importing farm plastic is collected, recovered or offered and made available for recovery as above

- obtain the use of a premises, provide containers and other equipment to ensure that farm plastic waste is collected, handled and stored in a manner that does not cause environmental pollution

- register and pay an annual fee to the local authority (£100) in whose functional area the producer operates in a form specified by that local authority and containing the information set out in Part 1of the Schedule

- apply for renewal of registration annually (not later than 31st January each year but not within six months of initial registration) in a form specified by that local authority and containing the information set out in Part 2of the Schedule

- submit a plan to the local authority on application and annually outlining the steps to be undertaken to comply with the Regulations containing the information set out in Part 4 of the Schedule and make available free of charge to any person who requests it

- the local authority may require the producer to supply specified information as appropriate to complying with the regulations and give notice of not less than 14 days to comply with the terms thereof

- compile, maintain and retain (for 1 year) information as set out in Part 3 of the Schedule and submit a monthly statement (within 10 days of the month end) to and as specified by the relevant local authority

- the producer must establish that the waste recovery operator is engaged in bone fide waste recovery activities

Approved Bodies

To become an approved body the procedure is set out in article 14 to 18 in the Regulation and is the same as the approval under the Waste Management (Packaging) Regulations and covered in Section 3.8 of this book. In the same way as with packaging waste, farm plastic manufacturers and importers will be exempt from many requirements of the Regulations by participating in an approved scheme for the collection and recovery of waste plastic. The Irish

Farms Films Group (a group established by the plastics industry and the Irish Farmers association) has been approved under the Regulations and will operate a national collection and recovery scheme for waste farm plastic.

4.4   New EMAS Regulation and IPC Licensing Initiative

The National Accreditation Board (NAB) and the Environmental Protection Agency (EPA) has recently formed an initiative to look at increasing coherence between Integrated Pollution Prevention and Control (IPPC) and EMAS. It is proposed that there would be a combined audit to EMAS and IPC Licensing. They would also have a common EMS and reporting format based on the EMAS Environmental Statement.

The NAB is an Accreditation Body. It accredits Bodies certifying to ISO 14001 and acting as EMAS Verifiers. The EPA as previously mentioned in Section 3.2 are responsible for IPC Licensing. IPC Licensing legislation is very similar to the IPCC Directive 96/61/EC.

The Benefits of the New Initiative between IPC and EMAS
The adoption of this initiative would have the following advantages:

- A combined audit for IPC and EMAS will be less costly than auditing both individually
- Environmental Reporting will have a common format leading to the EMAS Environmental Statement becoming the basis of Public Reporting. Also NAB has been appointed the National Competent Body for registration of sites participating in the EMAS Scheme.
- Environmental Management Systems are common to regulatory and voluntary activities and incorporated into mainstream management decision-making
- Greater level of environmental assurance
- Improved timeliness of reporting
- Better utilisation of resources with commonality of audits, reports and elements of both instruments
- More timely and coherent information flow to the public, regulators and the competent body.

Implementation of Initiative

Implementation will require agreement on certain specific issues and promulgation of a "Guidance Document" for sites and verifiers who are willing to adopt the proposed approach. Participation in the proposed approach will be voluntary. The 'coherent approach' will be implemented only in cases where both agencies are satisfied that their respective responsibilities will not be compromised.

5 ENVIRONMENTAL MANAGEMENT SYSTEM STANDARDS

5.1 Choice of an EMS Standard or EU Regulation

In 1972 the Ernst Winter & Sohn Company in Germany developed an EMS model known as the Winter Model. The Canadian Chemical Producers Association (CCPA) Responsible Care® program for chemical companies in 1984 developed its own Global Environmental Management Initiative (GEMI). In 1992 the Vienna Agreement was set up to ensure compatibility of standards at both European and International levels.

In the absence of European and International EMS standards, Standard Institutions in different countries have published their own standards in support of Article 12 of the Eco-Management and Audit Scheme (EMAS) regulation, which provides for the use of national, European and international standards.

Since March 1997 the British Standard BS 7750 has been withdrawn, due to adoption of ISO 14001 in the UK. This means that the accrediting Registrars in England will transfer registration of organisations that have BS 7750 to ISO 14001. Certificates for BS 7750 have remained valid up to the end of March.

The Irish EMS Standard, I.S. 310 has not yet been withdrawn in favour of ISO 14001. This is due to the National Standards Authority of Ireland opting to retain I.S. 310 until ISO 14001 complies fully with EMAS (which I.S. 310 does). There are currently some areas which ISO 14001 falls short of EMAS:

- Environmental reports - ISO 14001 does not require public declaration on environmental status
- Environmental policies, legal environmental proceedings and complaints.

At the moment it is not known when there will be conformity between ISO 14001 and EMAS. Bridging documents have been produced but so far have not been accepted. When harmony has been reached it is likely that I.S. 310 will be withdrawn.

Both I.S. 310 and BS 7750 will be of historical significance in understanding EMS Standards. Obviously, exposure to more than one EMS model gives one a greater understanding of environmental management systems. Some would argue that organisations who have been approved to I.S. 310 or BS 7750 and subsequently to ISO 14001 would have a much better system and would have benefited from this experience. So, although BS 7750 has been withdrawn and I.S. 310 will be once agreement between EMAS and ISO 14000 has been sanctioned, their relevance should not be dismissed, especially if ISO 14001 is updated at some future date.

The following will be dealt with in this text:

1. I.S. 310 - Irish EMS Standard
2. BS 7750 - British EMS Standard
3. EU ECO - Management and Audit Scheme
4. ISO 14000 Series

I.S. 310

The Irish Standard, I.S. 310, was published in January 1994 by the National Standards Authority of Ireland (NSAI) and the Environmental Standards Consultative Committee (ESCC). The standard was formally recognised by the European Commission in February 1996 as satisfying the corresponding requirements of the EMAS.

The standard is divided into:

(a) Part 1: Guiding Principles and Definitions
(b) Part 2: Requirements

The requirements for an EMS as defined in Part 2 of I.S. 310:1994 are as follows:

4.   Requirements
4.0 Environmental Management System
4.1 Management Commitment
4.2 General Review
4.3 Environmental Policy
    4.3.1   General
    4.3.2   Environmental Performance Objectives & Targets
    4.3.3   Environmental Policy Statement
4.4 Management Structure, Responsibilities & Accountability

4.4.1   Organisation Structure & Resources
4.4.2   Senior Manager
4.4.3   Awareness & Training
4.5 Environmental Management Programme
4.6 Environmental Performance Measurement & Register
4.7 Environmental Management Documentation
4.7.1   Environmental Management Manual
4.7.2   Control of Documentation
4.8 Operational Control
4.9 Operational Performance Verification
4.10 Corrective Action
4.11 Environmental Management Records
4.12 Environmental Management System Audits
4.13 Environmental Management System Review
4.14 Environmental Reports

According to the I.S. 310 Standard what is involved in registration to the standard is the provision by management of all the necessary elements of a reliable environmental protection system. The EMS must then be developed and implemented

These elements can be summarised as comprising the following viz.:

- A Company Policy relating to its own impact on the environment
- A Programme of measures for reducing that impact
- A management system to ensure, by appropriate organisation and procedures, that the Programme of measures is efficiently implemented.

BS 7750

This standard was originally published in March 1992. It was prepared by the Environment and Pollution Standards Policy Committee in response to increasing concerns about environmental protection and environmental performance. The standard provided a specification for an EMS, ensuring compliance with environmental policies and objectives, guidance on the specification and implementation within the organisation management system.

The standard was up-dated in 1994 to reflect the results of the BS 7750 pilot project and the Eco-management and Audit Scheme (EMAS).

The standard is divided into:

(a) Specification
(2) Annexes - A guide to EMS requirements

The following is a contents list to BS 7750:

Committees responsible
Forward
Specification

1 Scope
2 Informative References
3 Definitions
4 Environmental Management System Requirements
4.1 Environmental Management System
4.2 Environmental Policy
4.3 Organisation and Personnel
4.4 Environmental Effects
4.5 Environmental Objectives and Targets
4.6 Environmental Management Programme
4.7 Environmental Management Manual and Documentation
4.8 Operational Control
4.9 Environmental Management Records
4.10 Environmental Management Audits
4.11 Environmental Management Reviews

Contents list to BS 7750 Cont'd.

Annexes
A Guide to EMS Requirements
A.1 Environmental Management System
A.2 Environmental Policy
A.3 Organisation and Personnel
A.4 Environmental Effects
A.5 Environmental Objectives and Targets
A.6 Environmental Management Programme
A.7 Environmental Management Manual and Documentation

A.8 Operational Control

A.9 Environmental Management Records

A.10 Environmental Management Audits

A.11 Environmental Management Reviews

B Links to BS 5750 'Quality Systems'

C Links to the draft EC Eco-Audit Regulation

D Bibliography of glossaries and other sources
of general information on environmental matters

EMAS

The European Council adopted the Eco-management and audit regulation scheme in June 1993. The scheme was opened for voluntary participation by companies from April 1995. It's objective is to promote continuous environmental performance improvements of industrial activities. Industrial sites will commit themselves to evaluate and improve their environmental performance and provide relevant information to the public.

The Regulations complete title is:

"COUNCIL REGULATION (EEC) No 1836/93 of 29 June 1993 allowing voluntary participation by companies in the industrial sector in a Community Eco-Management and Audit Scheme". It is taken from the "Official Journal of the European Commission".

According to Article 3 for a site to participate in the scheme it must:

- adopt an environmental policy, (according to Annex I requirements) comply with the relevant environmental regulatory requirements, commit itself to continuous improvement of environmental performance and reduce environmental effects by economically viable application of best available technology;
- conduct an environmental review of the site on aspects referred to in Annex I, part C;
- introduce an environmental programme and environmental management system (EMS) for the site (the EMS must comply with Annex I requirements);
- carry out site environmental audits according to Article 4;
- set objectives aimed at continuous improvement of environmental performance in the light of audit results and

revise the environmental programme as appropriate to enable achievement of objectives;

- prepare an environmental statement in accordance with Article 5 and to include information referred to in Annex V;
- examine the environmental policy, programme, management system, review or audit procedure and environmental statement(s) to verify that they meet Regulation requirements and that environmental statements are validated (according to Article 4 and Annex III);
- the environmental statement must be validated by a competent body of the Member State where the site is located and disseminate it as appropriate to the public (according to article 8)

EMAS Requirements including articles and annexes are as follows:

Article Requirement
1. The Eco-Management and Audit Scheme and its Objectives
2. Definitions
3. Participation in the Scheme
4. Auditing and Validation
5. Environmental Statement
6. Accreditation and Supervision of Environmental Verifiers
7. List of Accredited Environmental Verifiers
8. Registration of Sites
9. Publication of a List of Registered Sites
10. Statement of Participation
11. Costs and Fees
12. Relationship with National, European and International Standards
13. Promotion of Companies' Participation, in Particular of Small and Medium-Sized Enterprises
14. Inclusion and Other Sectors
15. Information
16. Infringements
17. Annexes
18. Competent Bodies
19. Committee
20. Revision

Annex

I   REQUIREMENTS CONCERNING ENVIRONMENTAL POLICIES, PROGRAMMES AND MANAGEMENT SYSTEMS

A. Environmental Policies, Objectives and Programmes
    – Environmental Objectives
    – Environmental Programme for the Site
B. Environmental Management Systems
    – Organisation and Personnel
    – Environmental Effects
    – Operational Control
    – Environmental Management Documentation
C. Issues to be Covered
D. Good Management Practices

II REQUIREMENTS CONCERNING ENVIRONMENTAL AUDITING

A. Objectives
B. Scope
C. Organisation and Resources
D. Planning and Preparation for Site Audit
E. Audit Activities
F. Reporting Audit Findings and Conclusions
G. Audit Follow-up
H. Audit Frequency

III REQUIREMENTS CONCERNING THE ACCREDITATION OF ENVIRONMENTAL VERIFIERS

A. Requirements for the Accreditation of Environmental Verifiers
    – Accreditation Criteria
    – Accreditation of Individuals
    – Application for Accreditation
    – Accreditation Process
    – Supervision of Accredited Verifiers
    – Extension of Accredited Scope
B. The Function of Verifiers

Basic Guide to Implementing EMAS

The organisation must first establish that it is involved in the industrial activity as listed in "Council Regulation No. 3037/90" denoted by NACE classifications. The Revised Regulation for publication early in 1998 will open EMAS to most sectors.

The following actions might be useful in implementing EMAS:

- A complete site description and map should be provided showing the actual location and infrastructure of the site with boundaries marked in red.

- Prepare a file of all information applicable to the environment, including drawings, maps, emission/discharge points, procedures, plans, copies of planning permission, licenses etc.

- Prepare an Environmental Policy. This should demonstrate the organisation's commitment to environmental protection and should cover targets, objectives, compliance with legislation and continuous improvement of environmental performance.

- Carry out the Environmental Review. This is the initial identification and analysis of all the organisation's environmental effects.

- Establish an Environmental Programme. This will entail quantified targets and objectives and mechanisms to achieve and review these.

- Produce an Environmental Statement. This statement should be designed for the public and written in a concise and comprehensive form. According to the Article 5 of the Regulation it should include the following:

  ➢ a description of the company's activities at the site to be considered;
  ➢ an assessment of all the significant environmental issues of relevance to the activities concerned;
  ➢ a summary of the figures on pollutant emissions, waste generation, consumption of raw material, energy and water, noise and other significant environmental aspects, as appropriate;
  ➢ other factors regarding environmental performance;
  ➢ a presentation of the company's environmental policy, programme and management system implemented at the site considered;

➤ the deadline set for submission of the next statement;
➤ the name of the accredited environmental verifier.

- Have the Environmental Statement validated. This needs to be performed by an independent, accredited environmental verifier. Validation will involve an on-site assessment of the environmental policy, environmental programme, environmental management system, procedures to ensure that they meet EMAS requirements.

- Apply for site registration. The company must submit the following to the Competent Body for independent verification (the National Accreditation Board as the Competent Body will be responsible for accreditation of environmental verifiers):

  ➤ Completed Application Form
  ➤ Application Fee
  ➤ Validated Environmental Statement
  ➤ Information on the company as outlined in Annex V of the Regulation. This includes: name of the company, site name and location, description of site activities, name of accredited verifier, deadline for submission of next validated environmental statement, description of the sites EMS and auditing programme.

- Successfully registered sites will be awarded a Statement of Participation by the Competent Body, demonstrating their involvement in the scheme and allowing them to publicise this on company stationary and correspondence

5.2   The ISO 14000 Series

The Workings of Technical Committee (TC) 207

Within the International Standards Organisation (ISO) a technical committee ISO/TC 207 was formed in 1993. There were 500 delegates representing 47 countries. Their objective was to work towards the development of acceptable international environmental management standards. ISO/TC 207 was formed into sub committees and working groups. ISO/TC 207 Sub Committee 1 (SC1) deals with Environmental Management Systems and has two Working Groups WG1 and WG2. The Working Groups have prepared Committee Drafts and circulated these for agreement and ballot. In June 1995 the committee designated ISO 14001, Environmental Management System Specification draft international standard (DIS) status. In September 1, 1996, ISO 14001 and ISO 14004 were published as internationally accepted standards and are open to organisations for use.

The Significance of the New Standard

ISO 14001's purpose is to provide assistance to organisations in implementing or improving an EMS and is consistent with the goal of "Sustainable Development".

The ISO 14000 series contains the following published standards:

- ISO 14001 : EMS Specification and Guidance for Use
- ISO 14004 : EMS General Guidelines on Principles, Systems and Supporting Techniques
- ISO 14010 : Guidelines for Environmental Auditing-General Principles
- ISO 14011 : Guidelines for Environmental Auditing-Audit Procedures -Auditing of EMS
- ISO 14012 : Guidelines for Environmental Auditing - Qualification Criteria for Environmental Auditors.

The following ISO 14000 series standards are at various stages of development:

- ISO 14013 : Management of Environmental Audit Programmes
- ISO 14014 : Initial Reviews
- ISO 14015 : Environmental Site Assessment
- ISO 14020 : Goals and Principles of all Environmental Labelling
- ISO 14021 : Environmental Labelling-Self Declaration Environmental Claims-Terms and Definitions
- ISO 14022 : Environmental Labelling-Symbols
- ISO 14023 : Environmental Labelling-Testing and Verification
- ISO 14024 : Environmental Labelling - Guiding Principles, Practices and Criteria for Multiple Criteria-based Practitioner Programmes
- ISO 14031 : Environmental Performance Evaluation

- ISO 14040 : Life Cycle Assessment - Principles and Guidelines
- ISO 14041 : Life Cycle Assessment-Life Cycle Inventory Analysis
- ISO 14042 : Life Cycle Assessment-Impact Assessment
- ISO 14043 : Life Cycle Assessment - Interpretation
- ISO 14050 : Terms and Definitions-Guide on the Principles of ISO/TC/207/SC Terminology Work
- ISO Guide 64 :Guide for the Inclusion of Environmental Aspects of Product Standards

Because of the enormous success of International Standard ISO 9000 (Quality Management System) with over 70,000 registrations world-wide, it is believed that ISO 14001 will receive similar international acceptability. Consequently, there is an unprecedented international interest in the new standard. Indeed, many organisations have prepared for certification to ISO 14001 on the basis of the draft documentation in advance of the now published ISO 14001 standard.

Apart from the benefits associated with environmental management systems in controlling environmental aspects etc. (see section 2.1), there are other benefits in being certified to ISO 14001. These are:

- expected to achieve the world-wide acceptance as a standard that ISO 9000 has attained;
- will minimise trade barriers;
- multi-national organisations will have the possibility to have uniform acceptance of ISO 14001 throughout all their facilities (assuming that there will soon be agreement between ISO 14001 and EMAS);
- enhancement of public perception on a global scale;
- a single standard will ensure there is no conflict between interpretations of different EMS standards;
- as ISO 9000 has become a pre-requisite for doing business in many markets, ISO 14001 may also become a requirement for doing business;
- ISO 14001 may promote international trade.

Comparison of the ISO 14000 Series and ISO 9000 Series
Those organisation registered to ISO 9001 or ISO 9002 (Quality Management Series), will find many similarities with ISO 14001. In developing the ISO 14000 Series, ISO/TC 207 liaised with ISO/TC 176 which developed the ISO 9000 standard. Therefore ISO 9000 can be considered a good base for an organisation applying for ISO 14001. ISO 14001 has the same fundamental systems elements as ISO 9000, for example, documentation control, management system auditing, training, corrective action. Where both standards clearly differ is in the setting of objectives and targets, environmental aspects, legal and other requirements, internal and external communication. The operation of ISO 14001 calls for quantifying targets to reduce environmental impacts or aspects and continual improvement.

Annex B Tables B.1 and B.2 of ISO 14001:1996 shows correspondence between ISO 9001 and ISO 14001. To summarise the common elements between ISO 9001/ISO 14001:

- Organisation/Structure and Responsibility
- Quality Policy/Environmental Policy
- Management Review
- Document and Data Control/Document Control
- Control of Inspection, Measuring and Test Equipment/Monitoring and Measurement
- Corrective and Preventive Action/Non-conformance and Corrective and Preventive Action
- Control of Quality Records/Records
- Internal Quality Audits/EMS Audit
- Training/Training, Awareness and Competence

However, being certified to ISO 9000, does not guarantee product quality or being certified to ISO 14001 does not guarantee good environmental performance. To implement either standards, because a customer request them, is also a serious pitfall. Both ISO 9000 and ISO 14001 are management systems, designed to provide the structure for an organisation to achieve improved product quality and environmental improvement. Their requirement of the necessity for continuous improvement is likely to lead to better environmental and quality performance. The outcome should be a positive one.

With ISO 9000 product quality is a contractual arrangement between supplier and customer, where the customer specifies their needs and these are agreed with the supplier. ISO 14001 is much more intangible and has a much wider public where specifying environmental requirements is really taking the views of interested parties and formulating these into policy, objectives and targets. Assessment of an organisation's ability to prevent pollution and continually improve is difficult but is achieved by setting quantifiable objectives and targets.

The Content of ISO 14001
ISO 14004 defines the key principles for management in implementing an EMS as:

- Recognise that environmental management is among the highest priorities
- Establish and maintain communications with internal and external parties
- Determine the legislative requirements and environmental aspects associated with the organisation's activities, products and services
- Develop management and employee commitment to the protection of the environment, with clear assignment of accountability and responsibility
- Encourage environmental planning throughout the product or process life cycle
- Establish a disciplined management process for achieving targeted performance levels
- Provide appropriate and sufficient resources, including training, to achieve targeted performance levels on an ongoing basis
- Evaluate environmental performance against appropriate policies, objectives and targets and seek improvement where appropriate
- Establish a management process to review and audit the EMS and to identify opportunities for improvement of the system and resulting environmental performance
- Encourage contractors and suppliers to establish an EMS.

The structure of ISO 14001 is as follows:

Clause		Content
1		Scope
2		Normative references
3		Definitions
4		Environmental management system requirements
	4.1	General requirements
	4.2	Environmental policy
	4.3	Planning
		4.3.1 Environmental aspects
		4.3.2 Legal and other requirements
		4.3.3 Objectives and targets
		4.3.4 Environmental management programme(s)
	4.4	Implementation and operation
		4.4.1 Structure and responsibility
		4.4.2 Training, awareness and competence
		4.4.3 Communication
		4.4.4 EMS documentation
		4.4.5 Document control
		4.4.6 Operational control
		4.4.7 Emergency preparedness and response
	4.5	Checking and corrective action
		4.5.1 Monitoring and measurement
		4.5.2 Non-conformance, corrective & preventative action
		4.5.3 Records
		4.5.4 Environmental management system audit
	4.6	Management review

Annexes

A	Guidance on the use of the specification
B	Links between ISO 14001 and ISO 9001
C	Bibliography

Synopsis of the ISO 14001 Standard

Introduction: Gives an overview of the guideline, uses of the standard and a diagrammatic EMS model for ISO 14001 International Standard.

1. **Scope:** Explains that the standard specifies requirements for an EMS, applies to environmental aspects over which the organisation can control and be expected to influence and reasons for an organisation seeking to obtain the standard.

2. **Normative References:** Current editions of the standards are given but these are subject to revision. Currently there are no normative references.

3. **Definitions:** These are useful definitions of common environmental terminology applicable to the standard.

4. **Environmental Management System Requirements**

I.   **General Requirements:** An organisation shall establish and maintain an EMS in line with the requirements of Clause 4.

II. **Environmental Policy:** Outlines the requirements of the organisations environmental policy including:

   - Nature, scale and environmental impacts covering activities, products and services
   - Commitment to continual improvement and prevention of pollution
   - Compliance with legislation and other requirements of the organisation
   - Framework for setting and reviewing objectives and targets
   - Documented, implemented and maintained and communicated to employees
   - Available to the public

III. **Planning:**

4.3.1 Environmental Aspects:
   - Procedure(s) to identify environmental aspects of its activities, products or services
   - Determination of those that have a significant environmental impact

- Significant impacts must be considered when setting environmental objectives
- Information on environmental aspects must be kept up to date

4.3.2 Legal and other Requirements:
- Procedures should be maintained to identify, have access to legal and other requirements to which the organisation subscribes
- Applicable to environmental aspects of activities, products and services

4.3.3 Objectives and Targets:
- Establish/maintain at each relevant level within the organisation
- In establishing and reviewing, consider legal and other requirements, significant environmental aspects, technological options and organisation financial, operational and business requirements, and views of interested parties.
- Consistent with the environmental policy and indicate a commitment to prevention of pollution.

4.3.4 Environmental Management Programme(s):
- Programme to achieve its objectives and targets
- Designation of responsibility for objectives and targets at each function and level
- Means and time-frame for achieving objectives and targets
- Organisational changes should be reflected in the programme and environmental management applied to these projects

4.4 Implementation and Operation:

4.4.1 Structure and Responsibility:
- Roles, responsibility and authorities defined, documented and communicated
- Resources for human, specialised skills, technology and financial.

- Specific management representative(s) with authority to:
  a) establish and implement an EMS according to ISO 14001
  b) report on performance for review and improvement of the EMS

4.4.2 Training Awareness and Competence:

- Identify training needs
- Provide appropriate training/experience to those whose work creates a significant impact on the environment.
- Procedures and employee awareness must be undertaken on:
  a) importance of conformance to the environmental policy, procedure and the EMS requirements
  b) actual or potential significant environmental impacts and the benefits of improved personal performance;
  c) roles and responsibilities in achieving conformance with policy, EMS requirements including emergency preparedness and response requirements;
  d) potential consequences of a departure from specified operating procedures.
- Personnel competency based on education, training and/or experience.

4.4.3 Communication:

- Good internal communication process
- System to respond to relevant communication from external interested parties
- Consideration of processes for external communication on significant environmental aspects and records of decision.

4.4.4 Environmental Management System Documentation:

- Establish and maintain information in paper or electronic form
- Information to describe core elements of the management system and their interaction
- Provide direction to related documentation.

4.4.5 Document Control:

- Procedures required to control all ISO 14001 documents ensure that :
    a) they can be located
    b) periodically reviewed, revised and authorised approval
    c) current revisions at all locations
    d) obsolete documents removed from point of use
    e) any obsolete documents retained for legal and/or knowledge preservation purposes suitably identified
- Documentation legible, dated and readily identifiable
- Maintained in an orderly manner and retention time specified
- Procedures and responsibilities for document modification.

4.4.6 Operational Control:

- Identify operations and activities associated with significant environmental aspects
- Plant activities, including maintenance, to be carried out under controlled conditions
- Procedures to cover situations where there absence could lead to deviations from environmental policy and objectives and targets
- Operating criteria in procedures
- Communication of procedures and requirements to suppliers and contractors

4.4.7 Emergency Preparedness and Response:

- Procedures to identify potential for, response to accident and emergency situations associated environmental impacts
- Revise after occurrence of accidents or emergency situations
- Periodically test procedures where applicable

4.5   Checking and Corrective Action

4.5.1 Monitoring and measurement
- Procedures to monitor and measure key characteristics
- Record information to track performance, operational controls and environmental objectives and targets
- Calibrate monitoring equipment
- Periodically evaluate compliance with environmental legislation and regulations

4.5.2 Non-conformance and Corrective and Preventive Action
- Procedures for responsibility and authority to handle and investigate non-conformance, actions to mitigate impacts and for corrective and preventive action.
- Corrective and preventive action to eliminate cause of actual/potential non-conformance
- Implement and record any changes in procedures as result of corrective and preventive action

4.5.3 Records
- Procedures for identification, maintenance and disposition of environmental records
- Include training records, audit and review results
- Records legible, identifiable and traceable to activity, product or service
- Record retention times
- To demonstrate conformance to ISO 14001

4.5.4 Environmental Management System Audit
- Periodic EMS audits to be carried out, in order to:
    a) determine whether or not the EMS
        1) conformance and to planned environmental management and to ISO 14001
        2) properly implemented and maintained
    b) results of audits provided to management
- Audit programme and schedule based on environmental importance of activity
- Audit scope, frequency, methodologies, responsibilities and requirements to be included

4.6 Management Review
- Management to periodically review the EMS to ensure continuing suitability, adequacy and effectiveness

- Ensure necessary information is collected and document review
- Address possible need for changes to policy, objectives and elements of the EMS

Basic Guide to Implementing ISO 14001

- Senior management commitment is required before beginning with the ISO 14001 implementation project. A senior manager should be appointed, resources allocated to the project (financial and personnel resources), authority given to implement to the responsible person to implement the EMS requirements.
- Prepare a comprehensive initial environmental review by examining the organisation's aspects of it's activities from the site. Consider all relevant legislation, past and future activities and the environmental impacts of these.
- In identifying the environmental impacts, involve the views of interested parties who are concerned with the organisation's environmental performance.
- Define and document the organisation's environmental policy, demonstrating commitment to complying with regulations and legislation, pollution prevention and continual improvement.
- Communicate the environmental policy to all employees and involve them in the information gathering and improvement process.
- Make the environmental policy available publicly.
- Determine the organisation's environmental objectives, targets and decide on quantifiable measurements for these.
- Establish the environmental programme for how the goals and targets will be achieved and how improvements will be implemented.
- Implement the EMS by establishing procedures, controls for environmental impacts, implementing environmental policy, communication methods, audits, review etc. Auditing and review will enable continuous improvement.
- Measure progress by periodic monitoring of significant environmental impacts.

- Establish corrective and preventive action to deal with results of monitoring, complaints and application of legislation.
- Conduct management review to ensure continuing effectiveness of the EMS, environmental policy, environmental performance and future organisation needs.

ISO 14004

This is a guidance standard to provide assistance to organisations implementing or improving an EMS. Its not an auditable standard but rather lists the elements that should be considered as an aid to implementing an EMS. ISO 14004 is based on five principles as follows:

Principle 1 Commitment and Policy
- Define policy and ensure commitment to the EMS

Principle 2 Planning
- Formulate plan to fulfil policy

Principle 3 Implementation
- Develop necessary capabilities and support mechanisms to achieve policy, objectives and targets

Principle 4 Measurement and Evaluation
- Measure, monitor and evaluate environmental performance

Principle 5 Review and Improvement
- Review and continually improve the EMS to improve overall performance

Explanation of TC 207's Development of other Main Standards

Environmental Performance Evaluation (EPE) - ISO 14031
This standard is being developed to provide guidance in measuring the outputs of the EMS, relating to the organisation's control of the impact of its activities, products and services on the environment, based on its environmental policy, objectives and targets. The evaluation process involves disseminating performance data, determining how well objectives and targets are being met and making the data publicly available.

Environmental Auditing (EA) - DIS ISO 14010 - 14013

These standards provide guidance on principles for auditing, qualification criteria and how audits should be conducted. Audits should be conducted by competent individuals who are capable of maintaining objectivity, impartiality and determining conformity of the EMS with requirements.

Environmental Labelling (EL) - ISO 14020, CD ISO 14021/22, PWI ISO 14023/24

These standards are to provide guidance in environmental labelling symbols, test and verification, certification procedures etc. Currently eco-labels are used throughout the world, but there needs to be more control in the criteria used to define their use. The ISO standards will address requirements and harmonise a system whereby products can use environmental labelling.

Life Cycle Assessment (LCA) - WD ISO 14040/42, CD ISO 14041, PWI ISO 14043

These standards will ensure a systematic programme is used in the analysing and quantifying environmental impacts on products, processes and services during the entire product life cycle. In determining where environmental impacts occur, energy and material flows of products and processes are evaluated. After manufacture product distribution methods, disposal and recycling are examined to determine potential environmental impacts.

Environmental Aspects of Product Standards - WD ISO 14060

This standard is intended as a guidance for design elements that can affect the environment. It provides terminology and methods that can be used in new product development and how to assess how product standards can influence environment effects.

5.3   Responsible Care® Systems

Introduction

Responsible Care® originated in Canada and the USA. The first formal Responsible Care® programme in Europe was begun in 1989 by the Chemical Industries Association (CIA) in the UK, followed by the UIC in France in 1990. While Responsible Care® is the same fundamental system and has voluntary membership of chemical industries, each country is at a different stage of development and uses it to best suit their particular needs.

Responsible Care® in Ireland

The umbrella organisation for Responsible Care® in Ireland is the Irish Pharmaceutical and Chemical Manufacturers Federation (IPCMF). The chemical industries launched its Responsible Care® programme in 1992. As a member federation of CEFIC (European Chemical Industry Council), the industry association's Responsible Care®, guiding principles are based on CEFIC guidelines; however for reasons including the fact that many of the federation's members are subsidiaries/branches of US based companies, much of the federation's Responsible Care® programme is otherwise based on the US CMA approach.

Thus its 3 Codes of management practice, (Process Safety, Environment and Distribution) draw heavily on CMA codes. More significantly, as a first step in monitoring company performance with respect to Responsible Care®, the federation adopted the US approach of monitoring progress towards implementing each code. This was to be, and has been, replaced by more direct monitoring of performance. In the environmental area, for example, the federation subsequently adopted the CEFIC guideline on environmental monitoring in its entirety, and companies have been reporting emissions for 3 years. Emission data is shortly to be collected for 1995 and plans are for the combined data for the past 4 years to be published.

This text will explain the CMA and CIA approaches and the role of the CEFIC.

The CMA Approach:

CMA member companies pledge to manage their business according to the following Guiding Principles:

- To recognise and respond to community concerns about chemicals and our operations.
- To develop and produce chemicals that can be manufactured, transported, used and disposed of safely.

- To report promptly to officials, employees, customers and the public, information on chemical-related health and environmental hazards and to recommend protective measures.
- To make health, safety and environmental considerations a priority in our planning for all existing and new products and processes.
- To participate with government and others in creating responsible laws, regulations and standards to safeguard the community, workplace and environment.
- To counsel customers on the safe use, transportation and disposal of chemical products.
- To operate our plants and facilities in a manner that protects the environment and health and safety of our employees and the public.
- To extend knowledge by conducting or supporting research on the health, safety and environmental effects of our products, processes and waste materials.
- To work with others to resolve problems created by past handling and disposal of hazardous substances.
- To promote the principles and practices of Responsible Care® by sharing experiences and offering assistance to others who produce, handle and dispose of chemicals.

There are six Codes of Management Practices. CMA members and their partners must make good-faith efforts to attain the goals of each Code. The Codes are as follows:

1. Community Awareness and Emergency Response (CAER) Code. It brings together the chemical industry and local communities through communication and co-operative emergency planning. Management practices should include a programme for:
    - Community Awareness and Outreach
    - Emergency Response and Preparedness

2. Pollution prevention Code. It promotes industry efforts to protect human health and the environment by reducing waste generation and pollutant emissions. Management practices should include a programme for:

- Pollution Prevention

3. Process Safety Code. This code is designed to prevent fires, explosions and chemical releases by identifying areas where improvement in safety performance can be made from process design through continuous operation and routine maintenance. Management practices should include an on-going process safety programme and should cover:
   - Management Leadership
   - Technology
   - Facilities
   - Personnel

4. Distribution Code. This code is designed to help reduce the risk that transportation and storage of chemicals pose to the public, carriers, customers, contractors, employees and to the environment. Management practices should include:
   - Risk Management
   - Compliance review
   - Carrier safety
   - Handling and Storage
   - Emergency Preparedness

5. Employee Health and Safety Code. This protects and promotes the health and safety of those people working at or visiting CMA member company or Partner sites. Management practices should include an ongoing health and safety programme to cover the following:
   - Programme Management
   - Identification and Evaluation
   - Prevention and Control
   - Communications and Training

6. Product Stewardship Code. It is designed to make health, safety and environmental protection an integral part of designing, manufacturing, distributing, using, recycling and disposing of chemical products. Management practice should have an ongoing product stewardship process that demonstrates:
   - Management Leadership and Commitment
   - Information and Characterisation

- Risk Management

Other elements that embrace the CMA approach are its :

- Public Advisory Panel which assist the chemical industry in identifying and developing programmes and actions that are responsive to public concerns.
- Member Self Evaluations. Member companies and their partners are invited to submit reports annually to the CMA on their progress in implementing each of the Codes of Practice. The self-evaluations measure progress and are a valuable management tool in showing where areas need more assistance.
- Management System Verification. CMA members and Partners develop their own management systems around the six Codes of Management Practices. Over the past year a management system verification (MSV) process has been developed for reviewing the member companies polices and procedures.
- Measures of Performance. In order to earn public trust CMA members and Partners must show they are improving their overall health, safety and environmental performance through Responsible Care®. The CMA has established credible, external performance measures for each of the six Codes.
- Executive Leadership Groups. These provide a forum for management to discuss and advance Responsible Care® implementation.
- Mutual Assistance calls for member companies and Partners to work together in sharing information and experience to successfully implement Responsible Care®.
- Partnership Programme allows eligible, non-CMA companies and state or national trade associations to participate directly in Responsible Care®.
- Obligation of Membership requires member companies and Partners to participate in Responsible Care® as defined by the CMA Board of Directors.

Management System Verification (MSV)
This is a new tool developed to assist CMA members and Partners in the continuous improvement of their management and

implementation of Responsible Care®. This process gives those participating the advantage of an outside view of the company's progress.

The procedure in carrying out a Responsible Care® management system verification is as follows:

- CMA member company volunteers for MSV by notifying CMA Responsible Care® Department.
- Verification team leader and members are selected.
- Supporting contractor identified.
- Team leader (supported by contractor) requests information and supporting documentation from Responsible Care® Co-ordinator.
- The scope and conduct of the verification is determined, as well as list of individuals to be interviewed and which facilities will be visited by the team.
- A Company/Verifier legal agreement for protection of confidential business information and indemnification of participants is signed.
- Participating facilities identify appropriate public representative to accompany verification team on its visits.
- The team leader will contact the public representatives to ensure they are aware of the selection and understand the verification process.
- The verification begins with the team's visit to company's headquarters (unless MSV is site-specific) to interview the executive contact and senior staff.
- Team visits selected facilities to interview plant manager and appropriate staff and conducts plant tour.
- Team conducts closing meeting with Responsible Care® Co-ordinator and appropriate staff.
- Team develops its final narrative report (only the company receives a copy of the final report).
- Each team member will certify that all work papers and related information are collected and destroyed. All documents supplied to the team will be returned to the company.
- Team submits their expense reports to the CMA.
- CMA issues recognition of participation to company.

The MSV core elements are:
- Policy and Leadership
- Planning
- Implementation, Operation and Accountability
- Performance Measurement and Corrective Action
- Management Review and Reporting

Attributes are listed A1 to E4 are listed under each of the above elements as follows:

A. Policy and Leadership. Senior management participation in the creation and implementation of policy.
A.1 Relevant to nature of products and processes
A.2 Fosters openness and takes into account public and employee input
A.3 Commitment to continual improvement
A.4 Commitment to comply with regulations
A.5 Commitment to the Guiding Principles
A.6 Documented and communicated
A.7 Provides staffing and resources

B. Planning
B.1 Risk assessment process
B.2 Risk evaluation integrated with R&D
B.3 Product Risk Information system
B.4 Systematic review of relevant regulations
B.5 Documented objectives and accountabilities
B.6 Identification of needs and resource allocation
B.7 Assess community and employee concerns

C. Implementation, Operation and Accountability
C.1 Defined Responsibility and Accountability
C.2 Task specific training
C.3 Communication and dialogue with stakeholders
C.4 Employee involvement
C.5 Documented procedures and change processes
C.6 Written emergency response plans
C.7 Participation in community response planning
C.8 Distribution emergency response process
C.9 Guidance and information to commercial partners

C.10 Qualification of carriers and contractors
C.11 Emissions reduction and pollution prevention

D. Performance Measurement and Corrective Action
D.1 Tracking of emissions and releases
D.2 Performance review of commercial partners
D.3 Investigation of accidents and incidents
D.4 Data files
D.5 Compliance Audits
D.6 Effectiveness and communications

E. Management Review and Reporting
E.1 Periodic review of objectives and policies, resources and
    performances
E.2 Reporting to stakeholders
E.3 Benchmarking Responsible Care® management
E.5 Employee performance management.

A series of questions are asked under each of the above elements relating to each attribute (for reference and illustration) during interviews.

The CIA Approach:
Participating member companies in committing to the principles of Responsible Care® required continual improvement in all aspects of health, safety and environmental (HS&E) performance and to openness in communication about its activities and its achievements.

This meant (according to Responsible Care® - Improving health, safety and environmental performance in the chemical industry CIA publication) a rigorous programme of action in:

- Commitment by the CIA membership is total. Adherence to the principles and objectives of Responsible Care® is a condition of membership.
- Health, safety and environmental performance, measured by a consistent set of indicators, has clearly improved.
- Systems for mutual aid and sharing best practice are now in place through a national network of cells.

- Channels of communication to the public and its elected representatives are now extensive.

This programme is being enhanced by:
- development of guidance for management systems and procedures which underpin the Responsible Care® commitment
- recruitment of additional members to extend coverage within the chemical industry
- extension of reporting by sites to their neighbouring communities
- and partnership agreements with sectors allied to the chemical industry, chemical distribution and trading having being the first.

In 1992, the first edition of guidance was published: 'Responsible Care® Management Systems - Guidelines for certification to ISO 9001 - Health, Safety and Environmental Management Systems (and BS 7750 - Environmental Management Systems) in the chemical industry'.

These guidelines were based on ISO 9001 (1987) Quality Systems, BS 7750 (1992) Environmental Management Systems and the draft proposed Eco-Management and Audit Scheme (EMAS).

In 1993, the CIA participated in a BS 7750 Pilot Study. In 1994, two companies took part in joint trial assessments to BS 7750 and ISO 9001 using the 1992 guidelines.

In 1995, the second edition of guidance was published by the Management System Advisory Group entitled 'Responsible Care® Management Systems for Health, Safety and Environment'. These guidelines are based on changes to the other management standards outlined above, experience from the BS Pilot Study and commentary from the participating certification bodies.

The second edition guidance addresses the requirements of other management systems, namely:
- ISO 9000 series of standards (1994)
- BS 7550 (1994) Environmental Management Systems
- Eco-Management and Audit Scheme (1993) (EMAS)

- ISO 14001 Environmental Management Systems
- 'Successful Health and Safety Management' HS(G)65 (1991)

The guidance is very comprehensive and produced in a format that facilitates understanding. Guidance on the development of HS&E Management Systems and a cross-reference to the existing management systems documents appears on the right hand pages, while on the left hand pages examples are given which are intended to assist understanding of the guidance.

While the Responsible Care® guidelines have not been universally adopted as a formal standard, it should be given serious consideration by organisations developing health, safety and environmental systems or all of these.

The Responsible Care® Advisory are currently preparing a self-assessment questionnaire, which will enable companies to evaluate their progress in Responsible Care® Meanwhile, the Chemical Manufacturers Association (CMA) in the US and the Canadian Chemical Producers Association (CCPA) are both evaluating verification processes for implementing Responsible Care® programme by members.

Content of the Responsible Care® Systems for Health, Safety and Environment (Second Edition)
The contents are as follows:

GLOSSARY

INTRODUCTION

1.0   LEADERSHIP AND COMMITMENT

2.0   INITIAL REVIEW

3.0   POLICY AND OBJECTIVES
3.1 Policy
3.2 Objectives

4.0   ORGANISATION
4.1 Structure and Responsibility
4.2 Management Representative
4.3 Resources
4.4 Communication

4.5 Training
4.6 Documentation
4.7 Documentation Control
4.8 Document and Data Control

5.0   IDENTIFYING REQUIREMENTS
5.1 Assessing Significant HS&E Risks
5.2 Defining Screening Criteria
5.3 Identifying HS&E Requirements

6.0   SET TARGETS AND PLAN
6.1 Prioritising and Setting Targets for Improvement
6.2 Control
6.3 Performance Criteria and Indicators
6.4 Emergency/Incident Control

7.0   IMPLEMENTATION
7.1 People
7.2 Controls required by Regulation
7.3 Purchasing
7.4 Process Control
7.5 Management of Change
7.6 Outputs from the Manufacturing Process
7.7 Storage and Transportation

8.0   MONITORING
8.1 Assess Compliance, Strengths and Areas for Improvement
8.2 Corrective Action

9.0   MANAGEMENT REVIEW

The management system structure used by the Guidance is based on Deming's *Plan-Do-Check-Act* cycle.

Act:

Leadership and Commitment
To gain essential commitment from senior management to the HS&E programme.
Conduct Initial Review
To assess and review the strengths and weaknesses of the existing HS&E Management System in broad terms.

Plan:

Set Policy and Objectives

To define the organisations direction and long-term aims for HS&E in terms of performance and the conduct of its activities.

Define Organisation

To define the structure of the organisation and responsibilities, the type and extent of resources and the documentation required to implement the Policy and Objectives.

Identify Requirements

To obtain detailed information on HS&E hazards and consequences for activities and materials within the organisation's control and establish requirements based on their significance.

Set target and plan

To prioritise the significant requirements for improvement and control and to document plans to achieve the improvement programme.

Do:

Implement

To put the plans to meet the organisations policy and objectives and improvement programme into practice.

Check:

Monitor

To check the performance of the organisation in meeting its HS&E requirements to correct deficiencies and to audit the whole management system.

Review

To review the effectiveness and suitability of the management system in achieving the targets.

(c) The Role of the CEFIC

The CEFIC acts as an umbrella organisation in Europe for Responsible Care©. They have prepared CEFIC Guidelines for the Protection of the Environment for chemical companies as follows:

1. Prepare and regularly review at the highest management level, company policies and establish procedures for their implementation;

2. Foster among employees at all levels, an individual sense of responsibility fro environment and the need to be alert to potential source of pollution associated with the operations;
3. Assess in advance the environmental implications of new process and other activities and monitor the effects of current operations on the local environment;
4. /minimise adverse environmental affects of all activities, and monitor the effects of current operations on the local environment;
5. Take the necessary measures to prevent accidental releases;
6. In co-operation with public authorities, establish and maintain contingency procedures to minimise the effects of accidents that may nevertheless occur;
7. Provide the public with the information necessary to enable them to understand the potential environmental effects of the companies' operations and be prepared to respond positively to expressions of public concern;
8. Provide public authorities with relevant information and assist them in establishing well-founded environmental regulations;
9. Provide appropriate advice to customers on safe handling =, use and disposal of the companies products;
10. Ensure contractors working on the companies' behalf apply environmental standards equivalent to their own;
11. In transferring technology to another party, provide the information necessary to ensure that the environment can be adequately protected;
12. Promote research into the development of environmentally sound processes and products.

The companies commitment is expressed by adhering to the above guidelines. However, national chemical industry associations are free to establish their own set of Guiding Principles. This allows the following seven fundamental features of Responsible Care® to match national specificity's, cultures or legislative frameworks:

a)   A formal commitment on behalf of each company to a set of Guiding Principles signed, in the majority of cases, by the chief executive officer;
b)   A series of codes, guidance notes and checklists to assist

companies to implement the commitment;

c)   The progressive development of indicators against which improvements in performance can be measured;

d)   An ongoing process of communication on health, safety and environmental matters with interested parties outside industry;

e)   Provision of fora in which companies can share views and exchange experiences on implementation of the commitment;

f)   Adoption of a title and a logo which clearly identify national programmes as being consistent with and part of the concept of Responsible Care®;

g)   Consideration of how best to encourage all member companies to commit to and participate in Responsible Care®.

6   ENVIRONMENTAL RISK MANAGEMENT

Introduction

This section gives an overview of the Risk Management aspects attached to environmental risk exposure. This should give further credence to the ideal of developing an accredited environmental management system. Also considered are the legal and insurance aspects together with initiatives to reduce risk in line with the EMS objectives, i.e. a review programme and internal auditing of all environmental issues.

6.1   Risk Management

The corner-stone of risk management is managing pure risks such as flood, fire and accidental releases rather than speculative business risks such as markets, currency, production costs etc. Risk Management will however contribute to a more stable and profitable business in the long term by eliminating doubt and reducing the total cost of risk. Typically managing risk can be achieved by:

(i) **Risk transfer** - insuring against pure risks or contracting out high hazard operations such as coating or spraying.

(ii) **Loss Control Prevention** - measures designed to minimise or prevent catastrophic and less dramatic accidents.

Usually, companies use a combination of Loss Control and Risk Transfer. The better the level of control the more cost effective the insurance option. Larger Corporations are tending to self insure (in part at least) or form Captive Insurance companies which effectively means they take the risk "in-house". A philosophy which in turn raises the importance of loss control and prevention, due to the direct impact of any losses on the organisation. Of course the captive or self insurance programme will normally have an element of catastrophic cover (in the form of reinsurance) to safeguard the organisation, resembling the bookmaker off loading onerous bets.

Cost of Risk

In the area of health & safety of personnel in the workplace, studies in the US, UK and Ireland show that insurance compensation only covers a small proportion of the overall costs associated with accidents. Hidden costs such as lost production, retraining, absenteeism etc. are usually significant. These costs surely underscore the necessity for prevention of accidents in the first place. There is no reason to believe that the same would not apply to environmental incidents, furthermore the insurance compensation remedy may be more limited for environmental exposures, a topic dealt with in a later paragraph discussing insurance.

Organisations who have developed safe working environments and cultures can show significant reductions in the total cost of risk e.g. Dupont at international level and Waterford Stanley in Ireland. Of course, it is easier to show reduction in costs where there are a large number of incidents such as workplace accidents or where an organisation is so large that they would have a number of environmental or fire incidents throughout the world. For smaller organisations, benchmarking and reviewing industry trends is useful if analysing your current status. Already initiatives have been developed across industries which reduce risk, and often operating costs at the same time.

Co-ordinated Approach
A sound risk management strategy should look at all pure risks identifying common threads which will work across a number of areas e.g. solvent elimination or substitution means less chance of fire, toxicity to personnel and consequent damage to the environment. On the other hand be careful not to protect against one risk and increase another. Typically this could happen by increasing extraction rates for a harmful chemical process to reduce workplace exposure but at the same time polluting the external environment via excessive stack emissions. The converse is equally important and a happy medium is always possible or better still eliminating problems rather than looking for "end of pipe" solution. A good environmental management system will adopt a co-ordinated approach to tie in with other risk concerns necessary for protection of business

Let us now look at the legal situation both civil and statutory and consider some typical risk exposures.

6.2   The Legal Situation

The area of Statutory Regulations is dealt with in Part 3 and 4 of this book. Here we look at civil liabilities arising through civil actions (common law) and the relationship with Statutory Regulation. In Ireland the major legislation is the Environmental Protection Agency Act 1992 which covers the issuing and policing of integrated pollution control licences. The Act applies to major tier industries, others are covered by legislation including water pollution, air pollution, waste, noise and planning acts. Fines for breach of licence under EPA Act can be as much as IR£10m and may include imprisonment for directors and officers.

The foregoing represents the basic Statute Law but Civil Law holds the greatest exposure as virtually any claim could arise provided negligence is proven. The outcome of any civil case would of course be strongly influenced by Statute Law. Compared to the low level of fines currently imposed (other than the few companies thus far subject to EPA licensing) the awards under Common Law would generally far outweigh statutory fines. While Shell UK was fined £1m for an oil spill, it was found that clean up costs far outweighed the criminal penalty. A total bill exceeding £7m was incurred in clean up costs.

Apart from breach of Statutory Regulations, Civil or Common law remedies (based on precedent) are open to an injured party in respect of environmentally related causes and are summarised as follows:

- Nuisance e.g. noise or smells which interferes with the use or enjoyment of land/property.
- Trespass - this is where a material passes onto land without consent of the land owner. Such an incidence could result by way of airborne particles or liquid effluent streams.
- Ryland V. Fletcher 1868, is the foundation for legal principle which imposes strict liability (no onus to prove negligence or motive) on the occupier of land, from which anything dangerous escapes onto another persons land, if this results from a "non natural" use of the land from which it escapes e.g. damming a water course.
- Negligence - this is a Common Law duty that a person or company take reasonable care that their actions do not cause

harm to others. If damage is reasonably foreseeable, the injured party (ies) is entitled to compensation. This is a general principle not specific to environment.

It should also be noted that the present legal climate holds potentially responsible parties retro-actively liable for acts performed prior to Regulation being in existence. Significantly, clean-up costs for sites are spiralling.

Specific mention should be made of waste and the principle of "cradle to grave" and even "cradle to cradle" where recycling is involved. Basically the producer of the waste has a primary responsibility to see that the waste is safely disposed of and causes no harm to the environment. In Ireland we produce 80,000 tonnes of hazardous waste annually of which 13,000 tonnes is exported. There are special requirements for Transfrontier shipments. Also landfills will now be licensed under the new Waste Management Act.

Currently our Nation generates 7.4 million tonnes of municipal and industrial wastes. Cost of collection runs at about £42 per tonne and from £7 to £25 per tonne disposal cost. The use of the Landfill option will continue to be the case despite it being the least desirable option. The landfills will also become self financing further upping the cost. Basically liabilities and operating costs are increasing and so reduction of waste at source becomes highly attractive.

6.3   Standards

So what standards, norms, codes of practice should industries strive towards to avoid civil actions or prosecutions under Statute law, not to mention the adverse publicity which could impact at worst the future viability of a company. The EPA in granting a licence will stipulate maximum limits for air emissions, effluent, noise etc. and would require an EIS (Environmental Impact Statement) in relation to new projects falling within defined limits.

Other industries falling outside EPA licensing requirements would have limits set by local authorities who will invariably look to EPA standards. Until such time as agreed European limits are set out it is likely that German, US or UK standards will be followed. EPA Guidelines are now available for a number of industries. Regardless of which standards are required or adopted it seems the EPA requires certain principles:

"Policy of sustainable development"
"The polluter pays"
Batneec (best available technology not entailing excessive cost).

These principles are and will be applied to all scheduled activities when integrated pollution control licences are being sought.

Since these principles underpin the general functions of the agency granting IPC licences it is considered that there is a strong link between compliance and the necessity to have an environmental management system. Thus far these systems have been adopted on a voluntary basis and open only to industrial activities, although it is envisaged that they will become mandatory in the next few years.

The EMS should provide a sound basis for going forward as well as establishing any potential liabilities arising from previous use of site.

6.4   The Risk Environment

We are all familiar at this stage with the consequences of environmental disasters e.g. Chernobyl Russia, Sandoz Switzerland, pollution of Rhine river, Union Carbide, Bhopal India and Seveso, Italy. In Ireland, there has been and still is major controversy surrounding fires in August 1993 when in separate incidents large amounts of fire run off water with contaminants entered Cork harbour the centre of "chemical industry" in Ireland.

A less obvious problem was highlighted when, in 1992, in the aftermath of a major fire in an animal meats cold store, major costs were incurred in the disposal of the damaged stocks. Mad cow disease had diminished the possibility of recycling the burnt meats etc. These incidents were largely once off accidents and unforeseen (Loss Control Consultants might argue otherwise). Contamination of a town water supply in the mid south was in the news in 1996 and subject to much publicity. Recently a very busy petrol forecourt in South Dublin had to close down due to petroleum vapours in nearby residence. Aside from Business Interruption what about clean-up costs?

Liquid solvents can be particularly harmful, for example, one litre of solvent could contaminate 100 million litres of drinking water, remember Perrier and Benzene. One gallon of oil on water can cover an area twice the size of a football pitch. Volatile Organic Compounds (VOC's) can contribute to low level air pollution, global warming and if released accidentally cause immeasurable harm.

It is also important to realise that sugar, milk, salt etc. not normally regarded as hazardous can cause problems if released in great quantities e.g. during crises, fire, flooding.

Apart from sudden and unforeseen incidents gradual pollution poses a major problem which is not normally covered under insurance policies e.g. unintended leaking of oil or more toxic substances in the sub-soil from buried pipework, small overspills or air emissions containing minute toxic or eco-toxic substances. A whole aquifer or water supply system could be wiped out upon discovery of contaminant which could take weeks/months or years depending on sub-surface conditions. Think of how vulnerable would be a natural spring water bottler or whiskey distiller, not to mention a towns water supply if from a well or spring. Such gradual and often unnoticed pollution also poses problems for the purchasers and vendors of sites. A purchased site can become a financial liability rather than an asset with the costs of cleanup exceeding the bank value of the property.

The identification of contaminated land and the possibility for future uses are not yet strictly defined in Irish or Euro laws. Maximum allowable concentrations (MAC) can be derived from Dutch standards and UK guidelines which offer guidance albeit on a different basis. Environmental site assessments should therefore be undertaken involving intrusive or non intrusive techniques depending on past and intended uses. Due diligence studies should take account of the foregoing.

Remediation
Remediation is the action of cleaning the site contaminants which can be extremely costly and in some cases entirely prohibitive. Lately in Ireland, for example, hydro-carbon based contaminated

soil could be brought to a landfill at a reasonable cost and such an option has become increasingly costly due to decreasing availability of landfill sites. Ireland does not have a national incinerator.

Insurance

It seems insurance coverage for environmental exposures is quite limited. On Public Liability policies accidental and unforeseen damage usually occurring within the policy year is covered but then there are very often limitations such as the obvious one, i.e. limit of indemnity IR£2 million in many cases. Own site damage is not covered. Gradual pollution is basically excluded.

Property Damage and Business Interruption policies would not seem to cover the cost of remediation of soil and sub-soil. Limited cover is available but this usually entails an in-depth site investigation by insurance approved consultants with the costs being borne by the Insured.

Perhaps I am being simplistic but this type of cover seems a pretty safe bet for underwriters and is normally limited to IR£5 million. I think it is therefore safe to say that in terms of pure risk the environmental liability exposures are those which remain uninsured for most of Insurers clients.

Nevertheless, Public Liability still contains significant protection for pollution incidents especially for those organisations who represent higher exposure. Major Insurers are now seeking more information in relation to materials processed or stored in proximity to water courses, aquifers, residential areas or other environmentally sensitive surroundings. Insurers may insist on a site survey and it is likely that a sound EMS will be seen as a means of showing tangible commitment. Absence may inevitably lead to increased premiums or restricted cover including limited indemnity. Currently Insurers are sensitive in terms of sudden and unforeseen incidents and just one serious incident may trigger a knee jerk reaction. Following the PiperAlpha disaster at North Sea Oil Rig where claims exceeding £100 million were paid out on Employers Liability, Insurers subsequently set limits of £10 million on Employers Liability Policies only to be increased by request.

Another salient point is that, whether an organisation has an EMS or not the public are entitled under EC Directive 90-313 to have a wide range of information concerning the operation of a plant and the possible effects on the environment. The development of an EMS will inevitably highlight initiatives for continuous improvement which aside from ensuring greater protection should also in many cases lead to cost savings in operations and risk costs including insurance.

6.5   Loss Control Initiatives

We have seen thus far the many pressures brought to bear on industrialists in the area of environmental liability but lets not be all doom and gloom as it should be possible to control and manage liabilities and at the same time make a business more cost effective. In some instances solutions will be extremely technical and expensive in the short-term but offer payback in the long term. Others may be down to simple housekeeping measures and lead to immediate risk and cost reduction. Grants and award schemes may be available, take the example of Henkel Ireland who achieved European Better Environment Award for Industry in 1996 for a programme of measures designed to protect the environment including minimisation of waste and reduction of energy consumption as well as employee education. This included a recycling plant where 40 tonnes of Acetic acid is recovered each week.

There are three essential elements in good environmental risk management, i.e. evaluation, prioritisation and action by responsible individuals or teams by an assigned date. This ties in directly with the environmental management system where the Environmental Review evaluates all environmental effects, special consideration being given to emergency situations. The Environmental Programme describes specific objectives and the Internal Auditing Process helps to continually monitor environmental performance.

As mentioned earlier it may be worthwhile approaching initiatives on the environment in conjunction with Health, Safety, Property and Business Interruption protection. Information is available from a wide range of sources including Government Agencies e.g. ENFO, Department of the Environment, Forbairt, Environmental

Consultants, Insurance and Risk Management Consultants who will have access to international information and best practice.

The Environmental Technology Best Practice Programme running in the UK discusses some very practical solutions and of course your neighbours and companies who have been through IPC licensing or an EMS accreditation will normally be only too glad to provide information. Remember much of the information concerning environmental effects is now in the public domain by law.

Let us now explore some of the more common issues which should help to reduce environmental risk exposures.

Training and Education

Probably the single most important initiative. Implementation of sound environmental practices requires employee participation and understanding. Training can be on a very sophisticated level depending on needs or as simple as nurturing good housekeeping practices. Employees will then offer good feedback and help to identify risks and problems on an ongoing basis. They will also be well placed to deal with emergencies.

Example - An operator notices an oil leak on a machine, uses saw dust each day which in turn is removed to ordinary consumables, waste skip. There is no reporting procedure for leak and eventually considerable time and resources are spent. Not to mention the increased slip trip and fire risk and the possibility of potentially hazardous waste being disposed of in landfill.

Solution - Train and educate employee as to the risks involved and how they can help make the workplace more cost effective. Introduce record sheets to monitor all leaks. Issue absorbent mats and remedy most problematical equipment on preventative maintenance basis.

The philosophy is similar to tracking accident or incident records. Such a system will help to resolve problems at source and keep employees minds focused. Some useful videos and training packages are available from ENFO.

Energy Conservation
Simple means such as utilising efficient lighting systems, improving draught insulation and recycling of process heat can make significant contributions to energy conservation thus decreasing pollution levels and operating costs. The Irish Energy Centre runs the Energy Audit Grant Scheme, which provides grant assistance of up to 40% of the cost of conducting an energy audit and survey, to a maximum grant of £5,000. The aim of this initiative is to define and quantify a company's energy performance and monitors the achievement of specified targets. The audit checklist available from the Irish Energy Centre is still useful as an internal document for those who do not wish to participate in the grant scheme. The centre also has published a good practice guide in relation to Building Energy Management System (BEMS). Such a system is defined as a computerised control system which among other functions reduces energy consumption in the building by providing better control of energy consuming plants such as boilers, pumps, lighting, ventilation systems, air conditioning systems and hot water heaters. The BEMS can be expected to save up to 20% and occasionally more on energy consumption of the plant being controlled.

The BEMS is identified as an under-utilised technology and small and inexpensive systems are now available which means that systems can be justified in buildings where energy bills are as low as £10,000 annually. A correctly installed BEMS will also lead to a more comfortable and healthy environment. Nation-wide, and international recognition may be forthcoming for innovative solutions, contact Irish Energy Centre.

Disaster Management and Business Contingency Planning
It is essential that plans are in place to deal with the initial emergency e.g. evacuation/salvage, damage limitation, spill response teams, co-ordination with local emergency services, security, media and public relations as well as longer term issues such as relocating operations, sub-contracting, group support, replacement of vital plant and utilities. The plan should be tested at least on an annual basis and debriefing allowed to monitor and improve. The plan should even go so far as to consider the location of the emergency plan documentation and it's safety in the event of disaster.

Chemical Storage

Very often we see incompatible and reactive chemicals stored together e.g. acetylene and oxygen gases in the same compound or cage and organic solvents with highly corrosive acids or strong oxidising agents. Aside from chemical plants which require very special consideration, industrial plants should purchase purpose built chemical storage units or construct similar with incompatible chemicals stored separately. The stores should include containment or for very large quantities drainage to an effluent treatment plant capable of handling such chemicals. This building should be ideally detached and have adequate ventilation. Only working quantities should be brought into plant in the smallest possible safety containers. Racks are available with spillage containment. Special cementituous additives may be needed as ordinary concrete may be permeable to certain chemicals, check with manufacturers. For dispensing, use safety faucets which effectively have deadmans handles or use drums in the upright position with positive displacement pumps.

Bulk Storage with continuous welded pipe feeds to workplace may be another option. Safety cut-outs should be fitted to prevent overfill or to operate in the event of solvent/smoke/heat detection. NFPA 30 and Factory Mutual Guidelines give good information on the handling storage and use of flammable chemicals. An added benefit of having a detached chemical store is that the likelihood of ignition sources is minimised and in the unlikely event of fire, the liquid can usually be maintained within the compound. This has implications for fire water retention.

Fire Water Retention

The EPA have issued Draft Guidance Note to industry on the requirements for fire water retention facilities. This requires a risk assessment approach, for more hazardous industries and is quite comprehensive. Generally you should:

(i)   Establish outflows from all drains both foul and surface water and establish whether they can be confined.

(ii)   Identify specific areas such as chemical stores which are self contained.

(iii)   You will need to calculate expected fire water run-off based on automatic active systems such as fire water sprinklers and firewater used by public or private brigades.

(iv)   Existing effluent treatment plants may be used, consider on-line monitoring of VOC's or other likely contaminants such that uncontaminated water can be diverted to normal outflow. The site drains, yards etc. may be included in retention calculations provided outflows can be sealed. A pneumatic valve with remote activation may be useful.

Of course, detail should be discussed with the EPA and/or local fire authority.

Solvent Management

Look at source reduction/minimisation over "end of pipe" solutions. Reduced solvent emission will mean less expenses such as expensive abatement measures and could take you below IPC licensing threshold. Car manufacturers and/or suppliers have made significant inroads in solvent reduction. Companies that are prepared to invest some initial time, effort and money in implementing a solvent management system have been surprised at the amount of solvent that is lost from different processes and how they have achieved significant savings over a short period of time by implementing specific solvent reduction measures. Solvent management can be either a stand alone activity or part of a broader waste minimisation programme. A guide available from the Environmental Technology Best Practice Programme in the UK describes a six step solvent management framework.

Step 1 Having a first look at the solvent use; establishing an order of magnitude for solvent losses from the site or factory.

Step 2 Setting up a solvent management system; nominating a solvent manager and preparing a solvent management file.

Step 3 Keeping track of solvent use; compiling an inventory by examining solvent flows through individual processes. Auditing, measuring and simple mass balance calculations are used to improve the understanding of solvent use and identify opportunities for cost savings.

Step 4 Considering solvent reduction options; possible options for reducing solvent consumption and saving money are appraised against financial and business criteria.

Step 5 Showing a commitment to solvent management; objectives and targets are set and written into solvent reduction plan.

Step 6 Reviewing progress; time to take stock of your achievements before going on to further successes.

The guide describes how a surface finishing company in the south of England under pressure from it's largest customer replaced a solvent cleaning process with a an aqueous wash system which reduced overall solvent consumption from 20 tonne to just over 8 tonnes in one year. The new system had a very short-term payback of 6 months. The company is now saving around £7,000 per year in reduced operating costs. Further initiatives are underway.

Simple housekeeping measures can make significant savings e.g. replacing drums with 1 tonne IBC, they are easier and safer to move by forklifts, can be re-used and result in less residual waste.

Degreasing tanks come in for special mention and fitting of effective lids below the lip extraction can result in significant savings. Simple measures such as resealing lids, fitting of conservation vents on bulk tanks, painting tanks with reflective paint, using closed circuit distribution systems with continuous weld pipe, all help. Take conservation valves which can be particularly cost effective if using more volatile solvents such as MEK, Acetone and Methylene Chloride. A 4M tank containing acetone with an average vapour height space of 1.8M assuming an average temperature of 21°C and a diurnal temperature change of about I7°C to tank, will loose about 500kg of acetone per year, costing about £300. If the tank contained Methylene Chloride the loss would be greater at around 1,500 kg per year, costing approx. £750 per year. A £500 conservation valve can pay for itself in under a year.

Soil and Ground Water Sampling

The extent of soil and ground water sampling will very much depend on the site operations and those of neighbours e.g. residential area. For large plants in sensitive areas, a number of soil and ground water sampling points should be set up and regular readings taken. It is important to maintain records to avoid confusion in the event of future controversy. Smaller less hazardous sites would only require intermittent investigation but remember difficulties may arise in the event of divesting site. The idea is to create a benchmark for subsequent monitoring.

Maintenance of Records
Monitoring will occur across a range of activities but it is essential that records are meticulously maintained and inspected to show compliance, detect deviations, initiating necessary action and for use as defence in future possible legal proceedings. For waste transport and disposal, ensure adequate bonding of carrier, check with local authority. Check that the landfill site is licensed and request a "handback form" from the licensed site to confirm acceptance and disposal of waste. Note special requirements for transfrontier shipments, contact local authority. Again it is essential to maintain adequate records. The new Waste Management Act will require licensing of waste disposal sites.

Recycling
Oil is a typical example and there are several contractors who will collect oil from site or at collection point. On site recycling equipment is also available. ENFO provide a list of recycling companies. Encourage employee initiative on this subject.

Environmental Purchasing Policy
Ensure equipment or consumables that come on site have been reviewed by the environmental audit team consideration should be given to the most favourable environmental solution. Can lesser quantities be brought on site at a given time or indeed can operation be done elsewhere thus reducing risk? All alterations on site should also be reviewed for compliance with good environmental practice.

Control of Contractors
Ensure contractors on site are familiar with environmental best practices and any special permit systems in operation. This will clearly apply to general safety controls as contractors have been known to cause major disasters. A site can also be most vulnerable during extensive contract works.

Example - contractors cutting through foam insulated metal cladding in a cold store. Ignition of foam could cause total building and contents loss with severe environmental implications.

Spill Control
See Guidelines on Pollution Prevention (following).

Conclusion
Having a well defined and an operational EMS will benefit organisations in terms of legislation, litigation, Insurers, media, public and securing their own future viability. Quite apart from the fact that in most instances, the most progressive companies have shown operational cost savings.

6.6   Guidelines For Pollution Prevention

Site Drainage
Colour code manholes and grids
- BLUE: Surface Water (rainwater to river, stream, soakaways etc.)
- RED: Foul water (containing pollutants to sewage works).

Have available a comprehensive Drainage Plan of your site to accurately identify drains and to ensure there are no wrong connections either above or below ground.

Deliveries
- Before delivery, double-check storage tank levels
- Always supervise the delivery itself.
- Label all containers/tanks with the nature and volume of their contents to prevent overfilling.
- Ensure all storage tanks have well designed and constructed bund walls to safely contain any spillage.
- Have contingency plans in place to deal with any accidents and make sure all staff are aware of them.
- Ensure all loading and unloading areas are marked and isolated from the surface water drains.
- Provide catchpits for delivery points.

- Fit automatic cut-off valves on delivery pipes to prevent spillage's due to overfilling.
- Where possible site pipelines above ground. If a pipeline is to be installed underground it should be installed in a protective sleeve or duct and regularly inspected and tested.

Storage
- Regularly check that bund walls are secure - the wall and floor must be impermeable to the materials stored within it and there should be no drains or valves.
- Ensure that overflow pipes on all tanks discharge within the bunded area.
- Always store drums within a bunded area - preferably roofed.
- Use the appropriate containers for materials making sure they are sturdy, uncorroded and are not liable to leak.
- Regularly pump or bale out rainwater that may accumulate within bunded areas.
- Interceptors should be placed on any surface water drain at potential risk points such as fuelling and lorry parking areas. Inspect and regularly maintain the separators. Ensure they are properly designed and large enough to contain a spillage and that any water containing detergents are prevented from draining into them.
- Install security measures to guard against vandalism and theft - lockable valves should be fitted on all storage tanks. Secure fences, lock gates and doors and where possible store materials under cover.

Cleaning
- All washing operations should be carried out in designated kerbed areas which drain to the foul sewer. Bio-degradable detergents are not suitable for discharge to surface drains.
- Do not allow yard areas to be cleaned by hosing to the surface water drain.

Waste Storage and Disposal
- Consider methods of reducing the volume of waste.
- Ensure that waste contractors who remove it are registered and informed of its nature.

- All waste must be safely stored in designated areas which are completely isolated from surface water drains. The area should be bunded to contain spillage's.
- Rubbish compactors should be covered to prevent leaks of polluting liquids.
- Do not allow litter to enter a watercourse.

De-Watering (Building Sites Etc.)

- Silty water should never be pumped directly to a river, stream or surface water drain. Instead (as long as the silty water is not contaminated) it should be pumped to:
  - ➢ a foul sewer
  - ➢ a settlement tank
  - ➢ over a grassed area

Training

- Make sure all staff are aware of the importance of protecting the environment and the efforts made on site to prevent pollution.
- Give staff personal responsibility for regularly checking pollution prevention devices.
- Have a regular refresher programme of the initiatives taken.
- Ensure that all new employees receive environmental training.

Emergencies

- Have in place contingency plans to deal with emergencies.
- If in any doubt call the emergency services as appropriate and the EPA local contact.

7   MANAGEMENT OF ENVIRONMENTAL PERFORMANCE

7.1   Organisation

Description of the organisation.

The Environmental Review should begin with a complete description of the organisation. This should describe the entire scope of business activities in which the organisation is engaged. With more and more elements of manufacturing processes being "outsourced", it is important to define the boundaries to each activity, such as:

Is raw material purchased or manufactured?

Are sub-assemblies manufactured on site or elsewhere? etc.

These are important considerations in determining where there are potential environmental effects of activities.

Organisational Systems

The organisational structure and systems are then examined to decide how and where the environmental effects will be monitored and controlled as well as whether internal or external expertise is to be utilised.

The following activities will have to be integrated into the organisational systems:

- Environmental tasks and responsibility for the EMS.
- Environmental Policy
- Environmental Programme
- Training mechanisms
- Communication (internal and external)
- Monitoring and recording results of measurements
- Control of the EMS and corrective action
- Maintenance of Register of Environmental Regulations.

There will have to be an examination of sections or departments within the organisation to establish who can best handle the above issues and whether the expertise exists, if training is required or if external assistance is necessary.

Identification of responsibility and authority.

The organisation must be identify and designate responsibility by management for the various environmental activities (as above). This will demonstrate management commitment to the EMS and will ensure ongoing manageability. This is especially important if an EMS is being integrated into existing work routines without additional personnel resources being required. Environmental tasks must be undertaken on a continuous basis and cannot therefore be delegated to secondary importance.

A member of the management team must be given overall responsibility for environmental affairs and the EMS. This person must have the necessary commitment and be competent to carry out all the functions that are required. Direct responsibility to the Managing Director of the organisation should ensure independence and demonstrate the importance of this function throughout the organisation.

7.2   Planning

Location Considerations

Nowadays, there is increased public awareness of environmental issues and citizens tolerance is low resulting in a strong stand being taken on matters relating to new developments and their possible environmental effects. This is reflected in the rigours involved in attaining planning permission for new industry and the plethora of environmental regulations. The physical location of an organisation is therefore of great importance.

The organisation should examine the neighbourhood in which it is located or to be located. If it is an existing plant it will have little choice, but it can evaluate possible expansion opportunities. Emphasis should be placed on the possible negative effect of its activities on housing, schools, urban and recreational areas.

Details of planning needs to be examined. The organisation will need to conduct enquiries or investigations to see if they need, for example, air emission or effluent discharge licences.

Analysis of Current Situation

There are many issues which could constitute nuisance or disturbance when looked at from a legal perspective on behalf of a neighbourhood group. Examples of these include noise or vibration, odour, visually obtrusive objects e.g. signs, unsightly constructions, cables etc. The visual impact and aesthetic quality of an organisation is now a very important consideration. Organisations interested in implementing an EMS will seek to improve and maintain good visual impact of buildings and external equipment.

In analysing the current planning situation an organisation may find it helpful to note the following:

The legal status of the site e.g. has it got industrial zoning?, is there a Local Development Plan for the area where the site is located?

The Planning Acts will provide the legal framework for the proper physical planning and development of cities, towns and other areas. The Act details controls on development with emphasis on areas of particular relevance to the environment. The Planning Authorities, because of an amendment by the European Communities Regulations in 1994, have responsibility in the area of Environmental Impact Statements (EIS).

Organisations should be aware of any future amendments to the Planning Acts.

Organisations when considering reconstruction, extensions or expansion of plant should be aware that they may have to submit an EIS, when applying for planning permission. This will outline the environmental effects (impacts) on the surroundings, size of development and possible physical constraints. The company must liaise with the Local Planning Authority on the detail required in any EIS.

Compliance with the planning conditions re. expansions, changes in processes must have already taken place.

Copies of EIS will be available to the public through the Planning Authority.

Public notification must be given for any plant extensions requiring planning permission.

Any buildings constructed on site for the purposes of activities related to the operation of the plant must conform to the technical specifications of the building regulations. These include:

> Structure
> Fire Prevention, Control and Means of escape
> Site Preparation and Resistance to Moisture
> Materials and Workmanship
> Noise Output and Control
> Ventilation
> Hygiene
> Drainage and Waste Disposal
> Heat Producing Appliances
> Stairways, Ramps and Guards
> Conservation of Fuel and Energy
> Access for Disabled People.
> The environmental effects of organisation transportation on surrounding area.

Ongoing evaluation of Planning.
The extent of physical planning cannot be covered entirely in this text. An interested organisation would be wise to consider all details and aspects of planning, rather than realise the problems after certain activities have taken place and having to correct these at additional cost.

Planning needs to be evaluated at specified intervals in order to determine that plant development conforms to all regulations and that there is no negative effect on environmental surroundings. A Register of Environmental Regulations should be maintained and contain details of all applicable planning regulations.

7.3   Water
Ground Water Control
Those organisations who use ground water have a cheaper resource than tap water. Care must be taken in its use as its over exploitation or pollution will lead to depletion or destruction of a very valuable natural resource not only for the organisation but also for other

users. There must therefore be control of its quality and quantity used. Those organisations that use ground water should ensure that there are no potential risks of pollution. Reference should be made to the Local Government (Water Pollution) Regulations 1992 governing the discharge of dangerous substances to groundwater. A protection and conservation programme must be in existence. Ground water protection may be part of the soil protection programme.

Tap Water Control

Due to increased demand in usage of tap water by the public and by organisations, tap water needs to be protected from contamination at source and used as sparingly as possible. Some organisations may produce water for human consumption from ground water. Other organisational water supply may be used for production processes equipment, reactors, cooling purposes, hygiene and cleaning of facilities.

The starting point is to identify using a site map:
- Water receiving point on site
- Map the flow of water and the various connection points on the site network
- Mark drains and sewer networks
- Water availability points (fire hose reel) for potential fire fighting
- Water Meters.

The above will facilitate an effective maintenance for all taps and connection points. It will also allow pin-pointing possible sources of tap water contamination.

In order to monitor water usage, meters should be provided in the various production units throughout the plant. Consumption peaks can also be identified and controlled.

Conservation of Water Programme.

The aim of such a programme is to make people aware of the indirect environmental effects of water consumption, i.e. impact of treatment plant (energy, sludge) and of the need to conserve water throughout the organisation. The awareness is best communicated by structuring a programme which would include:

- Showing examples of current wastage e.g. leaking equipment
- Current water usage by various areas of the plant
- Identification of ways to reduce water consumption e.g. water saving taps, less water consuming equipment
- Individual responsibilities and awareness
- Setting and implementing objectives and goals
- Feedback of results.

Waste Water Discharges

Before examining waste water discharges, check the quality of raw water first as there may be some contaminants in it or deterioration in quality from time to time.

The legislation covering water pollution makes it an offence to cause or permit any pollutant matter to enter waters. There is a licensing system whereby certain discharges into water are permitted. Waste water discharges whether to waters or a sewer must then occur only in accordance with the conditions in the discharge licence. Monitoring records must also be maintained and submitted to the Regulatory Authority. The Regulatory Authority must be notified immediately of any process alterations or extensions with the possibility of a review of the licence. For discharges to waters there is legal provision for the public to examine documentation and make representation regarding a licence application or proposed licence. Reference should be made to the Local Government (Water Pollution) Act, 1977 on accidental discharges.

Application for a discharge licence should include:

- Plan of site with details marked and showing proposed drainage system
- Nature and composition of discharge (weight and volume)
- Method of treatment (if any)
- Times when discharges will be made
- Description of industrial process.

The granting of a discharge licence is subject to fulfilment of certain conditions. These may include:

- Times when discharges are made
- What effect the discharge will have?

- Discharge outlet construction
- Existence of meters, manholes, inspection points etc.
- Sampling of discharge, records and information supplied to the regulatory authority
- Preventative measures and emergency routines.

The consequences of accidental discharge and reporting of it is considered of particular importance if it enters external waters or sewer. The organisation must ensure that all potentially pollutant matter is contained on site. There must therefore be procedures in place for dealing with emergency situations, accidental spillage's, isolation and mop-up whether it is raw material or waste.

7.4   Air

The effects of pollution

Pollutants in the atmosphere, such as sulphur dioxide (SO2) and nitrogen oxides (NOx) from combustion of fossil fuels, are deposited later as acid rain. This can damage crops, trees and aquatic life. The main sources of air pollution are:

- Motor vehicle fumes (hydrocarbons)
- Power plants and incineration plants
- Agriculture (ammonia)
- Industry sources e.g. solvent and dust emissions, inorganic (Hcl,) fibres (wood, asbestos) and odour.

The most publicised effects of air pollution is global warming (greenhouse effect) and damage to the ozone layer on a global scale. On a local scale effects of pollution include carcinogenic and health effects e.g. increased lead levels in children and respiratory diseases are said to be caused by air pollution.

Industrial Air pollution control

As a significant amount of air pollution is caused by industrial plants, they will have a great responsibility in not causing it in the first place. The starting point is to mark all significant emission points on the site map. These may include:

- On-site energy production emission
- CFC's and "blacklisted" substances emission

- Solvent emission
- Dust emission
- Fume emission from heating processes
- Process emissions
- Cooling towers
- Abatement equipment used for reducing air emission e.g. filters, scrubbers etc.
- Services

The mapping will accommodate maintenance of emission equipment and monitoring emission points. In monitoring these consideration should be given to differentiate between normal operating conditions and start up/shutdown conditions.

Some organisations will be required to have a licence for their air emissions. This will have a statutory framework and be controlled by the regulatory authority. Reference should be made to the Air Pollution Act, 1987. All new activities are licensable, only certain existing activities are licensable. The licensing will cover emissions of smoke, gas, aerosols and dust with particular attention paid to the following emissions:

- Asbestos fibres, glass fibres and mineral fibres
- Carbon monoxide
- Chlorine and its compounds
- Fluorine and its compounds
- Heavy metals and their compounds
- Organic compounds
- Oxides of nitrogen and other nitrogen compounds
- Sulphur dioxide and other sulphur compounds

As part of planning permission requirements emission levels will be set by the planning authority. The limitations are based on current knowledge, economic cost and environmental requirements. For existing plants, the age of the facility is taken into consideration.

The general emission limits are set with reference to the German TA Lüft Standard. The organisation must ensure:

- The best available technology (BATNEEC) is being used.

- Air emissions do not cause a nuisance in terms of damage to health of local residents, damage to local flora and fauna or interference with local amenities.
- A licence review by the regulatory authority must be carried out before alterations or extensions that are likely to change the nature and composition or increase emission levels take place. Licensing arrangements must also be made where appropriate.
- Accidental emissions must be reported immediately to the regulatory authority.
- It is necessary to carry out a full on-going programme of monitoring and records made available to the regulatory authority.

References should be made to the EPA BATNEEC Guidance Notes and BPM (Best Practicable Means - UK).

Air emission reduction and monitoring programme

The responsible organisation will look at the chemicals used in its processes and endeavour to replace the more harmful ones where possible. Any improvements would have a positive effect on emissions.

Procedures should detail all equipment cleaning, maintenance, actions to be taken in the event of accidents, shut-downs etc.

Communications with regulatory authorities and the public as well as complaints processing should also be integrated into the EMS.

Monitoring of air emissions is usually performed by external consultants who have the necessary expertise to examine and analyse total particulate, VOC (volatile organic compounds), dust, cyclohexane soluble material etc. As a cost saving measure samples could be taken at various intervals by in-company personnel and then sent to a university or external company for analysis. External expertise will usually be used in defining how the monitoring should take place.

The procedure should identify:

- Frequency of sampling
- Parameters to be monitored
- Continuous monitoring or grab samples

- Sampling points
- Calibration of equipment
- Selectivity and sensitivity of equipment.

Method for Determination of Hazardous Substances (MDHS 47) and reference to OECD guidelines and TA Lüft Standard may be used in choosing standardised procedures. Recording of monitoring results should also be performed in a specified way. Not only should results be recorded but also details about equipment, production loading, maintenance's carried out, complaints received etc. This will allow better understanding of results analysis and trend identification.

7.5   Soil

Sources of soil pollution

Soil pollution has a negative environmental effect in the same way as discharges to water. In fact soil pollution can also lead to water pollution if it is not properly contained. The main sources of soil pollution are:

- Landfilling of wastes
- Leaking underground tanks, pipes and related equipment
- Overground tanks that leak
- Storage of hazardous material (raw material and wastes)
- Leaking during transportation of waste, chemicals and fuels and subsequent leakage in loading and unloading of operations.
- Incidents such as spillage's, explosions etc.
- Storage of PCB's, transformers or capacitors on site.

The emphasis with soil pollution should be on prevention as the cost of remediation of any pollution is usually very high. In addition cleaning and repair of damage may not be 100% successful. Liability for site clean-up will lie with the owner and in the event of sale of the site.

Soil pollution control

The responsible organisation will concern itself with the protection and improvement of soil on site and in the surrounding area. The following approach might be adapted in the early stages:

Examination of site history and past events. If the plant site was previously used for another organisation, it should be established if any activity had a negative effect on soil e.g. spillage's may have occurred or the site may have been used for landfilling of wastes etc. This needs to be an extensive examination as the present facility may have inherited environmental problems from the previous site occupiers.

Map all site equipment, storage locations, loading and unloading areas etc. that have a potential for polluting the soil. Internal and external activities (to site perimeter) should be considered.

Determine protection (e.g. bunding, spillage control and cleaning) and preventative measures for all potential sources of soil pollution.

Soil protection and monitoring programme.

Depending on the risks involved a protection and monitoring programme should be implemented to address these risks on an on-going basis. The extent of sample analysis and frequency of monitoring will depend on evaluation of risks.

It may be necessary for an organisation to carry out the following:

- Leakage testing on underground tanks or piping. If there is leakage found then replacement or protection of existing tank or pipe work (e.g. a bund or retaining dyke capable of containing the contents should be installed). Provision for detecting and repairing sources of leaks should be implemented at the design stage.
- Soil samples for analysis of possible pollutants.
- Chemical analysis of surface water for pollutants.

The soil protection and monitoring programme will depend on the results of the above. Counter-measures should be put in place to deal with any concerns identified.

Obviously, investment in soil protection e.g. adequate bunding, will reduce the cost of sampling and monitoring. In the event of alterations or extension to existing facilities due consideration should be given to suitable soil protection measures.

7.6   Noise

Noise Nuisance

Noise pollution has an adverse effect on the quality of life and the health and safety of the individual. It affects both hearing and behaviour. There is therefore widespread concern among a community or person experiencing high noise levels either intermittently or on an on-going basis. It is now easier for a person affected by noise nuisance to take legal action to have that noise mitigated.

Organisations should refer to the Local Government (Planning and Development) Act, 1992 and the Environmental Protection Agency Act 1992 and Noise Regulations, 1994.

Each organisation will have its own particular sources of noise from its various processes and facilities. These will be internal and external (outside the plant boundaries but within the site perimeter).

Because of changes within industrial plants (nowadays constant change in part of business), these bring their own noise sources e.g. construction activities, machine/process installations etc. Constant sources of noise usually emanate from existing production facilities and equipment.

From the health and safety aspect of an organisation, it is internal noise that is important and from the organisations environmental perspective it is that which is external that is of concern. Most organisations with noise problems will already be engaged in controlling noise and have implemented a noise reduction programme. Those interested in the effect of noise on the environment should extend this programme to include external noise.

Noise Measurement and Noise Control

The first steps to controlling and reducing noise levels might include the following routines:

- On a site map show all sources of noise (temporary, permanent, fluctuating and intermittent). This should include both indoor and outdoor sources. Reference should be made to day and night-time permissible dB(A).
- Record noise levels

- Record occurrences of noise
- Record duration of noise

External noise measurement should be performed at distances from the plant or nearest residence. This will allow analysis of the effect of plant noise on the neighbourhood and that which is likely to cause a nuisance.

The granting of planning permission can include conditions requiring the reduction or prevention of noise and vibration. These also extend to any structural changes in the plant. The regulatory authority may also have specific maximum noise levels for a particular plant depending on time of day etc. There is also EU Legislation on noise emissions during construction.

Noise Reduction Programme
The responsible organisation will concern itself with noise reduction and prevention. Noise can be :

- Prevented e.g. alternative technology. This may not be possible or may be too costly for some industries.

- Reduced at source by process improvement e.g. better layout, low noise emission machines and equipment etc.

- Reduced by noise-proof or noise absorbing materials.

- Reduced by better and more frequent maintenance of equipment and machinery, isolation of machine or personnel or personal protective equipment (PPE).

The purchasing policy of the company needs to emphasise the purchase of equipment and machines with low noise emission levels. EU Directives now require manufacturers to provide information regarding noise level of certain product.

Education and training is a vital part of noise reduction programmes. Employees can identify ways to reduce noise levels by awareness for example, they can switch off unnecessary noise emitting equipment, organise intermittently noisy activities to a time when they will have less noise nuisance impact on neighbours.

7.7   Chemicals

Environmental risks of chemicals

Accidents such as the 1976 Seveso (resulting in the Seveso Directive) dioxin release and the 1984 Bhopal release of poisonous gas have increased public and industry concern about the potentially adverse affects of chemicals on humans and harmful environmental risks associated with chemicals. The best approach is one of prevention by anticipation and control of risks and hazards.

While there is a vast number of chemicals on the market, information on their health effects, concentrations and environmental effects is not well known. This makes management of their risks difficult.

Chemical classification and labelling

In order to classify chemicals, identification of their environmental characteristics needs to be carried out e.g. toxicity in terms of carcinogenic (predisposes organisms to cancer), teratogenic (produces deformities in developing foetus) and mutagenic (can cause permanent changes in genetic material), dangerous to aquatic life, ozone depletion, "greenhouse" effects etc.

The following routine might be applied:

- List all chemicals on site and quantities used per day/week/month and year.
- On the site map mark the positions where all chemicals are stored, handled and used. This should include every substance that is chemically based. List all the chemicals used for classification to determine compatibility for storage adjacent to each other.
- Classify the chemicals used on-site according to their hazard, i.e. reactive, carcinogenic, toxic, ecotoxicity etc. Label chemicals accordingly.
- Ensure that all storage and handling areas are adequate to control chemicals in the event of leakage and that there is good ventilation, mop-up procedures and personal protective equipment.
- Draw-up and implement procedures for the control of chemicals. These should include acquisition of chemicals,

- delivery/transport, storage handling, disposal of containers etc.
- Identify and implement emergency procedures for chemicals e.g. spillage, fire etc.

The most important element of good classification and labelling of chemicals, is that there is good information available on each chemical. Those personnel who have been trained will have no doubt once they come in contact with chemicals as to the possible hazardous effects or risks associated with them and how to handle each in a safe way.

Chemical risk reduction
As described already preventive effort by an organisation will minimise the risks associated with the chemicals it uses.

The first steps of chemical risk reduction is complying with all the relevant legislation and phasing-out "blacklisted" chemicals.

Next, the organisation should concern itself with risk reduction of all chemicals, including better handling procedures and corrective actions when new legislation and other findings relating to hazards of chemicals are published.

On an on-going basis chemical usage should be monitored with a view to reduce emissions of waste and The emission of chemicals to waste water and air should also be monitored. The emphasis should be on providing as much data on the effects of chemicals as possible, identify all potential hazards and constantly improving methods for reducing the release of chemicals.

7.8   Waste
Waste Disposal
Population growth, increasing industrialisation, intensive farming and improved living standards has created vast amounts of a variety of wastes which poses a complex problem of disposal. Modern society is faced with the enormous problem of waste management and how to safeguard today's and tomorrow's generations from its health and environmental effects. The most common method of waste disposal is via landfill sites, these are being questioned on the

grounds of health and safety (e.g. build up of methane gas). Both disposal and treatment of waste is now expensive given the amount of handling, disposal etc. In addition society is less prepared to tolerate waste developments (treatment, disposal), which has given rise to terms such as "not in my back yard" and "not over there either".

Toxic waste presents a more complex problem for society. Currently, safe disposal of toxic waste is very inadequate and the sea has been used as to dilute and disperse it. Public concern for the environment is putting pressure on industry not to use the sea for dumping. So, there will have to be investigations into alternative disposal methods.

Industry needs to concern itself with:
- As far as possible recycling and re-using waste
- Reducing the volume of waste by minimisation programmes
- Use safe methods for disposal of waste
- Treatment methods
- Hierarchy of Controls (eliminate, substitute, isolate, personal protective equipment)

Classification of Waste
Waste can be classified in different ways according to:

physical characteristics, i.e. solid, liquid or gaseous

hazard potential, i.e. hazardous, non-hazardous, inert

type of operation that gives rise to the waste (such as listed in the EU directive 75/442/EEC Annex 1

sector that generated that it e.g. household, agricultural, mining etc.

Solid waste includes sludge's and other semi-solid wastes as well as large bulky items and finely divided materials. Liquid wastes include those liquids not normally disposed of to sewers or waters.

Traditionally wastes were classified and quantified by the sector from which it arose and was divided into the following main categories:
- Domestic or Household Waste - produced from households or institution of a similar nature

- Trade or Commercial waste - generated by shops, offices and hotels
- Industrial Waste - arising from industrial activities and processes
- Agricultural Waste - slurry, silage effluent, dirty water, animal carcasses and pesticides.
- Construction Waste - demolition waste, hard-core, soil etc.
- Extractive Industry Waste - mining, quarrying, coal mining etc.
- Waste Sludge - wastes from water and wastewater treatment plants
- Miscellaneous Waste - wastes outside the above categories e.g. abandoned vehicles, old washing machines, fridges, furniture, waste oil etc.

Domestic or trade waste is generally referred to as Municipal Solid Waste (MSW) and is classified as being primarily dry, solid, non-hazardous and non-toxic.

Hazardous waste is that which is likely to cause threat to humans and the environment. Waste may or may not be hazardous depending on how it is handled. Its behaviour will depend on such factors as chemical properties, physical form, physical properties, concentration, where it is left and under what conditions and how it is treated. Hazardous waste has at least one of the following characteristics:

- Flammable
- Corrosive
- Chemically reactive
- Infectious
- Toxic
- Radioactive
- Carcinogenic, Mutagenic or Teratogenic
- Explosive

Examples of industrial hazardous waste include:

- Waste from oils, solvents, laboratory, medical, heavy metals etc.

- Waste from treatment and abatement processes e.g. water, air, sludge etc.

Non-hazardous waste will comprise of bulk items which industry has to dispose of. These include:

- Plastic, paper, cardboard, wood, metal scrap, glass, some types of unfinished and finished products etc.
- Waste from canteens, construction activity waste etc.

It may be necessary for some organisations to have waste permits depending on the nature of the waste being generated and disposed of.

Waste Control and Minimisation

To begin, an organisation needs to look at the different stages in the life cycle of waste, i.e.:

➢ Generation - production, handling, labelling and short term storage of waste
➢ Transportation - from producer to processor/disposal agent
➢ Processing/disposal - storage, treatment and disposal of waste

The above is important in gaining an overview of waste in order to minimise it.

Organisations may also find it useful to consider the "hierarchy of waste management strategies". The priorities are as follows:

Prevention	**Highest Priority**
Minimisation	
Recovery/Reuse	
Treatment	
Disposal/Dilute and Disperse	**Lowest Priority**

This means that waste managers and those responsible for policy and legislation should consider higher order strategies first in dealing with wastes. At the upper end of the waste management strategies prevention and the "4 R's", i.e. Reduce, Reuse, Recycle (Reprocess), to dispose of waste in such a way that it can be Recovered (secondary materials or energy) and are largely applied by manufacturing industry while those at the lower end are practised by the waste industry.

The most important consideration in disposing waste is its effects on human health and environment.

It is therefore important that waste does:

> Not to risk water, air, soil, plants or animals
> Not to risk causing nuisance through noise of odours
> Not to cause adverse affect on the countryside

Consideration must be given to the type and the volume of waste precautions to be taken disposal sites and the method of disposal.

Organisations must also ensure:

- On-site operations are undertaken in such a way that does not cause litter nuisance or has a visually bad impact to the public.
- Storage of waste should not cause litter nuisance.
- Transporting of waste from the site to the disposal facility shouldn't cause litter nuisance.
- If waste is disposed of on-site/land, it must not cause damage to human health or the environment. This cannot be performed without a permit.
- Third party disposal companies must have a permit for the type of waste and the quantity which is to be disposed of.
- Waste minimisation and recycling should be an important element of the organisations waste management and continuous improvement system.

In relation to hazardous wastes the organisation should ensure:

- Toxic and dangerous substances are taken away by a suitable contractor and that their permit is in accordance with the type of waste being disposed of.
- Toxic and dangerous substances are stored, treated or disposed of in a manner which will not cause harm to human health or to the environment.
- Irrespective of whether the organisation disposes of toxic or dangerous waste itself or if a third part it must be undertaken in a manner that will not cause harm to human health or to the environment.

Hazardous waste is that which is likely to cause threat to humans and the environment e.g. wastes that are toxic, ecotoxic, carcinogenic etc.

To control and minimise waste the best available technology (not entailing excessive cost) should be utilised.

- Waste issues should be considered in:
- Purchasing new machinery and equipment
- Installing new processes and facilities
- Designing new products and tooling
- Storage
- Packaging
- Construction and cleaning activities (also sub-contractors)

Packaging waste needs to be looked at in context of EU Directives, the Waste Management (Packaging) Regulations, 1997 and the country to which products are being exported to.

In Council Directive on packaging and packaging waste 94/92/EC there are:

- Requirements on the manufacturing and composition of packaging
- Requirements specific to the Reusable Nature of Packaging.
- Requirements specific to the Recoverable Nature of Packaging.

These have been implemented in national legislation via the Waste Management Act, 1996 and the Waste Management (Packaging) Regulations, 1997, dealt with in Part 4 of this book.

The implications for organisations, means that, they are responsible for taking back packaging on their products or making arrangements with the countries of destination to recycle packaging or being part of a scheme such as REPAK that organises this on their behalf. They may also be required in future to change packaging so that it is more suitable for recycling.

7.9   Energy

Effects of Energy Usage

Energy is of great importance and is used in vast quantities by industry and services. It's use and over-use has a huge impact on human life and the global environment. The indirect environmental effects of energy usage is also of concern, for example, the potential effect on the environment from transportation, storage of raw materials used for energy etc. Therefore by reducing energy consumption we also reduce environmental effects in the supply chain.

Energy derived from fossil fuels has the following environmental repercussions:

- "Acid Rain" causing damage to aquatic life, vegetation and soil.
- Global warming from carbon dioxide emission.
- Coal production releasing heavy metals and smoke.
- Motor vehicles exhaust emissions of lead, NOx, HC Photochemical smog and O3.

The EU published it is proposed Save Programme in 1992. Its proposals included:

- Annual inspections of boilers
- Inspection of cars for energy efficiency
- Incentive to reduce energy consumption
- Energy certification and audit of buildings.

From the Save programme it's obvious that there will be increasing emphasis on decreased energy usage and improving efficiency.

Control and Reduction of Energy Consumption

The organisation should identify sources of energy usage. These may include energy for production processes, cooling, heating, ventilation and transport. A good way to communicate to employees the need for greater awareness and energy reduction is to show them:

- The current and past consumption
- The cost of energy consumption
- Examples of where savings were made/can be made by insulation, timers, sensor lighting, etc.

- Environmental pollutant level for kW of energy
- Look for suggestions where savings can be made from employees.

Trends need to be established to see the energy usage effects of times of the day, production volumes, freight and transport necessity on the energy consumption and costs. The information and data from this fact finding exercise should be used as a basis for action in creating awareness and re-education in energy reduction.

There are many changes which an organisation might consider in improving its energy efficiency and reducing its energy bill:

- Better heating by equipment maintenance and insulation
- Optimisation of process energy usage
- Better technology, machinery and equipment which is more energy efficient
- Low sodium bulbs and energy saving lighting
- On/off cycles for machinery and I.R. sensors for lighting of intermittently used areas.
- Changed transport patterns to eliminate unnecessary journeys
- Awareness Programmes.

Energy can be saved by employee by simple observation and action, i.e. if some equipment is not in use, switch it off and if van or truck engines are running while stopped, switch them off.

Energy Conservation Programme
By encouraging employees to use the same energy saving mentality within the organisation as they would within their own homes, substantial reductions can be made in the energy bill. Once employees see what improvements they can make they will be encouraged to look at further ways to conserve energy.

Employees can also be encouraged to use public transport, bicycles and share transport in order to reduce the effects of transport on the environment. In extending or changing product layout, organisations should look at the possible increased energy consumption and find ways by better utilisation to minimise the effect of these. Management decision making should be based on information about what the cost of running a machine, equipment and production section is. Suppliers of machinery and equipment need to provide information on their energy consumption.

The interested organisation should carry out regular energy audits to evaluate the effects of better energy efficiencies. The results should be the basis for on-going improvement projects.

Sustainable energy systems have been dealt with in Section 1.5 of this book.

7.10 Products and Packaging

Environmentally friendly products and packaging

Packaging accounts for about 50% of municipal solid waste (MSW). The challenge is to produce products which will have less waste and use less energy throughout their entire life cycle. This means the evaluation of a product from raw material acquisition to the eventual disposal or recycling at the end of its life. Industry must therefore produce more environmentally friendly products in response to consumer environmental awareness and preference.

Packaging materials must also be such that they do not cause damage to natural resources and cause waste which cannot be recycled.

Packaging should strike a good balance between packing requirements, costs and environmental aspects. ECO labelling of products indicates to the consumer that the product has environmentally friendly raw materials and that its total environmental impact has been addressed.

An organisation trying to produce environmentally friendly products and packaging may investigate the following:

- An environmentally favourable production system which minimises waste
- Using environmentally friendly raw materials with better ecological effects and which can be recycled.
- Using environmentally friendly packaging materials.
- Providing information on the health, safety and environmental effects of their products.

- Examining the total environmental impact of their products throughout their life cycle.
- Examining possibilities of recycling products and packaging

An example of a company currently working to help other companies meet obligations in terms of current and future legislation, is Chep Ireland. For instance they have developed a sector offer for packaging companies and now count Smurfit Corrugated Cases and Union Camp among their customers and are currently seeking to develop Returnable Transit Packaging, with retailers by developing a plastic tray pool.

Environmentally friendly programme
The responsible organisation should involve its workforce in identifying ways to improve existing packaging and product design in order to minimise its environmental effects.

It is necessary to be aware of environmentally improved raw materials and production methods which comply with all statutory regulations. All new developments in environmentally sensitive products and packaging should be considered on an on-going basis.

As part of the programme, information should be made available quantifying the energy and raw material consumed in packaging and product. In addition, the impact of product and packaging on emissions and discharges throughout the entire product life span should be established.

The effects on natural resources and potential environmental damage should also be identified.

The improvement process should evaluate and optimise raw materials and the production process to ensure good environmental management of products and their associated packaging requirements.

7.11   Occupational Health and Safety
Occupational Health Risks
There is a rising toll of serious injuries from accidents and diseases caused by machinery and exposure to toxic substances. As

knowledge of the effects of work on health increase, responsible management have improved systems which improve health, safety and environment. Organisations have a role in:

- providing training and information
- Identifying risks and initiating action.

Some of the most common causes of occupational health risks include:

- Accidents causing injury
- Excess workload, repetitive strain injury (RSI) and work associated stress
- Strain caused by display screen equipment (DSE)
- Chemical and agents (carcinogen, mutagen, teratogen)
- Physical (noise, vibration etc.) and biological (micro-organisms) agents.

Risk reduction
Short-term measures to address occupational health risk should be to provide appropriate information to workers on the dangers to their health of the above and ensure medical surveillance to monitor the effects on them. The long-term measures must be to avoid exposure to harmful agents and that which is likely to cause a health problem or keep exposure at a very low level.

An organisation in pursuing a risk reduction policy should utilise the hierarchy of control principle of: eliminate, substitute, isolate and use personal protective equipment.

Some occupational hazards will be identified under the EMS e.g. handling of chemical agents and carcinogenic agents and adequate measures must be taken to reduce the risks. For this reason hazard identification must be extended to include environmental health hazards.

An on-going risk reduction programme should include information and standard operating procedures to cover the following:

- Occupational health and safety policy integrated into management activity
- Information on hazards, changing circumstances and preventative measures

- Instructions on the use of protective equipment
- Records of accidents and incidents in the workplace
- Job specific occupational health and safety training.
- Consultation on occupational health and safety matters and corrective actions.
- Training and education of new and existing employees
- Health surveillance of employees.
- Hazard identification and risk management

7.12   External Safety

External Safety Obligations

Not only do organisations have obligations to ensure hazards are identified and risks reduced within the plant but also externally. Any activity on the site area should be considered in order to establish potential human injury and ecological impact.

Risk reduction and emergency planning

In particular the focus of attention should be on:

- Storage, usage, transportation and disposal of chemicals, fuels, solvents and waste
- Loading and unloading of these

In reducing the risks involved with the above, careful thought should go into ensuring facilities and equipment are adequately planned. Good training in emergency planning is crucial in controlling incidents that may occur and minimising their effect. This will mean that people will know their roles and act instinctively. They will make confident decisions and be in command of the situation. Emergency plans must be tested to determine their effectiveness and the level of preparedness among participants. Organisations should refer to the contents of the Seveso Directive in preparing and putting an emergency plan in place.

The emergency plan should cover events like leakage's, fire, explosives etc. It should cover:

- Containment and evacuation actions
- Information to employees concerning potential risks

- Details of the routine of the emergency plan
- Contingency planning e.g. water, protective equipment etc.
- External authority communication e.g. fire department
- Extent of training required

7.13   External Contractors

With more and more services being performed on-site by outside contractors this may increase the environmental risks for the organisation. Contractors must therefore be familiar with the EMS and environmental policy, environmental objectives and targets. They must be trained and know the effects of their work on health, safety and environment.

Examples of outside contractors services commissioned include:

- Electrical and mechanical services
- Construction workers
- Waste handling/collection
- Canteen food preparation/delivery
- Cleaning and hygiene services
- Certification and testing services

7.14   Environmental Impact Assessment (EIA)

Necessity of an EIA

The EU environmental impact assessment Directive 85/337/EEC requires that before consent is given by a Government Body, certain construction projects have to be subjected to an assessment of possible environmental impact. In 1994, amendments were put forward to define projects, their nature and evaluation of results of such studies.

EIA is intended to gather information necessary to enable planning and decision making about a project. It will be a detailed study of the future effects on the environment and health of people. It also considers the social consequences of the people who will be affected by the project.

Carrying out an EIA

An EIA must address all the queries and concerns of authorities and interested public. For them it is important to know fully what effect the project will have on the environment and quality of life.

The main steps of the EIA process are:

- Decide what the EIA should cover taking into account the nature, size and location. For example, if the area is one of natural beauty then there is likely to great environmental awareness among its citizens and hence the organisation must proceed very carefully taking all views of interested parties into account.
- Prepare and gather all scientific knowledge and make an analysis of the significance of the environmental impacts. The assessment should be carried out, verified or reviewed by professional independent expertise. This is important in ensuring impartiality and objectivity.
- Monitoring should take place to ensure that all the findings and conditions are being implemented on the project. This should preserve the quality of the environment which will be affected by the project.
- Environmental management practices should be audited. There must be no doubt about the organisations data collection and analysis. As a result of carrying out an EIA recommendations may be made and measures determined by all interested parties before the project goes ahead.

Measures proposed by an EIA might include:

- Equipment for controlling or preventing pollution e.g. emission abatement equipment.
- Reduction of visual impact of buildings and facilities/equipment. This may also entail planting of trees and site landscaping to enable the project to blend in better with its environment
- Minimising nuisance caused by noise, or stack emissions. This will be of special importance if there are residents living close to the organisations site.
- Alterations in the manufacturing process to reduce emissions

- There may be additional monitoring or sampling required to make a judgement on adverse impacts or to verify improvements made by countermeasures already implemented.

EIA is of enormous importance to any organisation planning a new or additional facility. The success or survival of any project depends on it. It is important that accurate and reliable information and data is provided by the organisation and that the organisation fulfils all its obligations and acts on any recommendations identified in the EIA.

8 PREPARATION OF AN EMS

8.1 Environmental Review

An Environmental Review is the mechanism by which an organisation should establish the current status of its environmental effects. It will identify the organisations environmental compliance and any potential shortcomings that need to be addressed. This will enable an in-depth analysis of the hazards and risks throughout the whole organisation.

An awareness should be developed of the normal and abnormal operation of the organisation relevant to environmental protection. Consideration should also be given to possible unforeseen events and emergency conditions (e.g. leaks) likely to arise.

An Environmental Review should cover four key areas:

- Legislative and regulatory requirements,
- An evaluation and documentation of significant environmental effects,
- An examination of all existing environmental management practices.
- An assessment of feedback from the investigation of previous incidents and emergencies.

The review is a critical examination of all site activities to identify where improvements can realistically be made. Complete data should be collected on all environmental issues. This will be best performed by:

- Examination of the physical site and a study of its environmental effects
- Taking the views of all the interested parties (employees, the public, authorities etc.)
- Inspection of all documents and ensuring their adequacy. This will include licences, regulations, policies, instructions etc.
- Examination of compliance with legislation and expected changes in regulations and legislation

- Compilation of results and assessment of potential environmental effect of the organisation (i.e. emissions, discharges, waste etc.)
- Identification of organisational systems to control environmental performance (i.e. environmental policy, environmental programme, standard operating procedures, training etc.)
- Establishment of an appropriate action programme to address the above issues.

The Environmental Review report should be comprehensively written and must highlight :

- The nature and extent of problems and deficiencies, and the
- priorities for rectifying them
- An improvement programme designed to ensure that the personnel and material resources required are identified and made available.

The Environmental Review should cover the following and are dealt with in Part7 of this book with the relevant sections noted below:

7.1	Organisation	7.8	Waste
7.2	Planning	7.9	Energy
7.3	Water	7.10	Products & Packaging
7.4	Air	7.11	Occupational Health & Safety
7.5	Soil	7.12	External Safety
7.6	Noise	7.13	External Contractors
7.7	Chemicals	7.14	Environmental Impact Assessment

Transportation should also be covered in the Environmental Review. Some specific industries may also consider biotechnology and ionising radiation effects as part of their Environmental Review and the EMS Audit.

8.2   Environmental Effects Register

It is the responsibility of the Environmental Manager/Co-ordinator to establish, maintain and update this Environmental Effects Register. This is a controlled document and should comply with the requirements of the document control procedure. All significant organisational environmental effects that pertain to operations should be included on this register. In deciding on the significance of effects the local and global environmental impact of each must be examined.

The Environmental Effects Register should include the following:

- Identification of adverse environmental effects
- List of legislation
- Outline of elimination, reduction/control and recycling programmes in line with severity of effects.
- Severity of environmental effects will determine what objectives and objectives and targets will be put in place to control the risks. The development of an emergency plan may also be required.

The register should distinguish between normal and abnormal operating conditions and emergency situations (e.g. fire) in evaluation of potential environmental effects.

Analysis of effects might include:

- emissions/discharges during normal production and start-up/shutdown times
- the effects on environment and health brought about by emergencies and accidents
- past activities, current activities and planned activities.

In compiling the register, it is important to use an understandable, well-organised system.

An assessment summary sheet could be used outlining:
- Significance of emission/discharge
- Legal reference
- Scientific evidence
- Public attitudes e.g. concerns, complaints/no complaints

In determining the significance of emissions/discharges comparisons can be made between the emissions/discharges of the organisation and from other sources of industry. Scientific evidence can be gained from research institutions and regulatory authorities regarding the current knowledge of the environmental effects of an emission/discharge.

Public awareness should not be underestimated and a good system of communication with external interested parties should be maintained for tracking the extent of concerns about emissions/discharges.

8.3   Register of Environmental Regulations

Environmental Legislation

Concern and awareness of the public about the quality of the environment has led to an increasing amount of laws, regulations and directives being drawn up and implemented. These may vary from country to country. However most directives are continually being introduced by the EU in the field of environmental protection.

In EU Member States those regulations and directives are the basis of most of the environmental legislation in force. On a European level, the EU formulates policy and objectives pertaining to Environmental protection. Examples of the European environmental movement include:

- The most recent "5th Action Programme" (1993-1998) deals with promoting sustainable development and the environmental/industry relationship.
- Enshrined in the "Treaty of Rome" is the "polluter pays principle", which means that those who affect the environment will cover the cost of restoring or preventing the damage caused.
- The "Green Paper" on environmental liability outlines that producers or polluters should be liable for the damage caused.

In the light of all legislation and civil liability, the implications for an organisation being found liable go beyond financial to the consequences of loss of reputation. Liability for non-compliance with regulations may fall on the management (officers) of the organisation and can be either civil or criminal.

Compiling the register of Environmental Regulations

The task is to compile legislative, regulatory and other policy requirements applicable to an organisation. These should apply to the following aspects of company activities, products and services:

- General Environmental Legislation

- Physical Planning
- Environmental Management
- Waste
- Air
- Water
- Noise
- Energy

The register is not meant to be legal interpretation of Acts of Government and Statutory Instruments but should be a summary of the legislation relevant to the organisation's activities.

The register may give the following information:

- Title of legislation
- Purpose
- Summary
- Implications for the organisations

Different legislation and regulations will apply to different types of industry operating in different countries. The following gives a list of the legislation which might apply to different aspects of an organisation's activities in Ireland:

General Environmental Legislation
Environmental Protection Agency Act, 1992
Access to Information on Environmental Regulations, 1993

Physical Planning
Local Government Acts (Planning & Development) 1963 and 1983
European Communities (Environmental Impact Assessment) Regulations 1989
Local Government (Planning and Development) Regulations, 1990
Building Regulations, 1991
European Communities (Environmental Impact Assessment) Amendment Regulations, 1994

Environmental Management
Council Regulation (EEC) Allowing Voluntary Participation by Companies in the Industrial Sector in a Community ECO-Management and Audit Scheme.

Waste

Local Government Sanitary services Act 1948
Public Health Ireland Act 1978 as amended by the Public Health Amendment Act 1907 Local Government Planning & Development Acts 1963-1983
Council Directive 91/156/EEC, amending Directive 75/442/EEC on waste
The European Communities (Waste) Regulations 1979
European Communities Toxic and dangerous waste Regulations 1982
European Communities (Waste Oil) Regulations 1984-1992
European Communities (Waste) Regulations (PCB) 1984
Directive on packaging and packaging waste 94/62/EC
Waste Management Act, 1996
Litter Act 1996
Waste Management (Packaging) Regulations, 1997
Waste Management (Farm Plastic) Regulations, 1997
Waste Management (Planning & Licensing) Regulations, 1997

Air

Air Pollution Act, 1987
Air Pollution Act (Licensing of Industrial Plant) Regulations, 1988

Water

The Fisheries Act, 1959
Local Government (Water Pollution) Act 1977 as amended by the water pollution (Amendment Act) 1990 and the Local Government (Water Pollution) Regulations, 1978
European Communities (Control of Water Pollution by Asbestos) Regulations, 1990 (S.I. No. 31 of 1990)
European Communities (Quality of Surface Water Intended for the abstraction of Drinking Water) Regulations, 1989. (S.I. No.294 of 1989)
European Communities (Use of Sewage Sludge in Agriculture) Regulations, 1991 (S.I. No. 183 of 1991)

Noise

Local Government (Planning and Development) Act, 1963

The Environmental Protection Agency Act 1992 (Noise) regulations, 1994

Energy
SAVE Programme
EC Draft Directive (93/76/EEC) to limit Carbon Dioxide emissions by improving Energy Efficiency (SAVE)

Chemicals
Dangerous Substances Act, 1972
The Safety, Health and Welfare at Work Act, 1989
The Safety in Industry Acts, 1955 & 1980
Regulations for Classification, packaging and Labelling of Dangerous Substances and Preparations (S.I. 77 of 1994, S.I. 393 of 1992
The Major Accident Hazards of Certain Industrial Activities Regulations, S.I. 292 of 1986, Amendments 1989 and 1992
Safety, Health and Welfare at Work (Chemical Agents) Regulations, S.I 445 of 1994)

Equivalent regulations will apply to the UK and Europe. Organisations may, if they wish, choose to contract the drawing-up and updating of the Register of Environmental Regulations to external expertise. Specialists expertise may be required in interpreting the implications for an organisation. It is important that the person who compiles the Register is aware of new directives, amendments to existing ones or new regulations and that they will update as changes take place.

8.4   ISO 14004

Environmental Management System (EMS) Principles and Elements - ISO 14004 Synopsis:

According to ISO 14004:1996 and as detailed in Section 2.12 (g) of this book, an EMS is based on 5 principles which is its organising framework. These are:

- Commitment and Policy
- Planning

- Implementation
- Measurement and Evaluation
- Review and Improvement

The clauses are as listed in ISO 14004.

4.1   Commitment and Policy

"Principle 1 - An organisation should define its policy and ensure commitment to its EMS".

4.1.1   General

Begin where there is obvious benefit e.g. regulatory compliance, limiting liability etc.

Later implement procedures, programmes and technologies to improve environmental performance.

Integrate environmental considerations into business decisions.

4.1.2   Top Management Commitment and Leadership

Top management commitment to improve environmental management from the start .

Ongoing commitment and leadership .

4.1.3   Initial Environmental Review

This establishes the current position with regard to the environment. It should cover:

- Legislative and regulatory requirements
- Environmental aspects of activities, products and services identifying those that have significant environmental impacts and liabilities
- Evaluation of performance to criteria, standards, codes of practice etc.
- Existing environmental management practices and procedures
- Existing policies and procedures for procurement and contracting
- Previous incidents of non-compliance
- Competitive advantage opportunities
- Views of interested parties
- Other organisational systems that enable or impede environmental performance.

Consideration must be given of the full range of operating conditions, potential incidents and emergency situations. The initial environmental review must be documented and opportunities for development of the EMS identified.

4.1.4 Environmental Policy

It establishes:

- Sense of direction
- Principles of action
- Goal of level of environmental responsibility
- Performance standard, set of values
- Responsibility of top management.

The policy should cover:

- Organisations mission, core values and beliefs
- Requirements and communication with interested parties
- Continual improvement
- Prevention of pollution
- Guiding principles
- Co-ordination with other policies, quality, safety etc.
- Local and regional conditions
- Compliance with environmental regulations, laws and other organisational criteria.

4.2 Planning

"Principle 2 - An organisation should formulate a plan to fulfil it environmental policy".

4.2.1 General

EMS elements relating to planning include:

- Environmental aspects and associated environmental impacts
- Legal requirements
- Environmental policy
- Internal performance criteria
- Environmental objectives and targets
- Environmental plans and management programme.

4.2.2   Identification of environmental aspects and evaluation of associated environmental impacts

- Environmental aspect is the element of an organisations activity, product or service that can have a beneficial or adverse impact on the environment. The organisation should determine their environmental aspects ensure that they are:
- Basis for environmental policy, objectives and targets
- Significant environmental impacts associated with aspects are considered when setting environmental objectives
- Determine past, current and potential organisational environmental impact
- Identify potential regulatory, legal, business exposure, health and safety impacts, and environmental risk assessment.

4.2.3   Legal and Other Requirements
The organisation should establish and maintain:

- Procedures to identify, have access and understand legal and other requirements
- These must be directly attributable to environmental aspects of its activities, products and services.

4.2.4   Internal Performance Criteria
Internal priorities and criteria where external standards do not meet the criteria of the organisation.
Assist the organisation in developing its own objectives and targets.

4.2.5   Environmental Objectives and Targets
The environmental objectives are:

- To meet the organisation's environmental policy
- Overall goals for environmental performance identified in the policy
- In establishing, consider environmental review findings, environmental aspects and their associated impacts.

The environmental targets are:

- Set to achieve environmental objectives within specified time-frame
- Specific and measurable.

When targets and objectives are set the organisation must consider:

- Establishing measurable environmental performance indicators
- Indicators can be basis for environmental performance evaluation and providing information on environmental management and the EMS
- Applying objectives and targets broadly across the organisation or narrowly to site-specific or individual activities
- Defining objectives at appropriate levels of management
- Reviewing and revising objectives and targets periodically considering the views of interested parties.

4.2.6   Environmental Management Programme (s)
- Establish to address all environmental objectives
- Integrate into organisations strategic plan for most effectiveness
- Programme should address, resources and responsibilities for achievement of environmental objectives and targets
- Identify specific action in order of their priority to the organisation
- Actions may deal with individual processes, projects, products, services, sites or facilities within a site.
- Programme is to help organisation to improve environmental performance
- Revise regularly to reflect any changes in objectives and targets.

4.3   Implementation
"Principle 3 - For effective implementation, an organisation should develop the capabilities and support mechanisms necessary to achieve its environmental policy, objectives and targets".

4.3.1   General
Capabilities and support required constantly evolve according to changing requirements of interested parties, dynamic business environment and process of continual improvement.
To achieve environmental objectives and targets the organisation most focus its people, systems, strategy, resources and structure.

Approach implementation in stages based on awareness of environmental requirements, aspects, expectations and beliefs and resource availability.

4.3.2   Ensuring Capability

4.3.2.1 Resources - Human, Physical and Financial
- Define and make available human, physical and financial resources to implement environmental policies and achieve objectives
- Procedures to track the benefits and costs of resources and their environmentally or related activities
- Include issues such as cost of pollution control, waste and disposal.

4.3.2.2 EMS Alignment and Integration
EMS elements should be aligned and integrated with existing management system elements. This will allow better management of environmental concerns and benefit management system elements as follows by their inclusion:

- Organisation policies
- Resource allocation
- Operational controls and documentation
- Information and support systems
- Training and development
- Organisation and accountability structure
- Reward and appraisal systems
- Measuring and monitoring systems
- Communication and reporting.

4.3.2.3 Accountability and Responsibility
- A senior person(s) or function(s) with authority, competence and resources responsible for the effectiveness of the EMS
- Defined responsibility and accountability of relevant personnel for implementation of an EMS and environmental performance
- All employees accountable for environmental performance and support of the EMS.

4.3.2.4 Environmental Awareness and Motivation

- Top management must build awareness and motivate employees by communicating environmental values and commitment to environmental policy
- Effectiveness of the EMS dependant on individual commitment and shared environmental values
- All employees should understand, accept, respond and be accountable for achieving environmental objectives and targets
- Improvement in environmental performance enhanced by employee motivation to continually improve and making suggestions.

4.3.2.5 Knowledge, Skills and Training
- Identify knowledge and skills required to achieve environmental objectives
- Consider these as part of personnel selection, training and development
- Provide training on the environmental policy, objectives and targets
- Knowledge training on the impact of employee activities on the environment if performed incorrectly
- Contractor evidence of knowledge and skills to work in an environmentally responsible manner
- Education and training on regulatory requirements, internal standards etc. Level of training dependant on task.

4.3.3   Support Action
4.3.3.1 Communication and Reporting
A communication process must be established to report internally and externally on environmental activities to:

- Demonstrate management commitment to the environment
- Deal with concerns and questions about environmental aspects of activities, products or services
- Raise awareness of environmental policies, objectives and targets
- Inform internal/external interested parties about the EMS and environmental performance

- Those responsible for environmental performance should be informed of the EMS monitoring, audit and management review
- Information to employees should motivate them to encourage public understanding and acceptance of the organisation's efforts to improve environmental performance.

4.3.3.2 EMS Documentation

The nature and extent of documentation will depend on the size and complexity of the organisation. Consider organising and maintaining a summary of documentation to:

- Collate environmental policy, objectives and targets
- Describe the means of achieving the objectives and targets
- Document key roles, responsibilities and procedures
- Provide direction to related documentation and other elements of the management system
- Demonstrate the implementation of appropriate EMS elements
- Serve as a reference to the implementation and maintenance of the EMS.

There should be a clear definition of all types of documents, operational procedures and control of these available. EMS documentation supports employee awareness of what is required to achieve objectives, evaluate the EMS and environmental performance.

4.3.3.3 Operational Control

Establish and maintain operational procedures and controls.
This ensures the environmental policy, objectives and targets can be met.

4.3.3.4 Emergency Preparedness and Response

Emergency plans and procedures must be prepared for unexpected or accidental incidents, environmental incidents and potential emergency situations. These should include:

- Accidental emissions to the atmosphere
- Accidental discharges to water and land
- Specific environment and ecosystem effects from accidental releases.

The procedures should consider incidents or potential incidents as a result of:

- Abnormal operating conditions
- Accidents and potential emergency situations.

4.4   Measurement and Evaluation

"Principle 4 - An organisation should measure, monitor and evaluate its environmental performance".

4.4.1   General

Measuring monitoring and evaluating are key activities of an EMS. Ensure organisation is performing in accordance with stated environmental management programme.

4.4.2   Measuring and Monitoring (Ongoing performance)

Measure and monitor actual performance against environmental objectives and targets:

- Evaluate compliance with environmental legislation and regulations
- Analyse results to determine success and identify activities for improvement
- Ensure reliability of data, such as calibration of instruments, test equipment, and software and hardware sampling
- Identify environmental performance indicators on an ongoing basis
- Indicators should be objective, verifiable, reproducible and consistent with the environmental policy, practical, cost effective and technologically feasible.

4.4.3   Corrective and Preventive Action

- Identify corrective and preventive actions resulting from findings, monitoring, audits and reviews of the EMS
- Ensure actions are implemented and there is systematic follow-up to ensure effectiveness.

4.4.4   EMS Records and Information Management

Records should cover:

- Legislative and regulatory requirements
- Permits
- Environmental aspects and their associated impacts

- Environmental training activity
- Inspection, calibration and maintenance activity
- Monitoring data
- Details of non-conformance, incidents, complaints and follow-up action
- Product identification, composition and property data
- Supplier and contractor information
- Environmental audits and management reviews.

Good environmental information management should include a means of identification, collection, indexing, filing, storage, maintenance, retrieval, retention, and disposition of pertinent EMS documentation and records.

4.4.5   Audits of the EMS
Conduct periodically to determine if the EMS conforms to planned arrangements, is properly implemented and maintained:

- Auditors should be trained in objectivity and impartiality
- Frequency of audits dependent on nature of the operation, environmental aspects and potential impacts
- EMS audit report according to the audit plan

4.5   Review and Improvement
"Principle 5 - An organisation should review and continually improve its EMS, with the objective of improving its overall environmental performance".

4.5.1   General
Apply a continual improvement process to the EMS to achieve overall improvement in environmental performance.

4.5.2   Review of the EMS
Review at appropriate interval to ensure continuing suitability and effectiveness of the EMS.
Broad in scope to cover environmental dimensions of all activities, products and services, including impact on financial performance and competitive position.

Review of the EMS should include:

- Review of environmental objectives, targets and environmental performance

- Findings of the EMS audits
- An evaluation of the effectiveness of the EMS
- Evaluation of the suitability of environmental policy and need for changes in the light of:
- Changing legislation
- Changing expectations and requirements of interested parties
- Changes in products or activities
- Advances in science and technology
- Lessons learned from environmental incidents
- Market preferences
- Reporting and communication.

4.5.3   Continual Improvement
- Embodied in the EMS
- Achieved by continually evaluating environmental performance of the EMS against the environmental policy, objectives and targets
- To identify opportunities for improvement.

The continual improvement process should:

- Identify areas of improvement in the EMS to improve environmental performance
- Determine root cause of non-conformance or deficiencies
- Develop and implement corrective and preventive action to address root cause
- Verify effectiveness of corrective and preventive actions
- Document any changes in procedures resulting from process improvement
- Make comparisons with objectives and targets.

8.5   Education and Training
Environmental Awareness Training
Investment by organisations in the education and training of their staff can be of great benefit in the successful introduction of an Environmental Management System. An awareness of the following is important:
- energy saving
- waste reduction

- recycling
- environmental effects of their activities
- improving environmental performance
- health and safety issues.

In industry, introductory or awareness training programmes may be needed for the following:

- Executive and management personnel to understand their Environmental Policy, the EMS and criteria for effectiveness.
- How other personnel can contribute to the EMS
- New employees assigned to new tasks, equipment and procedures.

The introductory and awareness programme should cover the following:

- Environmental Policy and the EMS
- Regulations, legislation and procedures
- Monitoring and data collection of environmental effects
- Waste
- Procedures and emergency procedures
- Communication etc.

In carrying out specialised environmental management functions, the organisation must decide whether to use outside expertise, recruit personnel with the necessary level of competence or to train existing personnel.

The organisation must regularly evaluate how effective its training programmes are in ensuring continued effectiveness of Environmental Management and the EMS. It is important to get good feedback from training programmes in order to determine how needs can best be met and continually improved. Training needs should also be tied into environmental management and effects improvements. The organisation will have different training needs depending on what stage of environmental management development it is at.

Initially an evaluation of the level of education and competence should be carried out. Once this has been determined, the task is to put in place a training programme to address the needs and gaps in knowledge and know-how.

General factory operatives whose activities have a direct or indirect environmental effect will need to become aware of their impacts. Thus training needs will probably be best served by an awareness programme.

A good example of this is the Danes, environmental awareness courses, through their Vocational Education Centres (AMU). Employees who participate in one such programme are asked to undertake projects in their homes which involves preparing the main family meal and measuring how much water, energy is consumed and how much waste (e.g. organic, packaging etc.) and waste water is generated during the exercise. In the workplace the same measurement approach can be applied to energy saving, waste reduction etc., an estimation can be made of how energy reduction can indirectly protect the environment by reduction of:

- emissions from power plants (CO_2, SO_2 and NO_x)
- disposal of ash from power plants
- electromagnetic radiation from electricity power lines
- transportation of fuels
- associated accidents and emergencies

The information and experiences are analysed with a view to the employees applying this in the work situation.

Many people believe that environmental training and awareness should begin earlier in the education system. In Ireland, while it is difficult to add environmental awareness as a full subject to the school curriculum it might be possible to introduce it as part of transition year studies. In fact, an Interdepartmental Working Group on Environmental Awareness has already reported on environmental awareness inclusion as pre-service and in-service education of primary and post-primary teachers.

As environmental work in an organisation will never be complete, training also needs to be on-going. Similar to Total Quality Management, which stresses involvement of all employees in the organisation, Environmental Management is most effective with total organisation involvement. It should therefore be part of the overall business strategy and resources allocated for environmental training.

Environmental Education

Traditionally environmental courses available in Ireland at third level have been in the environmental science area. Some of the first environmental science courses to become available were the Diploma in Environmental Science introduced by Sligo Regional Technical College in 1975, followed by, the Degree in Environmental Science and Technology in 1982 and Trinity Colleges Masters Degree in Environmental Science which began in 1981. The need for Sligo Regional College's courses came about as a result of 1972 being European Conservation Year and impending of the Local Government (Water Pollution) Act, 1977.

More recently,(i.e. 1990's) there are a variety of different third level college courses available to meet the upsurge in concern for environmental protection. Listed below are some of the colleges which provide environmental diploma and degree courses:

- Coleraine University
- Dundalk Regional Technical College
- Limerick Regional Technical College
- Queen's University
- Sligo Regional Technical College
- University College Cork
- University College Dublin
- University College Galway
- University of Limerick

The current trend in third level training is to provide courses within existing science disciplines but with the term "Environmental" preceding the existing course name. It is also common to find the names of new and already established departments preceded by the word "Environmental".

Environmental issues are now so broad that it is not possible for one type of course to provide training in all aspects of the environment. There is a role for environmental science practitioners and specialists and the spread of different courses available at third-level cater for these personnel needs.

There are also environmental courses available on a part-time basis. For example, Sligo Regional Technical College offer a Post Graduate Diploma/MSc in Environmental Protection which is designed for people at work who have environmental responsibilities but lack formal environmental training. This course is provided by distance learning and allows people to upgrade their skills and academic credentials with minimum disruption to their normal employment.

Other part-time courses are provided by Forbairt and IBEC. These courses are of short duration and are in specific environmental areas such as, legislation, waste management and EMS standards. They usually tend to be topical and deal with recent issues for example, the Waste Management Regulations, 1997. There are also courses available from other training institutions on environmental auditing allowing registration to the Environmental Auditors Registration Association (EARA), on their completion.

8.6   Information and Communication

The test of how effective the EMS and Environmental management are, is how the organisation communicates internally and externally. The best progress on environmental matters will not have been worthwhile if communication does not instil confidence in employees and the public. Information and communication must be comprehensive and such that people will trust the organisation. Too much information and communication is better than too little. Communication is the only way an organisation can discover the depth of feeling about their product or its environmental effects. It is therefore the most important element of Environmental Management.

Everything the organisation does and its employees environmental behaviour communicates a message to the public. Organisations must be very careful in examining how they communicate and motivate their employees in environmental goals. By focusing on the good internal communication within the organisation this will inadvertently improve the way employees will deal with the general public. They will communicate a positive message.

Internal communications should include regular information on the following:

- Environmental effects data following monitoring of emissions to air, water etc.
- Corrective measures following non-compliance with regulations and incidents.
- Organisation developments and investment plans

The organisation should demonstrate a commitment to identifying its environmental problems openly and to solving these.

Good organisation internal communications will ensure all employees are aware of the importance of compliance with legislation, environmental objectives and targets. They should know the impact of their work on environmental effects, their roles in achieving compliance and the consequence of non-compliance or deviations from procedures.

External communications should embrace all the interested public regulatory authorities, neighbouring community, suppliers and customers. Improvements in environmental performance will have a positive message for external audiences and will instil trust and confidence in the organisation. The organisation should be cautious in giving information which may be interpreted by the media in a negative way. This may not serve the best interests of the organisation. Organisations need to be aware that its environmental performance can have an influence on its commercial performance. Decisions on whether to buy products or not can depend on consumer perception of an organisation.

Environmental Reports need to be easily understood by their target audience. The extent of the target audience feelings should be known, as well as, the detail that should be supplied. The report should reflect the importance of the organisations environmental aspects.

9 ENVIRONMENTAL AUDITING

9.1 Introduction

With the recent advent of accredited environmental management systems, including BS7750 in 1992, I.S. 310 in 1994, EMAS in 1995 (open for registration) and the publication of the ISO 14001 standard in 1996, environmental auditing as an environmental management tool has greatly increased in importance.

This chapter is designed to provide the reader with a non-technical overview of the auditing process. It is not, however, a course in auditing, and is not intended to provide the reader with the skills and knowledge required to undertake a site audit. Rather, this chapter will provide a general introduction to environmental auditing, and outline the main reasons for undertaking an audit and the benefits which it can provide. The chapter will also familiarise the reader with both the jargon and practical steps necessary to undertake this process, which will forearm the company manager should he be seeking to commission an environmental audit himself.

9.2 What is Environmental Auditing?

Environmental auditing is a management tool used to check compliance with legislation and assess whether the systems in place are delivering the company's policies and goals effectively. In short, it is a tool to allow management to check that the company is doing what it should be doing.

An environmental audit will normally assess legal compliance - helping the company to ensure that its own operations are within the law, and that it is not liable to the threat of prosecution or litigation.

However, to suggest that an environmental audit is restricted to only assessing legal compliance would be short-sighted and would overlook many of the additional benefits the audit process can bring. More and more companies have found that undertaking an audit is a **profitable** activity, and it has commonly led to the identification of risks and/or cost saving opportunities within a company which may have previously gone unnoticed.

A *reactive* company, concerned with only doing the minimum legal requirement, will use an environmental audit just for ensuring legislative compliance. A *pro-active* company on the other hand, would be able to use an environmental audit for; identifying problems and possible corrective measures, measuring environmental performance, and pursuing eco-efficiency (eco-efficiency is the concept of obtaining economic benefits from ecological improvements). The audit process, if used properly, will also allow the company to examine new methods of gaining a competitive edge in the marketplace.

In this respect an environmental audit must be viewed as part of a process of continual improvement and will build upon the systems based approach already established in most companies. The environmental audit is not a one-off activity. It needs to be seen as an on-going programme where the audit is not only repeated periodically but developed in terms of scope and sophistication over time.

It is also important, however, not to view the environmental audit in isolation, nor to see it as the placebo for all environmental problems. The environmental audit is normally only one component, albeit the most important component, of a comprehensive environmental management system.

9.3   The Objectives of Environmental Auditing

The key objectives of an environmental audit are:

To verify compliance
One of the primary purposes of an audit is to verify compliance with local, national and international laws, regulations and standards, as well as ensuring that activities are adhering to the companies own policies and goals.

To identify problems
The audit will aim to detect any leakage, spills or emissions within the company's operations and production processes at an early stage. Deficiencies in the production process which emerge over time can also be traced through the audit process.

To measure environmental impact
The audit will indicate how the company's activities impact upon the environment, covering such issues as emissions to air and water, solid waste disposal, noise, energy use and health and safety.

To measure performance
An environmental audit provides a measure of the company's environmental performance, allowing management to benchmark the company's activities against competitors.

To confirm the effectiveness of the environmental management system
The audit gives an indication of how both the EMS and general management systems as a whole are performing within the company - it may also provide indications of how the systems can be improved.

To develop the company's environmental strategy
The results of the audit will aid management in developing the company's environmental policies, goals and long-term strategy.

9.4   Why Undertake an Environmental Audit?

The simple answer is that it is always important to check that what should be done, is being done. Since companies are legally required to comply with environmental legislation, it is important they check that they are actually in compliance. It is only through auditing that a company can discover whether any of its activities are in breach of the law and thus liable to prosecution or litigation.

The motivation for undertaking an environmental audit can vary in each company - some may be concerned with ensuring compliance with a growing body of environmental legislation, others may wish to improve their market competitiveness, or they may need to satisfy the demands of insurers, investors or their customers, or they may wish to capitalise on newly emerging 'green' markets. The environmental audit offers a structured approach to pursuing any or all of these goals.

The first experience many companies will have with an environmental audit will be through their attempts to establish an environmental management system. An environmental management system (EMS), whether informal or certified, is likely to become an increasingly important tool for management in the future. Recent IPC legislation for example has awoken many companies to the need for an effective EMS if they are to remain in business.

The primary benefits of the audit process are (1) to identify the environmental problems associated with the production of goods or services before they become liabilities; (2) to develop benchmarks of good practice; and (3) to act as the basis of an evolving corporate environmental strategy. In addition an environmental audit can also help to; increase awareness of environmental policies and responsibilities among the company's workforce, identify new working practices which can significantly reduce waste and energy use, and finally, evaluate the internal training programmes and identify training needs within the company.

While many of these benefits contribute to the internal management of a company, there are also a number of external incentives for undertaking the audit process, these include:

Insurance
The costs of remediation following a pollution incident have increased dramatically in recent years - managers can now be held personally accountable for pollution incidents and imprisonment is possible - the result is that both premiums and the number of exclusions from policies have increased sharply. There are now few insurance companies prepared to cover general pollution risks unless the company is undertaking a regular environmental audit.

Market forces
A consequence of growing public awareness of the environment is that consumers are increasingly willing to switch to 'greener' more 'eco-friendly' products. The growth of green consumerism has challenged existing companies to demonstrate that their products and processes are environmentally friendly, while also providing a major marketing opportunity for new 'green' products. In the past the validity of many company claims have been questioned, and recent national and European initiatives on eco-labelling are designed to reduce consumer confusion and prevent unscrupulous manufacturers and retailers from jumping on the green bandwagon.

Companies are also being pressurised from the financial markets with environmentally literate shareholders, employees, insurance companies and ethical investment funds all demanding improved environmental performance. In the face of such stakeholder demands the environmental audit remains one of the best ways for a firm to demonstrate its environmental credentials.

Provision of Information
Applications for discharge consents, an IPC licence or stakeholder demands can often require the completion of complex questionnaires - which is often impossible without the information produced by an environmental audit. Auditing will consider not only current compliance, but will also anticipate the impact of future legislation and regulatory demands.

While the benefits of environmental auditing can be clearly identified it is also important to note that the process itself may not be entirely problem free. There are commonly financial considerations to take into account, and the company must be prepared to meet the costs of both the audit process and the cost of complying with the audit findings.

There may also be hostility to the audit process from within the company. There may be a natural reluctance on the part of management and workers to see outsiders entering the company in order to assess their performance. Managers may be uncomfortable if they feel their lines of responsibility are being invaded, and the legitimacy of an audit team, which may not have the same level of knowledge of an industry as the employees, can be challenged. It is therefore essential for the success of the environmental audit that senior management are seen to be supportive of both the audit team and the process.

9.5   The Use of External Consultants
Many of the consultancies which undertook environmental auditing initially have grown out of quality assurance operations or developed skills acquired in Environmental Impact Assessment Studies. Environmental auditing however, requires skills which go beyond these fields and relies on a more interdisciplinary approach.

The use of external environmental consultants in the auditing process is likely to increase in the future because:

1)All but the very largest firms can afford to maintain the necessary in-house expertise to adequately cover the legal, scientific and technical skills required in an environmental audit. Training existing staff members is an option but may prove costly in the short to medium term, and even when finance is available, SMEs (Small to Medium- sized Enterprises) in particular may face difficulties freeing-up sufficient manpower without stretching existing workloads.

2)Both companies and regulatory bodies are increasingly looking for independent third party verification of the auditing process, and this is a requirement of both the EMAS and ISO14000 standards. External consultants can also bring a degree of objectivity and fresh thinking to a company's activities - which may be lacking in-house.

3)Traditionally the audit process has been site specific. However, there is now a growing tendency to assess the linkages between companies and determine the overall impact of a product throughout its entire life-cycle - the EC Eco-label scheme is just one example of this trend. Assessing the in-direct environmental impacts of a company's activities or products will require expertise and measurements beyond a single plant.

Some points to note:
When employing external consultants the company management will need to ensure that the audit team are able to demonstrate the necessary range of backgrounds and disciplines to undertake an audit. Audit teams are normally composed of between 3-5 members, although smaller companies may be able to reduce this number to a minimum of two auditors. In addition to possessing the knowledge, skills and expertise necessary to undertake the audit, ideally the team should also be able to demonstrate some knowledge of the relevant industrial activity/field.

The audit team/client relationship should be one of total confidentiality.

9.6   The Audit Process - Figure 9.1

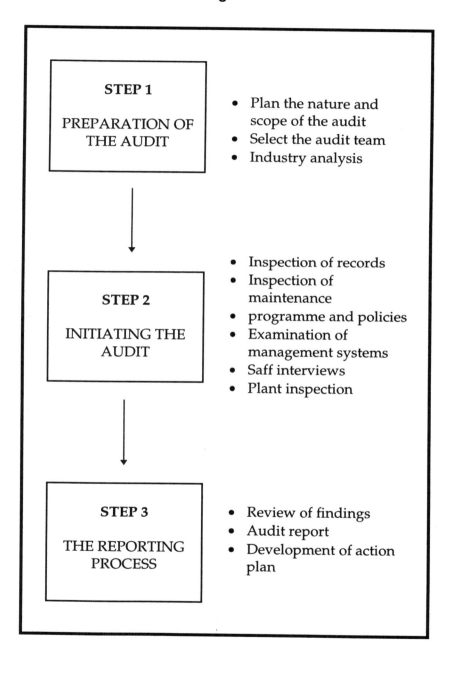

STEP 1

PREPARATION OF THE AUDIT

- Plan the nature and scope of the audit
- Select the audit team
- Industry analysis

STEP 2

INITIATING THE AUDIT

- Inspection of records
- Inspection of maintenance
- programme and policies
- Examination of management systems
- Saff interviews
- Plant inspection

STEP 3

THE REPORTING PROCESS

- Review of findings
- Audit report
- Development of action plan

Step 1 - Preparation of the Audit
I) Plan the scope and nature of the audit, and in doing so clearly
identify the subjects areas which will be included. It is important to
recognise the interdependence of environmental issues with all the
other key elements of company activity, and as such an audit will
often include many of the following areas:

- Occupational health
- Safety in the workplace
- Product safety
- Emergency procedures
- Security
- Transportation safety
- Transportation to and from the workplace
- Inventory control
- Housekeeping (both internal and external)
- Storage
- Production processes
- Procurement policies
- Corporate culture and policies
- Staff training

During the initial scoping phase of the audit, company management
will need to decide which of the company's operations or units will
be included in the study. A company's first attempts at an audit are
normally targeted at those units thought to have the greatest impact
upon the environment, with successive audits gradually widening
their scope to include more and more of the company's activities.
Managers will also need to consider which elements, if any, are to be
prioritised (e.g. air emissions, waste, soil contamination, effluent
discharges etc.) See Diagram 2 for suggestions.

II) Select the audit team - it is essential that members of the audit
team are independent and objective if the results of the exercise are
to be credible. Auditors must be free to provide management with
an honest and unbiased view of the company's activities, and their
findings should not be subservient to 'outside' issues such as
profitability, market share and production schedules. Even where a
company has suitably qualified in-house expertise, it is good practice

to ensure that at least one member of the team is external and independent of the company.

Figure 9.2

The Significant Impacts Commonly Associated
With Differing Industrial Sectors

Industrial Sector	Atmospheric Emissions	Water Use & Discharge	Solid Waste	Energy	The Natural Environment	Corporate/ Marketing Pressures	Human Health	Accidents/ Emergencies	Legislation
Agriculture, forestry & fishing	—	●	○	—	●	○	●	○	○
Energy & water supply	●	●	●	●	●	○	●	●	●
Minerals, metals, chemicals, plastics	●	●	●	●	○	●	●	●	●
Metal goods, engineering, vehicles	●	●	○	○	—	○	○	○	●
Food, drink, tobacco	—	●	—	○	—	●	●	—	○
Pulp & paper	○	●	●	○	●	●	○	○	○
Other manufacturing	○	○	○	○	—	—	—	—	○
Construction	—	—	○	○	●	○	—	●	○
Distribution & transport	●	—	—	●	○	—	—	○	○
Communications, printing, publishing	○	○	○	—	—	○	—	—	—
Banking, finance & insurance	—	—	—	○	—	○	—	—	—
Retail	—	—	○	○	—	●	○	—	○
Marketing, advertising	—	—	—	—	—	●	—	—	—

● = High Priority   ○ = Medium Priority   — = Low Priority
(Adapted from BiE 1991)

III) Industry Analysis - the audit team may provide a 'pre-survey' questionnaire, to be filled-in by the company management, in order to familiarise the audit team with the company, its activities, site and location.

Step 2 - Initiating the Audit
This will include:

I) Inspection of relevant records, certificates, discharge & disposal licenses, waste contractor permits etc.

II) Inspection of the company's maintenance programme and policies. The audit team will want to assess the strength of internal control mechanisms, and identify any risks associated with failure within the system.

III) Examination of management and their lines of responsibility, the competence of personnel, and the authorisation systems that exist.

IV) Confidential interviews with staff at all levels within the company.

V) Physical inspection of the plant, to examine working practices, management systems, safety equipment, sampling or monitoring procedures and energy use.

Step 3 - The Reporting Process
I) The audit team should confirm that there is sufficient evidence on which to base and justify their findings.

II) An official report based on the audit findings is presented to the company management. There is normally a formal 'review' of the audit report involving both the audit team and the company management to avoid any misunderstanding of the results.

III) The audit process will often conclude with the development of an 'action plan' to address the problems identified within the audit report. This will include identifying potential solutions, assigning responsibilities for action and establishing a timetable.

As the audit process, by its very nature, is reliant upon spot-checks and sampling the resultant report can only provide a snap-shot of the company's activities. There is therefore an element of uncertainty inherent in all environmental audits. By carefully scoping an audit and clearly defining its objectives in the initial stages, a professional audit team should be able to deliver a report which will provide a client with the confidence he requires in the findings.

PART 10: COMPANY PROFILES

10.1   Airport Services:

Aer Rianta: I.S. 310 and ISO 14001 Experience
by Mary O'Brien and John Murphy.

History Of Aer Rianta

Aer Rianta is a state company which first began operations in 1937. It's original task was to "operate lines of aerial conveyances directly or by means of Aer Lingus Teoranta". It was also charged with the development of aviation in general. The name Aer Rianta was derived from the translation "Air Ways" or "Air Tracks".

Aer Rianta is responsible for managing Ireland's major airports at Dublin, Shannon and Cork. The first flight from Dublin took place on 19 January, 1940. A record 9.1 million passengers passed through Dublin Airport in 1996 - over one million more than in 1995, giving the airport one of the highest rates of growth in it's history.

The birth of Shannon came about mainly as a result of it's strategic location as a transatlantic stop between Europe and America. In 1945 the first scheduled commercial flight passed through the airport. Shannon firmly established it's reputation as Europe's transatlantic gateway with the arrival also that year of TWA, Pan Am and BOAC. Perhaps, the most significant event in the history of Shannon came in 1947 when the world's first duty free shop was opened there. Cork Airport began operations on 16 October 1961 and although it is the smallest of Ireland's three main airports, it was the fastest growing of the airports through the 60's. As well as serving the important tourist areas of West Cork and Kerry it is also ideally located to service offshore gas and oil exploration work, off the south coast.

The period during the 1990s has seen the completion of a number of major capital investment schemes including the provision of improved passenger terminal facilities at all three airports, completion of a new IR£36m runway and the first phase of a IR£95m expansion of terminal facilities at Dublin Airport.

One important aspect of Aer Rianta's activities is to ensure passenger comfort and enjoyment in it's policy of "humanising" it's airports. It's famous Christmas lights display, extensive landscape programme, concert recitals and very successful "Arts Festival" are just some of the ways Aer Rianta attempts to fulfil it's ambition to be "the best organisation in the world in the field of managing airports and associated commercial activities".

Through the 80's and 90's Aer Rianta has broadened it's commercial activities with interests in the retailing, catering, hotel and tourism industries. In May 1988, "Aerofirst", a joint venture company set up by Aer Rianta and the Soviet airline, Aeroflot, opened new Duty Free shopping facilities at Moscow Airport on Aeroflot Flights.

From Aerofirst grew Lenrianta which provides duty free and catering services to Pulkova Airport in Leningrad. To support this overseas business, Aer Rianta set up a subsidiary, Aer Rianta International (ARI) which has and continues to oversee the development of many commercial ventures both within Russia and in countries in Eastern Europe, Asia and the Middle East.

In 1994 ARI was awarded the duty free contract for the prestigious Channel Tunnel. In 1996 the company became involved with the management of the Duty Free facility at Beijing International Airport. In 1997 Aer Rianta acquired a shareholding in Birmingham International Airport and in May of that year concluded an agreement to provide Duty Free Services at the new Chek Lap Kok Airport in Hong Kong.

Aer Rianta's success abroad has been mirrored by expansion at home. Aer Rianta acquired the business of a first class chain of hotels when Great Southern Hotels joined the Aer Rianta Group in 1990.

Dublin Airport
Dublin Airport has experienced significant growth over the last number of years. Over the last three years, the traffic figures have grown by about one million passengers per annum and it is expected that the airport will handle 11.3 million passengers by the year 2000. There are currently 22 airlines operating from Dublin Airport, servicing 59 destinations world-wide. Dublin Airport handled over 107,000 tonnes of cargo by 12 cargo carriers in 1996. As a consequence of the growth achieved in recent years, more attention is now being given to environmental issues. Despite the increase in traffic and the growth in the physical size of the airport facility, Aer Rianta has managed to

reduce energy consumption and water consumption with the introduction of sound environmental conservation measures.

Dublin Airport was awarded the ISO 14001 and IS 310 environmental management system standards in October 1996, making it the first Airport in the world to receive accreditation to these environmental standards.

Airports have become very dynamic enterprises and generators of jobs and wealth for the surrounding regions and their inhabitants. At the same time, their environmental impacts are giving rise to deep concern because of aircraft noise, engine emissions and air quality, soil and water contamination and waste management. The growth in air transport means that international airports nowadays represent major physical developments with a significant environmental footprint. Dublin Airport has installed a system, which effectively manages the environment and has introduced a programme of continuous improvement to ensure that the system will continue to meet the demands of both standards, while allowing for the physical development of the airport.

Environmental Issues At Dublin Airport

There are four categories of environmental issues for airport operators:

1. Those arising from the airports function as a landing and take-off point for aircraft.
2. Those arising from the transport of passengers and accompanying persons to the airport.
3. Commercial operations.
4. Airport related industries, such as aircraft maintenance, cargo handling and transport depots.

A complete environmental review of the Airport was undertaken and an environmental programme drawn up, which outlines a number of objectives and targets for Dublin Airport over the next few years.

- Sound environmental performance is increasingly seen by industry and business to have significant advantages. Protection of the environment and commercial growth are not mutually exclusive.

The main issues that concern Dublin Airport are as follows:

Air Quality

Emissions from airport sources may be broken down into four main categories:

- Aircraft operations
- Airside vehicular traffic
- Airport heating plant
- Landside vehicular traffic

Aircraft operations emissions arise during different modes of operation. Take off and landing studies over a number of years have indicated that hydrocarbons, which includes a large group of organic molecules containing hydrogen and carbon are of most interest. The fuel-derived benzene and toluene are normally included in any systematic analyses of air quality at airports. Oxides of Nitrogen (NOx) are also measured as they are emitted to the atmosphere during combustion through oxidation of fuel nitrogen.

Reduction in hydrocarbon emissions may be expected in the future through the use of aircraft engines with high combustion temperatures and compressors, however, this gain may be at the expense of high NOx emissions.

Dublin Airport measures the ambient air quality levels at two monitoring sites, once a quarter. The standard of air quality is satisfactory compared with World Health Organisation Standards. Nitrogen dioxide, volatile organic compounds (VOC), the specific organic compounds benzene, toluene and xylene are determined in ambient air. Particulate matter (PM-10 sampling) has recently been added to the monitoring programme.

The standard of air quality monitoring were generally good with Nitrogen Dioxide being normally within the rural range for this parameter of air quality.

Waste

Aer Rianta Dublin Airport handled over 9 million passengers in 1996 and this large passenger throughput produced almost two thousand tonnes of waste. The sources of this waste stream are varied and range from cardboard from the Duty Free operation to general office waste. An active effort has been made to separate easily recoverable waste, such as cardboard from Duty Free Shopping areas, by the installation of dedicated compactors. This approach has resulted in the collection of 235 tonnes of cardboard and paper for recycling (in 1996). Aer Rianta now sends 12% of total waste produced for recycling. A new innovation during 1997 was the collection of damaged timber pallets for re-use in the cardboard manufacturing industry.

Energy Management

One area that has developed significantly over the last number of years is the development of a comprehensive Energy Management programme. It is interesting to note that over the last 20 years the airport building has grown in area by 49%, the passenger figures have grown by 164%, but energy consumption has reduced by 30%.

The installation of a combined heat and effective energy management programme at Dublin Airport, have led to net savings IR£90,000 per annum. Dublin Airport is currently (1997) concentrating on the elimination of heat transmission losses by decentralising the main airport heating system. The main fuel has been changed form turf to natural gas. Water consumption has also been reduced by 23% in 20 years.

A Building Management System (BMS), the Satchwell BAS 2000 system, was installed at Dublin Airport in 1988. This started with 3 outstations in the Pavilion and was extended to the Passenger Terminal and Pier 'B' with 6 more outstations in 1989.

The BMS carries out the following functions:

- Automatic control of the heating and air conditioning systems to predetermined levels.
- Full monitoring and logging of conditions etc., on site.
- Semi-automatic control of Boilerhouses.
- Semi-automatic control of combined heat and power units.
- Monitoring of standby generator.
- Control of Terminal lighting levels with automatic switching if and when required.
- Monitoring of gas and fire alarms.
- Electrical and gas metering in selected areas.

Outstations service the following areas and all new alterations and installations are automatically added to the BMS system:

- Passenger Terminal
- Pier'B'
- Pavilion
- Link Building
- Pier 'A'
- Old Central Terminal Building
- Collinstown House
- Aer Lingus Cargo Building
- Aer Lingus Flight Kitchen
- Aer Turas Building
- Car Park Boilerhouse
- Red Brick Area (Maintenance)
- Pavilion Ground Power
- Water Reservoir

At present there are 43 outstations at Dublin Airport.
Future additions will include:

- Pier 'C'/Terminal West
- Terminal 6 Bay Extension
- Pier 'A' Extension North
- New Maintenance Complex
- New Hotel
- Energy Centre

Savings are hard to determine given the structured installation process which occurred at Dublin Airport. But given the system that was in place before BMS introduction there are undoubtedly huge savings.

Other energy saving projects carried out over the last number of years include:

- The decentralisation of the Central Boilerhouse into 4 separate remote boilerhouses has cut out distribution losses which were very high.
- Dublin Airport now has boilerhouses in the Passenger Terminal, Red Brick area, Flight Kitchen/Cargo, with the Car Park Boilerhouse only serving Aer Lingus Hangars.

- The Combined Heat and Power (CHP) Unit was installed in 1994. This is a 660kW machine driven by natural gas. Annual savings on this machine after costs amount to about IR£90,000.

- A second CHP unit of 1000kW output is to be installed in 1997. This unit will supply heat and air conditioning to Pier 'C' and Terminal West as well as electricity to the airport grid. Annual savings on this machine after running costs will amount to IR£100,000.

- The main Passenger Terminal standby generator 900kW has been fitted with a mains synchroniser panel which allows the machine to run during maximum demand periods in winter in parallel with incoming ESB supplies. This has the effect of saving about 9OOkW off maximum demand tariff. The bi-monthly savings achieved on winter maximum demand amount to IR£11,000 after running costs. There are plans to fit a synchroniser panel to more standby generators at Dublin Airport. These units range from 3OOkW to 450kW. Expected savings on these three units are about IR£14,000 per 2 monthly winter Optimum Maximum Demand bill.

- As mentioned previously a Terminal Lighting Panel has been fitted to the BMS system. This allows automatic switching-off of lights in non-populated areas of the Terminal at night. Local sensors allow timed on extensions for cleaners etc., when required.

- Manual switching-off of lighting is also a feature of this system whereby the Duty Office (which is operated on a 24 hour basis) can switch off areas by means of the BMS terminal. This is done from a central location.

- All new lighting fitted to Terminal areas in future will consist of high efficiency lights with high efficiency reflectors. Constant cleaning of light fittings is now a common feature.

- An awareness campaign in the form of switch off signs is in operation at Dublin Airport.

- Dublin Airport Dublin Airport is at present in the process of building a new Energy Centre. This centre will encompass the Boilerhouses for all of the Passenger Terminal areas and also cater for future expansions. The new 1000kW combined heat and power unit together with the new absorption chiller system for Pier 'C'/Terminal West will also form part of the Energy Centre.

- The biggest change to take place as part of the Energy Centre will be the rationalisation of the ESB supplies into one 38kW ring for Dublin Airport with a capacity for the future of 20MW. Aer Rianta will take ownership of this ring main with the effect of having lower electricity charges, demand penalties and the ability of adding new CHP Units at strategic points around the Airport site. When finished, the savings are expected to amount to about IR£140,000 per annum.

The net result of all the previously mentioned energy conservation measures has resulted in a reduction of over IR£100,000 per annum in the main ESB account which covers all passenger and airfield areas.

On the natural gas front, there has been a modest increase overall but when taken in context of combined heat and power being added to the natural gas account and also the dramatic increase in traffic figures and associated services huge savings have been achieved overall.

Noise Management

Aircraft noise and noise from associated ground vehicles are the most obvious issues facing airports. Dublin Airport is planning to install a noise monitoring system which will measure local noise levels and provide information to the airport, airlines and local communities on noise levels. Airlines have to follow designated flight paths to avoid causing noise over densely populated areas. There are plans in place to conduct a study of ambient noise levels in and around the aircraft parking area, where most of the airside ground vehicles operate.

Water

Water pollution at airports is ultimately the result of poor ground operational procedures creating more polluted water than waste water/run off water treatment facilities can cope with. Surface and ground water pollution at Dublin Airport can arise from the following causes:

- De-icing agents
- Anti-icing agents
- Fuel spillage's
- Oil spillage's
- Loss of containment of liquid or water soluble cargo

- Aircraft Cleaning
- Surplus fertilisers
- Pesticide residues
- Fire fighting material
- Aircraft maintenance
- Water treatment chemicals from boiler systems

There are 4 main streams running through Dublin Airport and 2 rivers. These are monitored by the Pollution Committee for Biochemical Oxygen Demand levels and appropriate action is taken as necessary. A major environmental review of the airport site is due to take place over the next three years which will include such topics as: fuel storage areas, underground fuel pipes, aircraft washing areas, waste storage area, maintenance areas and paint shop. An intrusive site investigation (including the excavation of a number of boreholes for the purposes of soil sample collection and for ground water and gas monitoring) will also take place.

The use of urea as an anti and de-icing agent is confined to the apron area and potassium acetate is used for runway and taxiway de-icing. This is the most environmentally acceptable de-icer on the market at the moment. Research is currently underway to examine the feasibility of changing to potassium formate, which has even better environmental characteristics.

Visual Impact
As part of it's overall commitment to the environment, Aer Rianta has made every effort to control the visual impact of the airport. Areas on the main approaches to the airport, within the Aer Rianta property boundary, are landscaped with woodland, shrubs and formal flowering bedding schemes. The design concept was to screen existing aviation industrial buildings and to enhance the visual aspect of the airports environs.

As part of the overall programme to improve the aesthetics of the airport there were 15,000 bulbs, 20,000 shrubs and 5,000 trees planted at Dublin Airport in 1996.

The Introduction of An Environmental Management System at Dublin Airport

The management of the environment at Dublin Airport is an integral part of the overall management system which has been previously accredited to the Irish Quality Mark and the International Quality Series ISO 9002. Aer Rianta built on these systems to take cognisance of the environmental effects of the operations at Dublin Airport. Environmental management is a priority and Dublin Airport decided to implement a formal Environmental Management System based the principles of ISO 14001 and I.S. 310 in order to lay down responsibilities and formalised procedures.

The full effect of the aviation industry on the environment is not fully known. A number of projects are underway world-wide to establish the full effects. Dublin Airport examined the primary activities that take place and established the environmental effects.

One of the most important aspects of implementing an environmental management system is to have a benchmark against which you compare your performance. In Dublin Airport's case, the Airports Council International, which is a professional body of International Airports was used in order to compare Dublin Airport's performance with that of leading Airports in the field of environmental management.

In developing the system a team of experts from within the organisation were gathered together to define the system and to develop programmes of improvement. Some of the benefits of the EMS have resulted in the following:

- IR£ 90,000 savings on Energy Bill
- Hydrant fuelling is being phased in on aircraft stands reducing the likelihood of spillage's and resulting in a reduction of emissions to the air.
- New compactors have been introduced to increase the volume of waste being recycled.
- The number and frequency of air quality monitoring stations has been increased.
- There has been a reduction in the amount of chemicals used in cleaning and an upgrading of arrangements for their storage and disposal.

- Almost 50% of all aircraft stands have fixed ground power, which reduces the need for APUs (Auxiliary Power Units), which are used to power the aircraft's air conditioning units before take off of aircraft. This reduces noise levels and reduces energy consumption.
- The use of CFCs have been phased out.
- New controls on the airside were introduced to reduce pollution and increase safety.
- The Fire Training Department now use natural gas instead of aviation fuel, to reduce pollution.
- Building Management Systems have been introduced to control the level of lighting and heating in the terminal building.

The main force behind Aer Rianta's drive towards continual improvement was not only to pre-empt regulatory forces, but also to show a commitment to the environment in which it operates and to show a commitment to the concept of sustainable development, which is enshrined in the European Fifth Action Programme for the Environment.

Other issues which concern Dublin Airport and the Environmental Programme for the future are as follows:

> Ground Transportation: to develop and improve transportation to and from the airport, in order to reduce pollution from ground vehicles.
> Material Usage: the reduction of non-renewable materials and the sourcing of alternative products which are more environmentally friendly.
> Effects on indigenous flora and fauna: studies have been undertaken on the wildlife surrounding Dublin Airport and the effect of the industry on them.

Conclusion

The 1990s have been challenging times for Dublin Airport, experiencing unprecedented growth in traffic figures over the last decade. The company has planned a major capital building programme of over IR£200 million in order to prepare for the 21st century. Nevertheless, Aer Rianta is confident that it is well placed to continue it's vital role in the development of aviation both in Ireland and abroad.

Dublin Airport has achieved significant benefits by installing an Environmental Management System, to effectively manage the operation of the airport. Improvements in waste management, energy management, water management and overall environmental awareness among operators and staff have been significant.

The challenge lies in continuing to meet demands for air travel and to effectively manage the corresponding burden on the environment by keeping up to date with latest technology and by continuing the monitoring of performance through ISO 14001 and continuous improvement programmes resulting from that standard.

10.2   Computer Software:

Symantec Ltd., BS 7750 & ISO 14001 Experience
by James Geaney.

The following paper considers the background and development of an Environmental Management System (EMS) registered to BS 7750 and ISO 14001. The document is based on the experience of the writer who headed the implementation team in the company where he is employed.

Some of the pitfalls and boundaries are discussed and some suggestions made. It is not intended to be a definitive 'how to do it' report, rather it is intended to provoke the reader's thought following the writers experience.

The company: Symantec Ltd.

Symantec is a wholly owned subsidiary of Symantec Corporation, the company is based in Blanchardstown, Dublin and manufactures computer software. The company operates a network partnership with disc manufactures, CD manufacturers and printers.

Intended and Unintended Products.

Each business, regardless of what it does produces two types of output, the intended product and the unintended product. In general, the focus is on the intended product as this is the 'thing' which generates the revenue and profits. However, if not given adequate attention the unintended product can have such a marked impact that the business can be prevented from operating. Consider two extreme examples,a rock concert where the intended product is enjoyment for the patrons, however, the local population has to put up with the unintended products of noise, traffic, waste, etc. At the opposite extreme the intended product of a nuclear power plant is electricity while the unintended products, radioactive material, are controlled by governments.

The growth of Quality Management Systems (QMS) registration to the ISO 9000 series of standards witnesses the focus on the intended product. As the buying public has become more affluent and conscious of the impact of the unintended products, so has the focus on what companies are doing in order to manufacture and distribute the intended product and what they are doing with the by-products. This is the realm of Environmental Management Systems where the company looks at the processes and the unintended products in the same critical light as for the intended products.

Basis of an Environmental Management Systems.
The basis of an Environmental Management System is the '4Rs':

- **REJECT:** why have the feature, is the packaging required?
- **REDUCE:** does it have to be as big, is so much required?
- **REUSE:** can the item have a second or third useful life?
- **RECYCLE:** can the material be recycled?

Given the above analysis has been done, in most cases, a company will see immediate benefit, in that assumptions made in the dim and distant past and the regular ad-hoc solutions have been challenged. Once challenged and found wanting then they can be fixed.

At this stage consider:

- How much extra packaging is used in your business, just in case?
- How many lights are left on during the day or overnight?
- If machines were oiled or covers closed would there be less noise?
- If steel were purchased in standard sizes, would there be less/more wastage?
- Is nickel plating required, could the item be made from stainless steel?
- How often is the company van serviced?
- Are all the company's activities meeting environmental legislation?

Regardless of the industry the short list above can be the basis for a more comprehensive list to be used for self assessment.

Registered Environmental Management System.
The basis of an EMS has been outlined above and in most cases economic benefit will be derived from even this simple analysis. In many cases people will seek to develop the work further. For those, there is good news in that there are currently four 'third party' documents against which the EMS can be built up and benchmarked, viz.:

- BS 7750   Specification for Environmental Management Systems.
- I.S. 310   Environmental Management Systems.
- EMAS   Environmental Management and Audit Scheme.

- ISO   Environmental Management Systems.
  14000

It is perfectly reasonable to limit a company's environmental programme to an in-house model, however, much benefit can be derived from adopting one of the above models.

Some of the benefits are:

- Third party document which has been produced by impartial experts.
- Using a formalised model removes the need to rationalise and justify assumptions.
- Third party registration is possible.

Once the EMS been built up around one of the above documents, then it is just a small step to having it formally audited and registered by a third party agency. Doing this draws the additional benefits:

- Assessment and registration are carried out by an impartial expert third party, this will be more acceptable to customers and insurers than a home grown self- certification system.
- There is an ongoing surveillance programme associated with the registration.
- The registration offers a positive company profile and thus a competitive advantage in the market place.
- Such a registration offers evidence of responsible behaviour and will thus attract ethical investors and customers.
- A built in discipline will be in place to monitor the legislative situation.
- Cost savings will accrue from the ongoing analysis.

When it comes to deciding which programme to develop, it is best to consider which matches the marketplace and relationships with any current registration body. For all practical purposes the above are equivalent and in general terms the registration agencies work to the same baselines.

Building up to a Registered Environmental Management System.
Some fundamental things need to be worked out first:

- Is an EMS relevant to the business, if so is the CEO committed. If the answer to either is no, the success of an EMS is doubtful.

- What is the scope of the registration? This needs to be relevant to the business, seeking registration on, say 25% of the business activity carried out on a site would seem a little less than plausible.
- What is the company's environmental policy? This needs to be set at the highest level in the company and personally endorsed by senior officers of the company. It needs to focus on features of the business which have an impact on the environment, thus a computer company focusing on the use of motor cars is less than meaningful.
- What is the current status? This is formally termed the 'Preparatory Review', in essence it requires the company to review it's past and current activities, identifying quantitatively it's impact on the environment. Below is an outline tableau listing, for illustration only, some of the possible effects which need to be considered. Additionally, these need to be considered under 'normal conditions' and 'abnormal operating conditions'.

	Road Haulier	Sheet Metal Shop	Print Shop
Solid Waste	Packaging	Metal trimmings	Paper trimmings
Liquid Waste	From cleaning	From cleaning	From cleaning
Gaseous Waste	Exhaust		
Electricity Use			
Water Use			
Oil			
Solvents			
Acids/Alkalis			
Road Traffic	1mKm per yr.		100 000 Km per yr.
Noise		60db in plant	
Dust			
Visual impact			

Odours	Diesel fumes	Grinding, Welding	
Radiation			

This is a dilemma, to what extent and how must the effects be analysed under normal and abnormal conditions. The first problem is definitions, in the majority of cases most definitions will be clear cut, however, this is not always the case.

Consider:

- Is a decaying load of food on a truck stuck in a port a normal or abnormal situation in the EMS.
- If a factory located in an residential area, is running a three shift system for a short period a normal or abnormal situation in the EMS.
- If odours are sensed near a factory only during hot weather, is this a normal or abnormal situation in the EMS.
- If security lighting is installed around a building and it impinges on the public roadway, is this a normal or abnormal situation in the EMS.
- If a company which has been doing seasonal work for say fifty years decides to import raw material and continue all year, is this a normal or abnormal situation in the EMS.

In the above cases the company needs to rationalise it's analysis, in over simplistic terms if it is not illegal it can be argued that it is normal operating conditions. However, exercise care, if a building goes on fire accidentally, this is certainly an abnormal condition but it is not illegal.

One of the most revealing tools in the EMS development is carrying out a life cycle analysis and gauging the potential impact the company has on the both the upstream and downstream activity. Consider the impact a software company has on a steel mill, well very little considering that the amount of metal used per disc is just a few grams. Now consider the life cycle of a product and the control a company has in terms of time. Current management tools such as Just In Time (JIT) can mean the raw material, processing and distribution can be done is a few hours, but does JIT mean any nett reduction in total inventory or does it simply mean inventory is stored elsewhere?

Now the next difficult problem, how must the analysis be done and to what extent. For most companies there will be a conflict between the 'science' and 'systems' people with each emphasising their point of view.

Consider:

- Company trucks: The science approach will advocate routine analysis of exhaust emissions while the systems approach will advocate type approval supported by an annual road certificate is adequate.
- Flue emissions: The science approach will advocate analysis of emissions and probably new technology while the systems approach will advocate monitoring and focus on compliance with legislation.
- Noise: The science approach will advocate monitoring stations at various points around the site while the systems approach will advocate 'common sense' i.e. if nothing can be heard 50m from the building then there is not a problem.

In practice a significant input from both is required though the balance will need to be worked out on a case by case basis. Of course such a major project will require input from many people in the organisation, great care must be taken in selecting the implementation team. The writer suggests that the team should not be bigger than five people because getting a larger team to stabilise and perform could become difficult and day to day pressures can blunt one's focus.

The extent of the analysis is further complicated by time, for what period must a retrospective analysis be done and what method should be used. There is no clear answer to this, however, good starting points are to examine old company records where they exist, discuss the past with older or retired employees i.e. the systems approach. Where these do not exist or are not possible, as will probably be the case, since many industrial sites change hands over time then analysis of the site becomes necessary. This can include taking soil cores, examining old drains and pipework, examining the building for asbestos, etc. Once problems are found the situation becomes more difficult as the company may have to 'pay for the sins of their fathers' and clean up the site to comply with local authority regulations, EMS apart.

Preparation of the documentation is the next major undertaking for the company. It is probably a fair assumption that any company working towards a registered EMS already has a registered QMS and Safety Statement. It is suggested that it is best to integrate the three, the hierarchy below has been used by the writer.

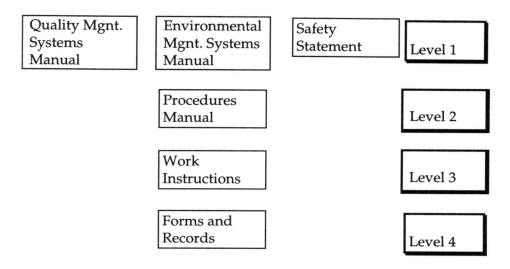

Some of the advantages of the above include:
- A unitary approach to documented management systems.
- The 'level' one documents can be used if different registration agencies are used, indeed the safety statement will need to be a standalone document.
- Revision control, distribution and use will be easier.
- This is a good basis for the upcoming QUENSH approach, referred to later.

One of the keystones on any documented system is the clarity and style of the technical writing. In most cases the documentation will be prepared by engineers, who despite the best of intentions are given to jargon, mostly the favoured TLA (Three Letter Acronym). While technical terms are required, the value of a document can be diminished by excess jargon and indifferent grammar. The writer advises that the documentation should be proof-read by a non-technical person and clarifications made.

The detail of the documentation must be sensible and reflect the level of knowledge and training of the people. Striking this balance right is usually a very difficult issue, indeed most companies that have put a QMS in place report having over-documented the system.

In preparing the documented system consideration must be given to the culture of the company, care must also be taken to avoid short-term aspirational programmes which will be abandoned once the glamour is gone from the programme. During the development of the system on which the writer worked some people advocated placing bird houses in the company's garden and feeding the birds with waste from the canteen. Against odds the writer prevented this being done as it would have been of effectively no environmental impact and would have been missed on the first wet day and subsequently abandoned due to lack of interest. On the other hand rodent control, though less glamorous is an integral part on the Health and Safety process. Other suggestions, such as, collecting used tea-bags and spreading the tea on the flower beds were stopped for the same reasons.

Improvement Objectives, the last major element of the EMS serve to tie the others together as is illustrated in the table below.

Current Situation	Route	Goal
Preparatory Review	Procedures	Policy
	Means	
	Objectives	

In the best management practice these objectives must be SMART:
- Specific
- Measurable
- Achievable
- Relevant
- Timely

These objectives need to relevant to the business, reflecting items which have a significant impact on the environment and of course reflect the policy. It would be of little meaning to set a twenty year objective for a company producing computers where the typical product life cycle is one year. However, a ten year objective may be quite acceptable for a power plant where the design life could be sixty years.

The writer recommends that the objectives are set at senior management level and the detail put on a Gantt chart supported by a narrative, listing:

- What the objective is, in quantifiable terms?
- How, where and by whom measurements will be made?
- How and by whom success will be determined?
- At what stage a sufficient level of success will be achieved to convert the objective to a standard process? Sometimes it may not be possible to improve, e.g. technological limitations or best practice is in place.

Training.
Over the last three years the situation on training has improved immensely, at present there are several excellent general training programmes on EMS, however, focused industrial training can be difficult to come by. A good source of information is the industry association to which your company belongs. Beware there are many trainers who have very little knowledge of and less experience on an EMS. An EMS is not simply an extension of a QMS it is an entity of it's own requiring industry specific knowledge. Both a 'systems and science' knowledge is required as discussed above.

In the last year a proliferation of manuals and journals has emerged offering advice, much of this is of limited benefit. The following are excellent sources of information:

- The index of the EPA act.
- The summary volumes of EU legislation, these may be inspected free of charge.
- Various texts published by Stanley Thorns Ltd.
- The Environmental Catalogue, published by HMSO.
- Information provided by registration bodies, including NSAI, BSI, NAB, SGS, Lloyds QA, etc.
- The Institute of Quality Assurance.
- Most of the above have WWW sites for people with access to the Internet. However, with other WWW sites caution is advised as much information is dubious and not accredited.

Steady State Operation of an Environment Management System.
In the early stages of the EMS frequent reviews and self audits are
necessary to establish the ongoing status. In most cases these can
parallel those of the QMS, however, a good knowledge of the science is
also required.

Probably one of the early outputs from the early EMS analysis is a
recycling process. While this will contribute to the process and will
motivate most people, at least short term, greatest benefit to both the
environment and the bottom line can be derived from the reject and the
reduce 'Rs'. Though of lower profile when these have become an
integral part of the organisation then the EMS is in steady state and
probably a very profitable 'product line'. The down side is the profit is
not seen though it's benefit is compounded year on year.

Third Party Registration.
Once the company is satisfied the EMS is adequate and has operated in
a stable manner for a period then application may be made for third
party registration. The point at which this registration should be sought
is a matter of judgement and varies from case to case, however, the
writer suggests that an absolute minimum of six months steady state
operation is required.

Following selection of the registration body application is made, as
with a QMS registration a desk audit of the documentation will be
carried out. If the documentation is found acceptable then a site audit
follows. Ultimately the day of the audit arrives, for this the company
needs to have the entire documentation set available and be able to
demonstrate the system in action, including a reasonable level of
technical competence specific to the industry.

It has been the writer's experience that the audit is both an exhausting
and learning exercise for the company and the auditors and while
auditors are critical in analysis they are objective in assessment. The
writer would be surprised if no issues cropped up during an
assessment audit, however, if these are not of major significance a
conditional registration will usually be given.

At this stage the work really starts, getting up the hill is difficult,
however, staying there is more difficult as other targets begin to acquire

urgency. This is where commitment from the CEO is critical as sustained resources are needed to support a process which has it's focus on what the company wants **'not to produce'**. The negativity and importance of the above statement must not be under estimated. The writer knows of at least four companies which have made failed starts on implementing an EMS, the failure happened due to the 'negativity' of the process.

The Future.
The Mobil Survey of 1995 reports nearly 100,000 companies registered to ISO 9000, given the general 'know-how' on registered systems, support for development of an EMS systems in the UK and growing public awareness it is reasonable to suggest that EMS's will have a faster rate of rise than QMS's.

In general a company name or brand name will give a customer confidence in the quality of a product, however, the same confidence will not follow on environmental issues. Indeed some of the finest Blue Chip names have had major industrial accidents, spanning pollution of the Rhine to dumping in third world countries. A registered EMS will thus be seen as a competitive advantage as 'Green Marketing' takes off, indeed it has arrived, consider some of the TV advertisements for German cars.

At present much work is being done on QUENSH management systems, consider the following from the British Standards Institution:

- Quality   ISO 9000 Quality Management Systems
- Environment   BS 7750 Environmental Management Systems
- Safety & Health BS 8800 Health and Safety Management Systems

Over the next few years there will be a growth in the level of Ethical Business, a preliminary scan of the business press or the Internet will show the significance which this is acquiring.

Conclusion.
The road to a registered EMS is a difficult one fraught with a dearth of good information and a proliferation of mis-information. The challenges are great but the rewards are worth the effort at both a personal and business level. Savings to the bottom line will be

compounded year on year and the image of the company will be enhanced.

In the final analysis the company will be seen by the stakeholders i.e. customers, employees, investors and suppliers as an organisation planning for the future.

10.3   Computer Hardware:

(a) IBM PCCO Greenock, ISO 14001 Experience
This company profile has been written with the assistance of Mr. Gordon Guthrie, Mr. David Chapman, Mr. Tony Quinlan and Mr. Barry Goodier. It draws on information from company brochures and previously written articles by the above.

The Company
When IBM arrived in Spango Valley, Greenock, in 1954, it was a rural area. Over forty years later, it retains it's rural character even though the facility has grown from 11,000 to 118,000 square metres and it's responsibilities have increased dramatically. The facility employs more than 3,000 people.

The formation of the IBM Personal Computer Company in 1992 gave Greenock added responsibility for the development and distribution of personal computers for the European, Middle Eastern and African market, having had responsibility for manufacture.

Yet as well as the facility, company land supports cows, sheep, mallards, coots and even a resident heron. This is not accidental. An environmental management system for the location is regularly updated to encourage this harmony. Both local and central government bodies are regularly consulted to ensure the facility stays ahead of requirements. Plant life also flourishes in and around the location.

Environmental Progress

The Facility
The IBM Corporation has set very high standards of performance for the manufacturing process. Waste water parameters are many more times demanding than legal minima, for example, on heavy metals, solvents, and oils.

The location has an environmental advisor and a dedicated environmental laboratory. The waste disposal contractors are regularly assessed by an independent consultant. Use of hazardous materials has been greatly reduced, so that Special Wastes produced have fallen to minimal levels.

Effluents, surface and groundwater are monitored meticulously and the results are reported annually, contributing to the corporate environmental management system.

Design
With $10 million invested in leading-edge quality and reliability test labs, IBM Personal Computer products are designed with high performance, high durability and long service in mind. The design of these products also places an important emphasis on minimising replacement and disposal costs.

All plastics used at the location conform to flame retardant standards although no polybrominated biphenyls or their oxides are used. Materials are chosen to ensure that volatile organic compounds are within regulatory and environmental health guidelines. A special "sniffer" laboratory analysis is carried out on all new plastic materials.

Manufacture
At the Greenock plant location you will find a corporate environmental policy which is translated into everyday practice. Everyone is encouraged to contribute to environmental management - right down to the recycling of plastic coffee cups and soft drinks cans.

Employees who make significant environmental contributions have since 1991, been recognised through IBM's Technical Excellence awards. In 1993 two Greenock employees received a Corporate award for a closed loop PVC recycling process, which is the first of its kind in the world for PVC.

All manufacturing processes have been CFC-free since 1990 and, since early 1993, have been free of all ozone depleting substances. Greenock was not just the first IBM European location to achieve this, but also the first in the industry.

In 1990 water replaced solvent, in cleaning printed circuit boards but even this method began to be phased out in 1994 with the introduction of "no-clean flux". This resulted in saving 12 million gallons of water a year, as well as the energy needed to clean the water. This is a vivid example of how good environmental practices can be cost effective - another benefit that it passes on to the customer.
Packaging

Packaging is increasingly environmentally important. Not only do you have to dispose of it from your site, the community has to dispose of it, this is often done in landfills.

All PC Company product packaging from the location conforms not only to European Union Directives but also to German recommendations, which are the toughest in Europe. Investing in test laboratories has allowed designing for precisely the level of protection needed, reducing the amount of packaging.

Plastics, such as polystyrene foam, have been cut by up to half for most products and eliminated completely on new keyboard packs. Plastic loose-fill material has been replaced with 100% recycled crushed paper. The corrugate used in cartons includes up to 65% recycled material.

Natural brown cardboard is used instead of white, which usually involves bleaching. Heavy metals - used in printing inks, for example - have also been completely eliminated.

In Operation

This is where electronic products directly affect your working environment on a daily basis. IBM Personal Computer products do not merely meet legislated standards in all countries where they are sold - they do much more. They exceed them.

The requirements of the EC Directive 89/336/EEC relating to electromagnetic compatibility have been followed in the design of equipment ever since it's issue - four years before it was due to become mandatory in January 1996. Most of the newer monitors also conform to the stringent Swedish guidelines on low frequency electric and magnetic fields known as MPR1 and MPR2. In fact, the IBM PC Company laboratory is one of only three in the world accredited to make MPR2 measurements. A technique developed by IBM further reduces electrical and magnetic fields, enabling various products to meet the even more stringent guidelines issued in 1991 by TCO, the Swedish Confederation of Professional Employees.

Reduced energy consumption has been achieved with the premium monitors which meet the US Environmental Protection Agency's

"Energy Star" standard of no more than 30 watts consumption when not in use.

The range of products with the Smart Energy System which manages energy consumption to ensure it is minimised, also meet the Energy Star standard.

A significant proportion of monitors also meet the ever stricter guidelines of the Swedish National Board for Industrial and Technical Development which specify less than 8 watts consumption when not in continuous use. In fact they typically use 4 or 5 watts.

Recycling
All packaging materials can be recycled and are marked with identification codes for easy sorting and recovery.

Product materials are also marked with recycling symbols for simple identification. Mixed or bonded materials, which make recycling virtually impossible, are avoided wherever it is feasible to do so.

Background To ISO 14001
The IBM PC Company site in Greenock, Scotland produces PC hardware for the EMEA geographies. The manufacturing processes 'on Site' and through an infrastructure of suppliers, produce Printed Circuit Boards of high complexity, and finished computers including: Servers, Desktops, Options and IBM Thinkpads, it's award-winning mobile computers.

Up until 1995 there had been a steady environmental improvement carried out through the elimination of CFC's, recycling of plastics and packaging, reduction in chemical usage, water based card wash processes and a switch to dry powder coatings as opposed to solvent based paints, etc.

Some of these activities had achieved excellence whilst other initiatives made lower impact, such as recycling of coffee cups, but all were done in an informal way with little opportunity for the synergy that could create a more focused effort had there been a vehicle available to promote this.

With more and more customers requesting information on the environmental policies and practice of the PCCo and it's products an

Environmental Brochure was produced in 1994. This was created with some difficulty since the author had to pull together all of the details of environmental achievement from all of these 'islands' of individual activity.

It was at this point that the need for an Environmental Management System and a steering committee was realised, and the concept of the Site Environmental Council was born.

Site Environmental Council (SEC)

The SEC in Greenock held it's inaugural meeting on the 9th February 1995. Attending the meeting were four managers with specific environmental responsibilities, plus three senior professionals with responsibilities in standards and management systems, health and safety, chemical and environmental control. The objectives of the SEC were agreed over two meetings, proposed to the Site Policy Group and set as follows:-

1. To implement an Environmental Management System and achieve certification to BS 7750, (later changed to ISO 14001) by 1996.
2. To advise the Site Policy Group on Environmental issues and strategy for the PCCo.
3. To ensure continued compliance with all mandatory requirements.
4. To communicate on behalf of the site on environmental matters, both internally and externally.

The SEC meets every month. It covers items on a standard agenda and addresses new issues as they arise.

Certification To ISO 14001

Pre Assessment Preparation

In mid 1995, the SEC agreed a schedule for achieving EMS certification to ISO 14001. This covered training of selective professionals in ISO 14001, choosing of the Assessment Agency, self assessment/readiness and preparation of the elements of the new 'system'.

The existing Greenock Quality Management System with the associated document control system was used as the framework on which to build the Environmental Management System.

At this stage, thirteen new Environmental procedures were created for the site covering Document Control, Emergency Readiness, Training, Waste Management, Audit Procedures, Deviation Control, External Requirements, etc.

After contact with, and estimated costs from, four agencies had been completed, the Assessment Agency selected was Bureau Veritas Quality International (BVQI). The date set for the initial assessment was 25th September 1995.

Initial Assessment
Two assessors from BVQI visited the site for one day. After a detailed investigation into environmental documentation, controls and practice, five major non-conformances, four minor and one observation against the standard were reported.

In general, the EMS in Greenock was not sufficiently 'mature' and had not been derived from 'first principles'. This meant going back and deriving the 'significant environmental aspects' of the site looking beyond the boundaries of the site geography and the products, to take account of all impacts to the environment.

At this point IBM Greenock now had six months in which to address the non-conformances and implement the EMS across all facets of business. The dates for the formal assessment were set for 15/18th January 1996 at which time the assessment team from BVQI would audit the Site EMS to ISO 14001.

Development and Implementation of the EMS to 1SO 14001
Throughout the intervening time, a further five procedures were generated to cover Waste Minimisation Targets and Measurements, Legislation and Regulations, plus Environmental Aspects.

Other requirements of the standard which were addressed during this time were :-

Training	Awareness training for new recruits. Formal certificated education plan with local university.
PCCo Policy	Statement published in local and national press.
Audit Program	Internal program started.

General   Procedures/controls/practice.

The readiness team met each week and worked with the Site Environmental Council to close out any issues. They also ensured the whole site was involved in the implementation of the EMS, and would be ready to demonstrate this to the Assessment Agency.

Formal Assessment

The result of the formal assessment again highlighted areas of inadequacy in the Site EMS. A number of minor non-conformance's were reported at the conclusion of the assessment covering :-

- Environmental aspects / selection / significant / insignificant.
- Transport / Waste improvement targets.
- Documentation.
- Housekeeping in certain areas of the manufacturing processes.

BVQI however confirmed that these would not have resulted in the loss of certification had it already been granted, and that IBM Greenock now had until the end of February to close these out.

All items were addressed at weekly reviews and as corrective action was completed, the details were sent by BVQI.

The date for the final visit was set for the 29th February when two auditors would visit IBM for one day to verify closure of outstanding items and check for any other areas of non-conformance.

Completion

After the visit on the 29th February, all previous non-conformance's were agreed to be closed although two others were opened. These covered a) calibration of the flue gas monitor in the site boiler house and b) the list of all environmental legislation affecting the site.

These were both promptly closed out and BVQI confirmed that the PCCo Manufacturing Site in Greenock does have an Environmental Management System that meets the standard of ISO 14001.

On The 9th April Mr Barry May, Chairman and Chief Executive of BVQI UK Ltd presented the certificate to the Greenock Site Director, Mr Ian J Crawford. Mr May confirmed that IBM Greenock was the first Company in the UK to achieve this registration in this manner, although a small number of others had been certified via the UK standard BS 7750. ISO also confirmed that IBM Greenock was the first PC manufacturing site World Wide to achieve certification to ISO 14001 from a standing start.

Linkage With Corporate Policy 139a

In developing and implementing an Environmental Management System that meets the requirements of ISO 14001, the PCCo in Greenock is meeting the requirements of CP 139A; since the aspects of 139A cover many of the requirements of the standard.

In particular where ISO 14001 and CP139A have led the Greenock EMS and the SEC to formalise local practice are :-

- Environmental and employee training in place. Four levels of formal education to be developed and delivered in 1996 by local academia.
- Effect on the community in terms of transport through urban areas, emissions to air and the River Clyde estuary monitored, measured and reported.
- Natural resources respected in terms of recycling of plastics, paper, wood, metal and other waste.
- Conducting a rigorous 'self assessment' that is based on analysis of mapped environmental processes and key questions that they themselves have re-visited to ensure the scrutiny of performance is maintained at a high level.
- Areas where secondary pollution to the environment is possible is avoided with direct action. Examples are where water used to wash fork lift trucks is contained and shipped to be treated to remove solids/chemicals; rainwater from the Site car parks is filtered to remove oil and sludge from employees' vehicles.
- Meeting of the highest standards of Environmental Practice.

Deliverables

In 1995 through the work of the Site Environmental Council and as a result of developing a formal Environmental Management System the following were achieved :-

- Effective communication channels now in place with Employees, Customers and Third Parties in the Community.

- Significant progress made on re-cycling of all types of waste, from domestic to process and product.
- Savings based on environmental improvements achieved and further improvements planned.
  - ➢ Energy consumption reduction
  - ➢ Waste minimisation
  - ➢ Compressed air
  - ➢ Etc.
- Conversion to Product Environmental Profiles (PEP) implemented for new products, ahead of Corporate schedules.
- Self Assessment program in place that meets the requirements of the Standard and also reports to Management on the Control status of the Site.
- Site readiness to deal with any environmental incident.
- A commitment to Continual Ongoing Environmental Improvement.

Business Advantages

The IBM PCCo in Greenock is the first PC Manufacturer in the EMEA marketplace to achieve this certification by developing an EMS from basics. This puts the PCCo in a strong leadership position that others will plan to attain in the next two years.

With virtually all 'Invitations To Tender' from major accounts now containing sections with environmental questions, the fact that IBM has it's EMS registered to ISO 14001 gives a decided marketing edge.

This will be used by the PCCo M&S Organisations to demonstrate IBM's leadership to Customers.

Future

With the IBM Corporation committed to implementing ISO 14001 across the Divisions, initially having completed a 'gap analysis' in 1996, IBM Greenock is ready to assist other locations in the development of their Environmental Management Systems by using the lessons learned and experience gained in the Greenock certification achievement.

b) Intel Ireland
BS 7750 & ISO 14001 Experience
This Company Profile was written with the assistance of the Mr. Neil Coghlan and Ms. Deborah Brennan of Intel. It has been compiled largely from the Intel company brochure, 1995 & 1996 Environmental Health and Safety Reports and the "The Design and Implementation of an Environmental Management System to ISO 14001 at Intel Ireland" Intel document by Deborah Brennan, Ciara Lynch and Fiachra Mullet.

Irish Manufacturing Facilities
Intel's needs little introduction. It is the world's most successful computer chip company commanding an enviable 80% market share. It's name is synonymous with computing and communication systems world-wide. Intel's Irish operation is very significant employing directly some 3,000 people. In addition, some 800 people are employed on-site by companies providing services to Intel under long term contracts.

Intel Ireland is situated just outside the village of Leixlip in County Kildare. The complex comprises of two microelectronic facilities and a third under construction:

- Fab 10 - an 8 inch integrated circuit manufacturing facility working at 0.6 micron technology.
- ESSM, the European Site Systems Manufacturing facility, makes system and board building blocks for the computer industry.
- Fab 14, will be the Europe's leading factory for the manufacture of advanced logic products. It comes into production in 1998 and will utilise 0.25 micron technology.

Intel's Products and Market
Intel products are instantly recognisable by the Intel Inside® identification. Recent products include processors Pentium®, Pentium Pro®, the latest MMX™ technology and recently announced Pentium II®.

Intel supplies the computing industry with the chips, boards, systems and software that are the "ingredients" of computer architecture.

These products are used by industry members to create advanced computing systems. Intel's mission is to be the preeminent building block supplier to the new computing industry worldwide.

Processor products:

- Microprocessors, also called central processing units (CPUs) or chips, are the "brains" of a computer.
- Chipsets perform essential logic functions in managing the data flow between the processor, main memory and peripherals.
- Motherboards, combine with Intel microprocessors and chipsets to form the basic subsystem of a PC.
- Networking and communications products enhance the capabilities of PC systems and networks.

Computer enhancement products:

- Flash memory provides reprogrammable memory for computers, mobile phones and other products.
- Embedded control chips are designed to perform specific functions in industrial, commercial and home based applications.

Original equipment manufacturers of computer systems and peripherals:

- PC users use Intel's PC enhancements, business communications and networking products.

Intel Ireland Manufacturing Processes
The process begins with silicon. Intel itself does not manufacture silicon wafers but purchases blank, polished wafers from outside sources and then begins the delicate process of building complex integrated circuits on them.

Fab 10: The 8 Inch Integrated Circuit Manufacturing Facility
The manufacturing process is as follows:

- An insulating layer of silicon dioxide is "grown" on top of the polished silicon wafer. The wafer is then coated with a substance called photoresist, which becomes soluble when exposed to ultraviolet light.

Masking

- Masks that were created during the design phase of the microprocessor are used to define the circuit pattern on each layer of a chip. The mask is placed over the photoresist layer. Ultraviolet (UV) light shines through the clear spaces in the mask, exposing portions of the photoresist which then becomes soluble.

Etching

- The exposed portions of photoresist are removed, revealing a portion of the silicon-dioxide layer underneath. This revealed silicon dioxide is etched away. Then the remaining photoresist is removed, leaving a pattern of silicon dioxide on the silicon wafer.

Adding layers

- Additional materials such as polysilicon, which conducts electricity, are deposited on the wafer by further masking and etching. Each layer of material has a unique pattern. Together they will form the chip's circuitry in a three-dimensional structure.

Doping

- In an operation called doping, the exposed areas of the silicon wafer are precisely targeted with various chemical "impurities" (like arsenic, boron or phosphorous in the form of ions of these ultra pure elements), thereby altering the way the silicon in these areas conducts electricity.

Creating Windows

- To provide a link to the additional layers put on the wafer, 'windows' are formed by repeating masking and etching steps.

Adding Metal

- Aluminium is applied to fill the windows, forming electrical connections between the chip's layers.

The Completed Transistor

- A wafer contains hundreds of chips, each of which may contain millions of transistors.
- The previous sequence of steps describes the photolithography process for building only one transistor. In reality, the process builds all the circuit components simultaneously on each mask. There are up to 20 masking layers and 300 process and checking steps to fabricate the complete wafer. The completed wafers are tested functionally to identify the good, fully working dies before shipment to Intel's assembly and test factories in Malaysia and the USA.

ESSM

This consists of two factories.

PC Boards Factory

The major products built by the motherboards factory are Pentium®
and Pentium Pro® motherboards.

The process flow is as follows:

Screen Printing of Solder 'Paste'

- This is for surface mount components onto the bare printed circuit board. The solder is tin-lead in paste form using the latest in 'no clean' fluxes which avoid the need for washing boards.

Surface Mounting

- High speed surface mount component placement machines pick individual components from reels or carriers and place them with extreme precision into the paste on the printed circuit board.

Infra-Red Reflow Soldering

- The oven melts the tin-lead in the solder paste which flows between the printed circuit board and the component contacts to form a bond. It solidifies as the board cools down.

Manual Insertion

- This involves insertion of 'pin through hole' components used for connectors, sockets and other components, whose size and shape make them unsuitable for machine placement.

'Wave' Soldering

- Soldering of 'pin through hole' components takes place as the board flows over a wave of molten solder. The pins and holes are filled with molten solder which solidifies as the board cools down.

Automated Testing

- Testing of individual components 'in circuit' then takes place. The complete board is tested functionally by running software programmes testing all of the functions and providing details of any failures.
- An intelligent conveyor system transports all boards through the process steps in a continuous flow.

PC Platforms Factory

In the PC platforms factory, the major products are PC's and Servers.

The process flow is as follows:

Collect a Set of Modules into a 'Kit'

- The 'kit' required to assemble depends on the specific version of the PC.

Assembly

- This is a manual assembly process which finishes with the PC ready to be tested.

'First test'

- This consists of running software, under the control of an operator, to exercise all the functions of the PC.

Extended test

- At this stage PCs undergo continuous self-controlled testing and are then loaded with software, ready to run.

Inspection & Packing

- PC's are then ready to be shipped to European PC manufacturers.

Background to EMS in Intel
In 1994 of the Environmental Protection Agency and integrated pollution control licensing (IPCL) came into existence. Intel Ireland had a system for environmental management however to meet the future requirements of an IPCL a robust EMS was needed. The EMS was designed to meet the needs of both BS 7750 and the then draft ISO 14001.

Intel Ireland took this proactive step to position itself ahead of potential European legal requirements and to place themselves in the forefront of best international practice. They became one of the first significant electronics facilities in Ireland and Europe to achieve registration to the ISO 14001 standard. They have benefited significantly from third party registration to ISO 14001 & BS 7750 EMS. The EMS provided confirmation that the organisation is managing it's environmental affairs, in accordance with an internationally recognised standard.

Design of the EMS

The design of the system was broken into two distinct areas. Operationally the system was driven by the site Environmental Policy and list of prioritised or significant environmental effects, Fig.10.1.

Operational Design

- Environmental Policy. It embodies the Intel Ireland environmental values and objectives which drive the EMS. It is consistent with the core principles of the Corporate Environmental Health and Safety Policy.
- Site Environmental Management Manual. This is a high level reference manual that describes the operational and administrative structures within the EMS. It also details roles and responsibilities within the EMS as well as the methods adopted for implementing, reviewing, updating and maintaining each element of the EMS. It's goal is to provide a route map to the different levels of the EMS and to describe how each element of the ISO 14001 standard has been integrated into Intel management structures.
- Register of Environmental Effects. It identifies and examines all direct and indirect effects associated with Intel Ireland operations. A screening procedure is built into the register, this facilitates the evaluation of the effects and determines those of greatest environmental significance. Effects are screened into four categories and targeted for operational control.

Figure 10.1. Intel Ireland Environmental Management System Operational Structure:

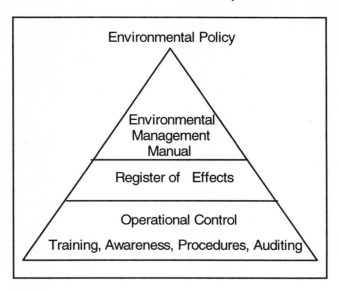

- Legal Register. It is a list of all legal requirements pertaining to Intel Ireland. The register includes applicable legislation, planning consents, environmental permits and corporate environmental health and safety guidelines. The legal register is tied to the register of effects in that any significant changes in legal requirements are automatically entered into the effects register and tracked to operational control.

Administrative Design

Administratively the EMS was based on the Intel Ireland safety organisational structure Fig. 10.2. Strategic direction for the site is set by site Environmental Ops group. This is the group who are ultimately responsible for the EMS. Management review of the system is undertaken periodically by the Environmental Ops. The aims and objectives of Environmental Ops are :

- Communication to site managers of:
- Environmental information, including audit results, trends, legal updates, future plans.
- Review of EMS Improvement Plan and performance against plans by the business units.
- Ratification body for Environmental Self Assessment results, policy & decisions made at EMS coreteam level.

- To provide leadership and direction on environmental matters as necessary.

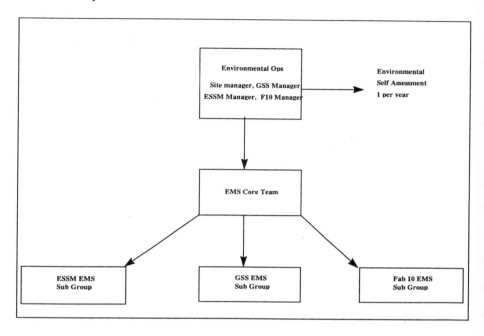

Figure 10.2. Intel Ireland Environmental Management System Administration Structure.

Once per year, Environmental Self Assessment is completed by the Environmental Ops group. The procedure is similar to Safety Self Assessment, the self assessment criteria are the administrative and operational elements of an EMS as laid down by ISO 14001 EMS. The process allows the site management team to review progress against environmental objectives and targets on an annual basis as well as the effectiveness of the EMS itself.

The next level of the management structure is the EMS coreteam. The team is composed of cross site personnel who represent their areas. They were key in the design, implementation and certification of the EMS to ISO 14001 at Intel Ireland. Their responsibilities are to work with the Environmental Engineer in the development of annual goals

252 Successful Environmental Management

and objectives and to work those goals and objectives in their areas.

Day to day operational work takes place at the sub group level, whereas EMS updates are covered at the quarterly coreteam meeting. The goal of the coreteam and the sub groups are to put environmental effects into operational control. This is achieved through environmental audits, awareness training and environmental pass downs and presentations. They ensure that the environmental content of their specs, procedures and programmes are appropriate to the EMS. They are the backbone of the EMS.

Implementation

Where possible the requirements of the EMS were to be built into existing processes or were to be designed in such a way that they could be merged with an existing system at a later date. For example, the Ireland Environmental Management Incident (EMI) system, which is used to investigate an environmental incident or environmental SBI (Safety Bulletin Incident) has exactly the same structure as the SBI programme.

Intel's first step in the implementation of an EMS to the standard set by ISO 14001 was to draft a Site Specific Environmental Policy. The Site Policy is in keeping with the principles of Intel's Corporate EMS Policy. Following that, resources for the EMS coreteam were negotiated with site management and the coreteam was established. The coreteam were given environmental awareness and EMS awareness training to bring them all to the same level of environmental knowledge.

The Environmental Team had developed a draft Register of Environmental Effects for the site. The information to develop the register came from a number of sources including the Fab 10 and Fab 10e, Environmental Impact Assessments, incident reports, environmental licence applications and various other environmental documents.

Following identification of the effects a screening tool was developed. The screening tool poses a number of questions to determine if an effect is in operational control.

The EMS coreteam verified the effects and classification of the effects for their areas. The goal of the coreteam was to put the effects identified in their area into operational control.

The EMS coreteam and the Environmental team applied targets and objectives to each effect to ensure it is brought into operational control. Most effects identified in 1996 related to strengthening permit/licence compliance systems. Existing management systems were used to achieve operational control.

The final element in Intel's implementation programme was an environmental auditing programme. The auditors were trained in environmental awareness, EMS and auditing. The programme is based on the safety auditing programme except that the frequency of environmental audits relates to potential environmental effect.

Registration to ISO 14001
The final element of the Intel Ireland process was Environmental Self Assessment, where the site managers reviewed the work to date, revised the Intel Ireland Policy, agreed the areas for improvement for the following year and committed to continuous improvement.

Following Environmental Self Assessment, the assessment for registration to ISO14001 took place. The assessment process had three distinct phases:

- Firstly, a preliminary assessment was completed. The focus of the assessment was to ensure that the methodology used to develop the register of effects was acceptable and that the EMS itself was auditable.
- The second phase was a literature review.
- The final phase, the main assessment, consisted of a document review, plant audits and interviews with site managers, coreteam, super supplier personnel and employees.

Benefits
Intel Ireland benefited significantly from third party registration to ISO 14001 and BS 7750. It has provided confirmation that the organisation is managing it's environmental affairs, in accordance with internationally recognised standards. The improved

management programme allows better supervision and control of activities that can impact on the environment and gives a mechanism which fosters the philosophy of continuous improvement throughout the organisation.

Environmental awareness was raised through all levels of the organisation. There is an integrated environmental responsibility built into business operations. Environmental considerations are an integral part of new projects, construction or process change. Employees take ownership for environmental matters in their areas.

Through the EMI Intel have a formalised system for analysis of the root cause of environmental incidents and near misses. This improved procedure has given the site, a better tool to investigate and fix any weaknesses in control and management Systems.

By using the register of effects and the screening mechanism, a systematic method was put in place to identify the most significant environmental effects. These effects became priorities and were worked on until operational control had been achieved. The method enables projects to be prioritised for capital submissions in terms of environmental impact.

Intel Ireland now have an independent, authoritative statement of conformity to the standards. By using independent assessors it is also positive where site public affairs is concerned. Feedback from the Community Advisory Panel and peers in industry has been positive. EMS is a platform for Environmental Excellence at Intel Ireland.

Environmental Reporting At Intel Ireland
Intel Ireland prepare an annual Environment, Health and Safety Report which is available to the public. The report details environmental, health and safety information including results, achievements, plans, emergency preparedness & response etc.
The following are examples of some initiatives undertaken:

- River Rye Enhancement. This was aimed at improving the River Rye habitat. Intel worked with the Office of Public Works, the Dept. of Zoology, UCD, the Central Fisheries Board and the Leixlip and District Angling Association. The project resulted in a 115%

Increase in Salmon.
- Fab 14 Excavation Re-use. To avoid extensive vehicle traffic and the use of off-site landfill, Intel undertook to use the 250,000 cubic meters of excavated rock and soil from Fab 14 within it's own site.
- External Safety Relationships. In 1994 Intel was awarded from the Construction Industry Federation for the Safest Construction Project during the building of Fab 10. In 1995 Intel Ireland received the 'Best New Entrant' Award in the National Irish Safety Organisation (NISO) safety competition. More recently, Intel Ireland received the British Safety Council Award for the electronics industry sector.
- In 1996 Intel Ireland achieved a recycling rate of 36%, for non-hazardous materials such as plastics, timber, metal cans and paper. The 1996 goal was 55%, double the national industry 5 year goal of 25%.
- Sulphate Reduction. A reduction in sulphuric acid consumption of 200 tons/annum was achieved and effluent sulphate concentration was reduced from 300mg/l to 140 mg/l.
- Noise Reduction. A plan was put in place to target the primary noise sources and a number of engineering upgrades were implemented with a consequent reduction in noise levels of up to 5dB.
- Salt Reduction. Using exhaustive laboratory testing Intel engineered a process change water treatment plant which allowed the company to improve treatment efficiency and achieve a greater than 30% reduction in salt discharges.
- Non Aqueous Cleaning. The process of producing printed circuit boards, in the ESSM factory, has been radically changed and upgraded to a dry process, eliminating the requirement to rinse boards clean after assembly, halving water consumption and reducing Lead, Copper and Zinc in waste water.

Future Initiatives
Intel Ireland have identified the following key areas of environmental development on which to concentrate and dedicate their resources in 1997:
- Training
- IPC Licensing

In the first half of 1997 Intel will focus on the training of the EMS coreteam. This will entail improving the standard and competency level of coreteam members.

Environmental awareness training will be developed for the Intel general site population. In addition, Fab 14 will be brought into the EMS process as the factory comes on line in 1998.

10.4   Chemicals/Fibres:

DuPont (UK) Ltd., Responsible Care® Experience

This company profile has been written with the assistance of Ms. Patricia Shaw of DuPont UK Ltd. It draws on information from company brochures, company information and annual reports.

The Company

Late in 1957, DuPont Company (United Kingdom) Limited announced it's plans to build a large Neoprene synthetic rubber plant on the site of an old Naval airfield at Maydown. Maydown is situated five miles north-east of the City of Derry on the shores of Lough Foyle, with the River Faughan skirting it to the east. The site occupies 416 acres of which about 120 acres are laid out as gardens around the manufacturing areas, forming an attractive landscape. This includes a wildlife pond and butterfly garden. Beside the plant DuPont are currently developing a nature trail and an interpretative centre for use by employees, their families and local schools and colleges. Displays in the centre will tell the history of the DuPont company, with special emphasis being given to the Maydown site.

Construction of the Neoprene plant started in 1957 and the first product was produced on May 12th, 1960. Since that time the plant has been expanded and modernised. The site began to manufacture Lycra® (DuPont's Registered Trademark for it's elastane fibre) in 1969 and has been continuously expanded since that time. It continues to be a thriving part of the business at Maydown.

The most recent addition to the Maydown product line is Kevlar® (DuPont's Registered Trademark for it's aramid fibre). It is one of the worlds strongest synthetic fibres.

The Maydown works currently has 960 employees and 250 sub-contractors employed.

Products and Processes

The UK market accounts for 12% of DuPont's products, while 88% is exported outside of the UK.

1. Neoprene

Neoprene was the first general purpose rubber to be commercially manufactured.

It is one of the most versatile synthetic elastomers on the market. Properly compounded Neoprene synthetic rubber resists deterioration from oil, grease, oxygen, ozone, chemicals, abrasion, sunlight, weather and fire. The customers include many household names in the rubber industry.

Neoprene is used to make conveyor belts, hoses, seals and expansion joints, power cables, wet suits and inflatable boats.

In the Latex form, it goes into rubber gloves, protective clothing, adhesives, sound-proofing and fire-resistant furnishings.

Neoprene FB, which is made only at Maydown, is used as a lining for the solid fuel rocket launchers in the Space Shuttle Programme.

Manufacturing Process

The manufacture of Neoprene is simple in principle and extremely complex in practice. It is manufactured as a multi-stage process.

The raw materials, butadiene and chlorine, are combined to form a dichlorobutene. This is refined and reacted under the influence of a catalyst, to form chlorobutadiene which is then polymerised.

Chlorobutadiene is a very small molecule, normally a mobile liquid. The process of polymerisation is similar to going from the single bead to a string, many thousands of beads long. It is this step which converts a simple chemical, chlorobutadiene, into a rubber.

The polymerisation is carried out by suspending the single molecules of chlorobutadiene in water and catalytically causing the single molecules to unite in long threadlike molecules.

The rubber is isolated by a freeze role process which was introduced in 1987. Here the film is formed by freeze coagulation onto a cold drum. The film is then washed and surplus water removed by squeeze rolls followed by hot air oven drying. The film is formed into ropes which are cut into "Chips", put into bags and sent to customers. The product is also sold in the emulsion form as Neoprene Latex and Neoprene FB.

2. Lycra®

Lycra® elastane fibre, invented in the DuPont laboratories has been revolutionary because it adds new dimensions to the concept of stretch. Lycra® is a man-made fibre which has special properties of stretch and recovery superior to those of rubber. The first of the group of fibres generically called elastane, Lycra® weighs a third less than a conventional elastic thread, but is considerably stronger, wears longer and provides two to three times the restraining power, so vital in foundation garments, swimwear and intimate apparel. Just 2 or 3% of Lycra® in a fabric can give 25% or more stretch.

Lycra® in weaves and knits for leisure and fashion wear, improves the drape and shape retention and recovery from wrinkles. Lycra® swimwear, innerwear and active sportswear give lasting fit and comfort and freedom of movement, and the use of Lycra® in sheer hosiery, where it brings improved comfort, wrinkle free fit and luxurious feel.

Manufacturing Process

The chemical structure of Lycra® is technically known as a segmented polyurethane where the stretch properties derive from a molecular chain structure built of "hard" and "soft" segments. The raw materials, to give this segmented structure, are mixed with solvent and reagents to form a polymer solution. Pigments and other enhancers are then mixed with the polymer to augment it's whiteness and dyeability, and to tailor it's properties for specific end use conditions.

The solution is then filtered and routed to storage tanks before the polymer is formed into a fibre in spinning. The spinning of Lycra® yarn is accomplished in production units called 'cells'.

Filtered solution is accurately metered to and forced through spinnerets (flat metal discs containing a pattern of minute holes) emerging into the spinning cell in fine streams. As the streams pass down the cell, the solvent is evaporated and each stream solidifies into a filament. At the base of each cell, the resulting fibre is wound on to tubes to form "cakes" of Lycra®.

Every cake is inspected and tests are done to ensure that Lycra® specifications are met before the product is packaged and shipped.

Further downstream processing can also be completed if necessary to meet specific customer requirements. For example, the Lycra® from a great many cakes can be wound together on a flat threadsheet, known as a beam, for use in warp knitting.

3. Kevlar®

Kevlar® aramid fibre was discovered in 1965 and was first introduced by DuPont in 1971. Kevlar® is the world's strongest synthetic fibre. It has the highest specific tensile strength of any fibre commercially available. Weight for weight, Kevlar® is five times stronger than steel. It offers excellent thermal stability and has a low elongation of break, plus excellent dielectric properties.

Kevlar® is available in a filament yarn, staple, pulp and fabric forms to serve a variety of industries and applications. It is ideal for applications requiring high strength at low weight and resistance to corrosion, heat and chemical attack. It is used extensively in marine, aerospace, automotive and sports composites, ropes and cables in the offshore oil industry. It is also used in safety apparel.

Kevlar's® abrasion resistance, compounding properties and high temperature performance have made it an ideal material for brake pads and gaskets. Kevlar® continues as the preferred reinforcement in high performance tyres, and is utilised to reinforce conveyor belts and flexible tubings.

Manufacturing Process

Kevlar® aramid yarn is made from an aromatic polyamide polymer. To produce the fibre, the polymer is mixed with a solvent to form a solution of controlled concentration and viscosity. The solution is then filtered, passed through spinnerets and quenched to form a filament yarn. The filaments are then washed with water, neutralised and dried. The bundle of filaments are then wound onto tubes to form bobbins of Kevlar®. Advanced process control techniques are extensively used to assure the high quality standards required for this fibre.

Environmental Protection

DuPont is located on the shores of Lough Foyle, an area of environmental importance, and the company is keenly aware of it's responsibilities.

The DuPont Company and the Maydown Works are committed to being 'a good citizen' in the community and this includes the protection of the environment.

Traditionally, DuPont has been a leader in the chemical industry in developing and applying environmental control technology and has supported sound environmental legislation.

The Maydown Works currently has an investment of nearly $10 million in environmental control facilities and spends about $2 million each year to operate the facilities. This includes the equivalent of more than 30 people full-time to operate and maintain the equipment and perform other functions required for environmental control.

Environmental projects at Maydown receive a priority listing in terms of funding and prompt implementation. They are very actively engaged in a "Responsible Care®" approach, which is aimed at continually improving environmental performance.

The River and Estuary Quality Survey carried out by the Department of Environment in Northern Ireland covering chemical and biological monitoring showed the Faughan and the Foyle to be of a high quality.

Organisation of Safety, Health and Environment
The site's Safety, Health and Environmental Affairs Group (S.H.E.A.), part of the Technical and Commercial Services Department, has, as it's primary concern, the safety and health of all site personnel. It provides resourcing and leadership in the areas of safe practices, fire protection, environmental protection and the safe handling and shipment of plant materials. Additionally, it consults and advises plant management and line organisation in matters pertaining to compliance with government regulations concerning clean air, clean water and occupational health and safety.

> **"We will not make, handle, use, sell, transport or dispose of a product unless we can do so safely and in an environmentally sound manner."**

These words help to reflect a commitment to safety which began in 1811 when the first safety rules were posted in the company's original powder mills. It is difficult to assess how much time is dedicated to the safety programme but it is a never-ending task in which each individual employee, in accepting a job, assumes the responsibility for working safely as a condition of employment.

Eleven main safety committees and many more sub-committees exist to review and update procedures and develop programmes which create employee interest both on and off-the-job site safety. As a result of these efforts, and the commitment of each individual employee, workers at the Maydown Works are 100 times safer than the average-employee in the chemical industry.

Over the years, the Maydown Works has received twenty-two International Department awards in recognition of having achieved goals for periods of excellent safety performance.

Maydown Works has also won the prestigious RoSPA Award (Royal Society for Prevention of Accidents), the Sir George Earle Trophy, on each of the three occasions that they entered - 1978, 1985, 1992 - and also the Weilness Award in 1994, in recognition of the efforts and achievements in improving the health and well-being of all employees.

DuPont's Commitment

Maydown's challenge is to meet the goal of zero waste, zero emissions and zero injuries. Their commitment is as follows:

> "We affirm to all our stakeholders, including our employees, customers, shareholders and the public, that we will conduct our business with respect and care for the environment.
>
> We will implement those strategies that build successful businesses and achieve the greatest benefit for all our stakeholders without compromising the ability of future generations to meet their needs.
>
> We will continuously improve our practices in light of advances in technology and new understandings in safety, health and environmental science.
>
> We will make consistent, measurable progress in implementing this commitment throughout our world-wide operations".

DuPont supports the chemical industry's Responsible Care® and the oil industry's strategies for today's environmental partnership as key programmes to achieve this commitment.

The main elements of the commitment are:
- Highest standards of performance and business excellence.
- Goal of zero injuries, illnesses and incidents.
- Goal of zero waste and emissions.
- Conservation of energy, natural resources and habitat enhancement.
- Continuously improving processes, practices and products.
- Open, public discussion and influence on public policy.
- Management and employee commitment and accountability.

Environmental Targets and Objectives
As part of DuPont's world-wide strategy for improvement, the Maydown site is committed to contribute to the following environmental goals:

- Packaging - World-wide across all businesses, DuPont is driving towards zero packaging waste, with interim targets to reduce by 35% by 1998 and 50% by 2000. This supports EU and UK government initiatives.
- Energy Efficiency - Improve energy used per kg of product produced- A 15% reduction of 1991 rate by the year 2000 is expected.
- Air Quality - Reduce priority air emissions and air carcinogens by 90% by the year 2000 (based on 1990).
- Water - Reduce the quantity of water consumed per kg of product.
- Hazardous waste - Reduce all hazardous waste at source.
- Wildlife - Enhance wildlife habitat at all manufacturing sites.

The specific site objectives for the Maydown Site include:
- Respect the external authority consent limits for discharge to water and air 100% of the time.
- Increase local community awareness of site operations including discharge information.

- Improve access to our ecology area for community interest groups.

Responsible Care® Programme
Responsible Care® is the international chemical industry's programme for continuous improvement in all aspects of safety, health and environmental protection. A network of working groups at Maydown involves personnel at all levels in Responsible Care®.

DuPont applies six codes of practice world-wide:
- Product stewardship.
- Process safety management.
- Distribution safety.
- Employee health and safety.
- Pollution prevention.
- Community awareness and Emergency Response.

Product stewardship
Product stewardship covers safety and environmental protection throughout the lifecycle of manufactured products - from initial production to end-use and recovery.

Product stewardship within DuPont is rooted not just in the company's ethical commitment and good corporate citizenship, but also in sound business common sense and the commitment to helping customers and end-users.

The commitment at Maydown has included the development of a new packaging material for synthetic rubber product, Neoprene. Traditionally, Neoprene was packaged in paper sacks. After using Neoprene, customers had to dispose of the waste paper. A new packaging material of specialised plastic has been developed. Now the packaging and the Neoprene are added together in the customers mixers. The waste problem simply disappears. This innovation won the Eco-Design category in this year's Better Environmental Awards for Industry, sponsored by the Irish Government agency, Forbairt.

DuPont believe that every employee can make a contribution towards protecting the environment during their involvement with the lifecycle of DuPont's products.

DuPont's commitment includes:

- Inventories and environmental assessments of raw materials, energy and water.
- Assessment of the safety, health and environmental impact of their products.
- A clearance system ensures that new and modified products meet or exceed in-house and external safety and environmental requirements.

At Maydown they are exploring various options for product recovery and disposal and have committed significant resources in working for the minimisation of waste.

Process Safety Management
DuPont has a long history of developing, building and operating safe facilities. The commitment to process safety and process hazards management continues as they integrate this code with everyday operating procedures. The Commitment has been shared with contractors and regular audits have-been carried out of their activities.

Frequent Process Safety Management audits are conducted both by plant personnel and off-site resources in order to measure safety performance using the standards required by the Responsible Care® Code.

A comprehensive Process Safety Management audit programme helps to ensure that high standards are maintained and improved.

In 1995, a lecture series on the subject of Process Safety Management (PSM), developed between the Maydown site and The Queens University of Belfast, won a Judges Special Award in the Institution of Chemical Engineers 'Excellence in Safety and Environmental Awards'.

The Maydown PSM committee created course material for the second year Chemical Engineering (Honours) students at Queen's and it was conceived as a significant step towards the development of engineers who would enter employment aware of the skills required for the safe management of Design, Installation, Process Operation and System Changes.

The National Vocational Qualification (NVQ) system is being implemented at Maydown. The NVQ system supports the requirements of the Responsible Care® Code to ensure that employees reach and maintain proficiency in safe work practices and the skills and knowledge necessary to perform their jobs.

Distribution Safety

This Responsible Care® Code is concerned with the transportation of hazardous goods. Maydown works closely with it's suppliers to ensure safe transport of raw materials.

As a service to the community, the Maydown site, which is a registered DuChem Response Centre, operates 24 hours per day to respond to any local or national distribution incident involving hazardous products or materials by any company.

The Emergency Services can contact Maydown and obtain vital information which will allow them to handle the incident safely.

The site has a special committee to raise awareness of distribution safety and provide effective management of the system.

There is a comprehensive inspection programme of incoming goods vehicles which is considered to be an exemplar for the whole of Europe, Middle East and Africa region.

Employee Health and Safety

The Health and Safety group:

- Has an established ergonomics programme with production area teams to minimise all the risks where people and machinery are concerned.
- Includes an introduction to our safety rules as part of the welcome to visitors and contractors to the site. For example, new contractors are shown a training video to give them a clearer understanding of our safe working practices.
- Promotes safety awareness while away from work, discussing off-the-job injuries and running a quarterly competition with cash prizes for charity.
- Reviews, and will continually audit and review, all safety equipment used throughout the factory.

- Organises and prepares training for on site employees on a regular basis. This includes briefing packages on specific Safety, Health and Environmental (SHE) topics.

To protect the health of employees, Maydown has a Non-Smoking Policy and actively encourages employees to stop smoking. Support is offered through the Site Medical Unit in the form of individual counselling and subsidised nicotine replacement 'remedies'.

'Health Horizons' is DuPont's name for it's corporate Health Promotion Programme. As the name implies, the programme not only focuses on the immediate health concerns of all employees, but also looks towards future health risks associated with an individual's lifestyle.

If employees choose to participate, they are asked to complete a Health Risk Survey concerning their health habits. Based on this, each employee receives an individualised, confidential health risk appraisal, indicating those habits which may contribute to good health and those which may work against it, the overall aim being to eliminate or reduce particular risk factors in order to prevent associated disease.

Emergency Response

As a chemical plant handling hazardous materials, it is absolutely essential that there are systems in place to deal with emergencies. Therefore, a trained team of Emergency Response personnel on each shift is available at all times to respond to any incident on-site. The initial response to any emergency is by the Plant Fire Crew supported by the ambulance and First Aid Team and the Emergency Repair tender. At the critical first stages of response, they will support the overall plan for the site and can prevent an incident becoming an emergency. The Northern Ireland Fire Authority will also respond. Plans to centralise the existing off-site Freight Emergency Response kits, which are currently held by the three on-site businesses, Kevlar®, Lycra® and Neoprene, into one central kit, are well advanced. This kit will be available to any site team responding to off-site Freight Emergency involving DuPont products or raw materials being shipped to or from the plant. Strong links exist between the Plant Emergency Response teams, the local Fire Authority and community emergency services. There are also strong links with corporate experts throughout the world. In the event of a fume release, the plant's Control Centre will receive details of the fume release by phone and will enter these via a dedicated computer terminal into the SAFER (Systematic Approach For Emergency Response) system.

SAFER is a sophisticated computer programme which models the behaviour of a release. It takes into account the topography of the area, the characteristics of the substances that might be released, the weather conditions and, of course, the best mathematical equations which describe fume dispersion behaviour. Within two minutes a map of the prediction is displayed on a colour monitor and a copy is logged on a printer to provide a permanent record of the incident. The benefits of planning for Emergency Response includes a raised level of safety and environmental awareness, both of those involved and others within the plant's work teams. This results in greater commitment of the entire workforce to meet goals of Safety, Health and Environmental (SHE) standards and best practices.

Pollution Prevention

Water Discharge
Effluent from various points throughout the plant is continually sampled and analysed daily to confirm quality. A large proportion of this effluent consists of sea water which does not come into contact with any process.

The Department of the Environment (DOE) regularly audit for effluent discharge.

Power Plant Emissions
Maydown Works operate a Power plant on the site. This generates both electricity and steam.

Emissions from the plant are Carbon Monoxide (CO), Sulphur Oxides (SOx) and Nitrogen Oxides (NOx), Hydrogen Chloride (HCl) and particulates.

Particulates Emissions
During 1993/1994 two bag house filters, at a cost of £2 million, were fitted to reduce particulates. By using a low sulphur grade of coal, there has been a reduction in sulphur dioxide emissions below that of oil-fired boilers, which were formerly used at the factory. Energy

conservation programmes have also helped to lower Power plant emissions.

Energy Conservation

In addition to being a member of the DuPont European Energy 2000 committee, Maydown has formed it's own E2000 sub-committee, which consists of employees from all areas with the mission of energy consumption reduction on the site.

Process Air Emissions

Process Air Emissions represent air emissions to the atmosphere from the manufacturing plants. They are made up of Volatile Organic Compounds (VOC's). Maydown will continue to work to reduce these emissions.

Waste For Landfill

Material for on-site landfilling consists of paper and cardboard not suitable for recycling, normal domestic waste and waste rubber which is non-hazardous. A new landfill, needed because of current landfill is almost full, has been designed to the highest standards by a group of expert consultants working with DuPont site engineers.

Waste For Incineration

Most of Maydown's liquid hazardous waste is disposed of by an on-site incinerator, a form of which has been operational since plant start-up, to dispose of the locally produced DuPont waste. This meets all it's permits' requirements and is audited regularly by the Government's Alkali Inspectorate. Solid hazardous waste is transported off- site for disposal.

The amount of waste generated is closely related to rate of production and to the particular type of product being produced.

There is work ongoing to investigate the best way to try to recover more of this waste for recycling. Regular audits of waste contractors and disposal location sites are made.

The European Waste Audit committee reviews the audit reports and advises sites on the 'Best of Best' contractors to do business with in the future, i.e. those that have adopted the best environmental practices and are committed to a process of continuous improvement.

Other Environmental Programmes:

Waste Management

The site's Environmental Excellence Committee has been actively pursuing a programme of waste minimisation which includes discharges to air and water.

Several on-site recycling programmes create financial aid for local charities. In an environmental audit, independently conducted by the Department of the Environment, the site was complimented on it's environmental performance and on it's environmental control systems.

Commitment to the community

To develop a 5-10 year plan for habitat enhancement, the company held a seminar for wildlife specialists from both sides of the border with representatives from the Royal Society for the Protection of Birds, Conservation Volunteers NI, the Ulster Wildlife Trust, Wildfowl Wetlands Trust, Foyle Fisheries Commission, local district councils and the Department of the Environment.

At DuPont's Maydown site, there is a move towards receiving certification by The Wildlife Habitat Council, a United States group which provides environmental protection and habitat enhancement on private lands. As a coalition of both corporate and environmental groups, it certifies corporate wildlife programmes as a form of third party validation of environmental stewardship.

To date, The Wildlife Habitat Council has certified a total of 137 sites in the US and 6 other countries, with 22 of the US sites belonging to DuPont.

Achieving better environmental awareness is important to DuPont and the site participates in the national Earth Week by running events for employees. their families and local school children.

Maydown has always had strong links with educationalists - primary, secondary and tertiary levels. Site visits for the students and reciprocal visits to schools and colleges by DuPont people have helped students' understanding of its industry.

Maydown have taken the opportunity to show visitors from the community, customers and suppliers, how the factory operates and over the last two years the number of these visitors has been steadily increasing.

This year a Community Advisory Panel (CAP) in which DuPont have joined industrial and residential neighbours, local community leaders and authorities to share their common hopes, concerns and aspirations.

Future Commitments
Maydown has committed to apply for registration to the Eco-Management and Accreditation Scheme (EMAS) and the ISO 14000/BS 7750 certification for environmental standards. The Kevlar® Plant at Maydown has achieved certification to ISO 14001 in April 1997 and the other plants are working towards that goal.

The fundamental objective of EMAS is to stimulate management commitment and action towards continuous improvement in environmental performance and make available to the public, relevant information on a site environmental statement which has been subject to independent verification.

Environmental progress is an increasing priority at DuPont and they are prepared to back that commitment by spending £140 million on their European plants over the next two years.

The company is currently working on a range of specific initiatives through its plants including:

Recycling:
DuPont operates 11 industrial plastics recycling plants world-wide and reprocesses nearly 1/2 million tonnes of material annually. The waste material is treated, upgraded and sometimes blended with virgin material before it is reused.

Improved Waste Management:
The company has launched EWE - European Waste Management Enterprise - to promote and develop the benefits of waste management in environmental planning.

Phasing Out Chlorofluorocarbons (CFC's):
Over £60 million has been allocated to the world-wide conversion programme to remove CFC's. Of this amount £8 million is being spent in Europe. Maydown has converted to non-CFC technology.

10.5 Engineering:

a) G. Bruss GmbH, I.S. 310 & ISO 14001 Experience
This company profile has been written with the assistance of Mr. Bernard Geoghegan of G. Bruss GmbH.

The Company and it's Markets
G. Bruss GmbH., Finisklin Road, Sligo, is a subsidiary of G. Bruss GmbH & Co. KG., Hamburg, Germany. The company was established in Sligo in 1981 and commenced manufacturing radial symmetric seals, precision rubber formparts and gaskets for the export market in March 1982. The 95,800 sq. ft. site area (75,000 sq. ft. of buildings) employs 350 people. The market is the automotive industry and it's suppliers, of which 90% is within EU countries and 10% outside of EU. The main customers include:

Automotive Industry
VW, Audi, Mercedes Benz, Ford, General Motors, BMW, Nissan, MAN, Saab Scania, Volvo and Porsche

Others
Valeo, Bosch, Behr, Knecht and ZF

The company has achieved success through providing innovative product development, working closely with it's customers on respective applications and in developing complete sealing modules. Elastomeric compounds are developed in line with the application requirements.

The main product range is as follows:

- O-Rings
- Oil seals - engine/transmission seals
- Cassette type radial oil seals - hub/pinion seals
- Gaskets - oil pan gaskets for engines and transmissions, rocker cover gaskets, cam cover gaskets and other cover gaskets
- Gaskets for heat exchangers and radiators
- Lip seals and bonded pistons - for automatic transmission
- Bellows - for automotive application and household appliances
- Boots - for axles and cardan shaft

- Modules and composite seals - retainers with integrated oil seal and gasket, rocker covers with fixing elements, gaskets, and noise insulation.

In satisfying customer requirements it has been necessary to reduce product cost while at the same time improving quality and just-in-time delivery. This has been achieved by changing from large scale batch production to making as the customer requires in manufacturing cells using Kan Ban.

Kan Ban is a highly visible simple discipline to manage tool changes, product changes, material purchasing and planning. It replaces Material Requirement Planning MRP, an expensive software system to manage manufacturing resources. Kan Ban reduces stocks and work-in-progress.

Cell manufacturing enables versatile work teams to manage the total production within one unit, known as a cell. It reduces raw material and work in progress movements.

Raw Material
The only raw materials are rubber compound in strip and sheet form imported from our parent Company. In Hamburg, Germany the types of synthetic rubber used are:

- Nitrile rubber
- Fluor rubber
- Polyacrylic
- EPDM

The other principal ingredients that are used to make the compound are fillers, which in the case of nitrile rubber and polyacrylic consists of carbon black.

Description of the Manufacturing Process
The following is an outline of the process involved in the manufacture of products:

Raw Material Preparation in Germany:
(a) Raw material developed in the laboratory

(b) Raw material manufactured to laboratory specification.
The manufacturing process consists of mixing and processing in a Bambury Mixer to make a rubber compound. The company produces approximately 60 compounds and approximately 20 of these are used most frequently.

The compound is produced in sheets and strips that are tested by the Quality Department in the Laboratory. These are then exported to the Sligo facility.

Manufacturing Processes in Ireland:
- Milling. The sheets of compound received from the parent company will have hardened and must be put through a mill that warms and softens the material for presentation to the pre-forming operations.
- Extrusion. Strips are fed into extrusion machines which produce basic pre-forms, e.g. seals, O-Rings etc.
- Pre-forming. Some products require a further hand operated pre-forming process. In particular for forming larger rings.
- Moulding. Two types of hydraulic press are in use, compression moulding machines and injection moulding machines. The injection moulding machines do not require the pre-formed parts. The moulding process, known as vulcanisation, is as follows:
    - ➢ Preforms are placed in the compression machine
      or
      strips are fed to the injection machine
    - ➢ The press is closed and heat applied
    - ➢ After a required time, depending on the product and the compound, the press is opened
    - ➢ The parts are removed by hand or blown off by compressed air.
    - ➢ The parts are roughly de-flashed, whereby the surplus material is removed by hand, trimmed and checked as required.
- Shot Blasting. Parts are frozen by liquid nitrogen and the excess material is removed by plastic or metal shot.
- Tempering. Parts are tempered in an oven at varying temperatures and times to allow them to achieve characteristics of hardness, elongation etc. suitable for end use.

- Inspection. Parts that have not been checked by the machine operator are inspected and faulty parts removed.
- Packing. Parts are then packed to order.

Change Management

To survive in global marketplace of the 1990's meant challenging and changing the way that business had been carried out since the beginning. What made it all the more difficult to see the need for change, was the success and profits that had been enjoyed since setting up in Ireland. The change management timescale was as follows:

- 1990   —ISO 9002 Quality System Standard
- 1992   —Cell Manufacturing
- 1993   —Total Quality Management (TQM)/Deming
                     Management Method
                     —Kan Ban & J.I.T.
- 1994   —Start of Customer Direct Deliveries
- 1996   —I.S. 310
- 1997   —QS 9000 (Automotive Industry Standard)
- 1997   —ISO 14001

The most fundamental change for the organisation was TQM and organising teams to carry out day-to-day activities and projects. TQM means providing:

- Goods and services, Defect free, Which will delight customers

It means changing organisational behaviour to facilitate:
- Treating employees as a resource, not a cost
- Finding the causes of mistakes, not the guilty
- Preventing mistakes, instead of detecting them
- Leading by involvement, not delegation
- Facts instead of assumptions
- Working on the process, not the department
- More open and better communication

In following the teachings of Dr. Edwards Deming, the company strove to create a culture which integrated his 14 Points into day-to-day activity.

Having implemented modern 'Lean Production' methods and benefited from coherent and goal-directed teams, the next management objective focused on achieving good environmental management.

Benefits of Environmental Management

While good environmental practice had been an integral part of the business, the following reasons were identified and were to justify implementation of an environmental management system:

- Customers were concerned about the content of raw materials and how environmentally benign processes were. Customers like VW and Mercedes Benz have set targets of recyclability for cars and reduced emissions. This would also affect their suppliers.
- To reduce energy usage and costs
- To reduce losses e.g. waste
- To comply with EU legislation
- To market products as having been manufactured under an environmental management system. This would hopefully add value to products.
- To gain competitive advantage over competitors by having an accredited environmental standard
- To further improve what we do.

Implementation of Environmental Management System (EMS)

The company already had a successful Quality System accredited to ISO 9002 Standard. Instead of implementing a new Environmental Management System on its own, it was decided early on to build on the success of that Quality System structure, by integrating Quality, Occupational Health, Safety and Environment. What emerged was a Quality, Occupational Health, Safety and Environmental Management System (QHS&E).

The General Review was undertaken and written before any work was undertaken in writing the Environmental Policy or initiating the Environmental Programme or System.

The manufacturing site was then examined to get a physical impression of the site and it's environmental performance. This included a study of documents e.g. licences, instructions and policies. Interviews with managers and employees then took place which involved critical examination of the operations on the site in order to identify areas for improvement to assist in meeting the EMS requirements.

A project Specification was drawn up which outlined the steering group, team members, project objective etc. This was to be the framework mechanism by which the requirements of I.S. 310 with the QHS&E Management System would be implemented.

There followed Occupational Health, Safety and Environmental (HSE) team meetings. Internal and external environmental issues were considered and these included:

> Legislation
> Physical Planning
> Soil
> Air Emission
> Drinking water
> Waste water
> Energy
> Occupational Health & Safety

> Outside Contractors
> External Safety
> Noise
> Packaging
> Chemicals
> Waste
> Environmental Aspects - Products

In carrying out the General Review the above primary issues were reviewed and actions implemented where appropriate.

In implementing the EMS the most difficult document to compile was the Environmental Effects Register. This took a lot of consideration by the environmental team. It meant coming to terms with definitions of:

• direct and indirect environmental effects
• normal and abnormal conditions
• controlled and uncontrolled emissions/discharges

For each environmental effect in the register there was an introductory page included which detailed the activity giving rise to the effect, methodology used in the assessment, relevant legislation, procedures reference, internal responsibility and also made reference to records which are associated with the effect.

Following the introduction page there is an assessment summary sheet which detailed the significance of the emission/discharge, referred to scientific evidence found either internally or from external sources and provided a means for recording public attitudes (concerns they may have with site processes, products or services).

A summary table included at the end of the register showed evaluation of significant environmental effects. This used an assessment rating figure for each environmental effect, which ranged from 1 - 4 (negligible - major).

In evaluating environmental effects the following were examined:

- Controlled/uncontrolled emissions to atmosphere
- Controlled/uncontrolled discharges to water
- Disposal of wastes
- Contamination of land
- Use of natural resources i.e. land, water, fuels and energy
- Noise, odour, dust and visual impact
- Effect on natural environment and ecosystems
- Local and global impact of effects
- Past current and planned activities on site

As there was already a good Quality Manual in existence, this was then up-dated to explain the Quality, Health, Safety and Environmental system. What was important was to show the interaction between all of these within one integrated system. To facilitate clarity due to the extent of documentation required, an EMS documentation overview was included in the manual. In addition an organisation chart showed division of responsibilities.

Other EMS documentation included:

- Register of Regulations
- Procedures Manual
- EMS Review
- Environmental Target Action Programme
- Environmental Audit Reports
- Environmental Concern Action Reports
- Environmental Records
- Responsibility Matrices

The most important aspect of this documentation was that it is easy to follow. Auditors must know what leads to what. Cross-referencing and overview diagrams makes this more comprehensive for them.

The Future

The route to implementing an environmental management system has been very beneficial to the organisation. The company personnel were awakened to a new approach to managing, recovering losses and optimising processes. Decision making is based on pollution prevention at source by better technology and practices rather than end-of-pipe solutions.

Achieving I.S. 310 is only a very short step on the journey of continual environmental improvement. The company will adopt new philosophies and standards to enable continuation on this journey and motivate all stakeholders (i.e. those internally and externally involved in our operations) to assist in this regard. The business is in constant flux or change mode, but the organisation must be fluid and flexible to adapt to new realities in the marketplace.

As an automotive component supplier Bruss are conscious of the car manufacturers drive towards recyclable cars and zero emissions. This cascades down to every level of supplier base in helping them achieve their goals.

While ISO 14001 was a draft international standard it was adopted by the Americans in January 1996. The U.S. Automotive makers had already considered applying it to their suppliers. The likelihood is that European manufacturers may adopt a similar strategy towards their suppliers.

At present Bruss are interested in all new developments in standards. Bruss has become registered to ISO 14001, QS 9000 and are considering the benefits of becoming registered to EMAS. The company are watchful of developments in Health and Safety standards and may at some time in the future pursue accreditation to one of these. This standard would be fully integrated into the Quality, Health, Safety and Environmental System.

b) EG&G Sealol, EMAS and BS 7750 Experience

This company profile was made possible with the assistance of Mr. Barry Carey of EG&G Sealol Ltd.. It draws on information provided by the company and their environmental statement.

The Company and it's Markets

EG&G Sealol is a subsidiary of EG&G Corporation of Cranston Road Island, USA. The Irish facility, EG&G Sealol, Shannon was established in 1974 and is located in Shannon Industrial Estate Co. Clare. The 85,000 sq. ft. Shannon plant employs 150 people and is the main European manufacturing facility of the American Corporation, from where sales are made to approximately 30 countries worldwide.

The facility uses the most advanced manufacturing techniques available to produce the high quality seals which it brings to the global market. The designs are some of the most advanced in the industry.

The components produced in-house can be categorised into three main groups:

1. **Welded Metal Bellows Mechanical Seals** - provide high performance capabilities for a vast variety of shaft sealing applications involving high-temperature, corrosive and/or abrasive media. They are designed for consistently smooth, life-long operation.
2. **Type 43 Rubber Bellows Mechanical Seals** - designed for high volume production and reliable service. Typical uses include hot and cold water pumps and motors, air and refrigeration compressors and mild chemicals.
3. **Sealide (Silicon Carbide) Components** - was introduced in 1972 in response to a growing need for a seal face material which could provide optimum performance and service life on virtually all centrifugal pump sealing applications. It is recommended for sealing slurries, silting materials, solvents, gasses, acids, strong caustics and high temperature water (over 250F/120C).

The products range from a water pump costing pennies to a sophisticated mainshaft seal for nuclear submarines. Applications for Sealol products include, for example: jet engine main shaft seals used in commercial and military aircraft, seals for pumps and compressors, elastomer-free seals for fluid applications up to 800F degrees, spring driven pump seals for process and marine service, high speed aircraft accessory drive seals etc.

The Manufacturing Process

The activities involved in the manufacture of Sealol Products may be grouped under the following ten processes. It should be noted that not all processes apply to each product line, but the following sequence is generally typical of the production processes:

- **Metal Machining.** (turning, drilling, milling and tapping). Metal bars/tubes are machined to form component parts for both welded metal bellows and Type 43 seals.
- **Metal Pressing.** This process involves stamping 'bellows plates' from metal foil on hydraulic presses
- **Metal Acid Picking.** This is a cleaning process involving immersion of metal 'bellows plates' in an acid solution prior to their being welded together.
- **Metal Computerised Tig Welding**. Metal 'bellows plates' are welded together to form the 'bellows stack'. Bellows 'ends' (from the metal machining process) are then welded to the bellows stack.
- **Sealide** (silicon carbide) / **Carbon/ Ceramic Machining** (grinding and slotting). These materials are machined to from the sealing faces for all three product groups.
- **Lapping and polishing of metal, sealide** (silicon carbide), **carbon and ceramic components.** This process produces a smooth (lapped) surface finish by abrasively removing (lapping) material from the sealing faces of metal, sealide (silicon carbide), carbon and ceramic components.
- **Assembly.** There are two assembly areas relating to Welded Metal Bellows and Type 43 seals respectively. These areas, as the name suggests, are where the final assembly of the product is carried out prior to packing and shipping.
- **Packing / Shipping / Receiving.** All products and components entering, or leaving, the facility pass through this area.
- **Administration.** This activity collectively groups the functions of Sales Administration, Documentation Control and Quality Assurance Administration.

- **Miscellaneous.** This heading covers any activity or process not covered under previous headings (e.g. gardening, window cleaning, painting etc.)

Development of EG&E Sealol and Achievement of Environmental Management Standards BS 7750 and EMAS

EG&G Sealol International Ltd., established the Shannon plant with five employees operating a single product line on 2,500 sq. ft. facility in 1974. In 1977 the company relocated to a 10,000 sq. ft. factory and expanded it's workforce to 20 employees. The next five years saw the number of employees increase to forty five.

In 1982 the company again relocated within the Shannon Industrial Estate to a 40,000 sq. ft. facility. Through the recession of the 1980's, the company tightened it's belt and devoted it's efforts to minimising waste and cross-training of it's workforce. This commitment to advancing the capabilities of it's workers, together with implementing 'Just-in-Time' philosophy, has not only avoided redundancies, but ensured that the company was ideally prepared to take advantage of the recovery forecasted for the 1990's.

In 1990 the company added to it's manufacturing facility two adjoining factory bays resulting in an increase in area to it's present day 85,000 sq. ft. Employment levels have also kept pace with expansion.

The company prides itself on it's commitment to 'Total Quality', 'Customer is King' and 'Environmental Awareness' philosophies. It was the development of these philosophies that initially encouraged the company to seek accreditation to ISO 9002 Quality Standard which was achieved in February 1993. This international standard focuses on the quality assurances systems of manufacturing facilities.

Astute management at this time recognised that ISO 9002 Standard lacked a formal commitment to environmental issues of which the company had an acute awareness. Research indicated that the development of BS 7750 Environmental Standard complimented the ISO 9002 Standard in addressing these issues.

BS 7750, published by the British Standards Institute, was the first ever environmental management standard. It confirmed that a

company was controlling all relevant environmental issues, such as
air emissions, effluent discharges, waste, nuisance and noise. It also
demonstrated care in the use of materials and energy, in management
of health and safety of staff and in matters of product and public
safety.

Having been successfully audited, by Swiss certification agency SGS,
in August 1993 EG&G Sealol, Shannon, became the world's first
mechanical engineering company to be presented with the Green
Dove Award for having implemented an environmental management
system meeting the requirements of BS 7750 and the EC Eco-audit
regulation (EMAS).

Formal presentation to BS 7750 Standard was confirmed in March
1995.

Not satisfied with this accolade, the company then sought to promote
environmental awareness beyond the confines of it's own facility. It
was awarded the EG&G WARP (Waste Reduction Pays) Award and
is today cited as the environmental benchmark within the EG&G
Corporation world-wide.

It is also cited as an environmental benchmark company in the Eco
Management Guide developed with the financial support from the
European Commission.

EG&G Sealol, Shannon's certification to EMAS in December 1995 was
yet another jewel in the company's crown. It was the first company in
Ireland to have achieved this standard and was the first mechanical
engineering company in the world to be registered under this scheme
in Brussels.

EMAS goes a stage further than BS 7750 Standard in that the company
must publish a Site Environmental Statement detailing it's
environmental goals and it's performance against these stated
objectives, 'warts and all'. It invites constructive criticism in order to
develop better environmental policies, targets and awareness.

Environmental Management System Implementation
The underlying concepts governing EG&G Sealol, Shannon's
environmental performance are; commitment, awareness and
involvement by all from top management through all levels of

employees and, beyond, to contractors and suppliers. All must be educated to the principals of the 3 R's (i.e. Replace, Reduce and Recycle):

REPLACE - Use more environmentally friendly products and processes.

- All purchased paper and cardboard products are manufactured from recycled material and are themselves recycled in turn.
- Freon (an ozone depleting CFC) was replaced as a cleaning agent with an aqueous based detergent (1993).
- Polystyrene was replaced as a packaging medium with purpose designed recycled paper packing (1994).
- Soluble oil coolant was replaced with an aqueous based coolant (1993).
- Cleaning solvents were replaced with citrus based cleaning solution (1993).

REDUCE - Energy, materials and waste.

- The company achieved a 75% reduction in abrasive powder (1992), a 50% reduction in acids (1993) and a 30% reduction in lapping sludge (comprising of oil alumina oxide resulting from the grinding processes and containing trace elements of mercury and other heavy metals) (1994).
- Initial streamlining of paper processes resulted in significant savings.

RECYCLE - Where possible

- During 1994 the company recycled 24 tons of metal, 5.5 tons of paper, 3 tons of cardboard, 1 ton of tea-bags (recycled as garden compost) and 1 ton of aluminium drink cans.
- In the same year, refining, filtration and re-use achieved a reduction of 1,710 gallons of rust inhibitor, 350 gallons of mineral oil and 360 gallons of soluble oil.

Far from costing money, installation costs of environmental procedures were recouped within twelve months of implementation and further significant cost savings are on-going. Additional benefits include a cleaner and safer work environment, and increased environmental awareness amongst employees and their families, customers, suppliers and contractors.

The company's existing ISO 9002 and BS 7750 management systems provided the framework for EMAS with a considerable number of systems and controls already in place.

The most difficult aspect of developing any environmental management system is the identification and classification of environmental effects. Once this is achieved procedures can be put in place to address these issues.

All direct and indirect environmental effects, and potential effects, were identified and categorised by EG&G Sealol. The criteria used for rating the significance of direct and indirect environmental effects are:

- The degree of the hazard of the effect being considered. This is a function of the chemical/physical properties of the substance(s) (toxicity, flammability, etc.) and the amounts being used.
- The potential effect involved. This will be determined by the existence of targets and their sensitivity.

Environmental effects were then classified under three categories:

1. Class A - Major Environmental Effect
2. Class B - Intermediate Environmental Effect
3. Class C - Minor Environmental Effect

All effects falling within Class A are deemed significant for the purposes of EMAS. All environmental effects were documented in detail in the Environmental Register of Regulations and Effects. A tabulation was provided listing the main environmental effects relating to the twelve manufacturing processes.

This included the following headings:

- Process
- Effect
- Class
- Methods Addressing these Effects
- Manual/Procedure Reference

These effects, regarded as significant, were then reported in this format in the EMAS Site Environmental Statement.

The preparation of the Site Environmental Statement was regarded as the single greatest addition to the existing environmental management system with the format, wording and content all coming under individual scrutiny during the certification audit. It's content comprised of:

- Site Map - Showing exact site location and surrounding neighbourhood.
- Industrial Activities - Description of the facility, growth and product range.
- Manufacturing Processes - All activities involved in the manufacture of the product.
- Environmental Effects - Tabulated listing of all significant environmental effects, class, and method of addressing these for each process.
- Performance Figures - These have been documented under the following headings:
  - Toxic / Hazardous Waste
  - Utilities
  - Recycling
  - Emissions
  - Discharges
  - Results of Waste Minimisation Priority List
  - Performance with respect to other significant effects

- Other Factors - Regarding Environmental Policy.
- Company Policy.
- Management Programme - Explanation of the environmental programme and management system implemented.
- Next Environmental Statement - This sets a deadline for submission of the next statement. EG&G Sealol propose to report the findings, following an audit to EMAS annually.
- Verification - An accredited environmental verifier's services has been engaged to verify that the environmental management system and statement conform to the EMAS regulation.

The achievement of EMAS certification provides third part corroboration that the company has identified and is managing all critical environmental issues under a best code of practice.

The Way Forward
EG&G Sealol has embarked on a pro-active approach toward environmental issues and is encouraging both customers and suppliers to do likewise. Company policy is to seek out and actively encourage environmentally conscious suppliers, while seeking to eliminate from it's supplier base those who are not.

Future trends indicate that other companies will adopt the same approach and that, within a relatively short time frame, all companies will be compelled to adopt an EMS in order to survive. Many of the relevant environmental issues are already law, all of the staff health and safety regulations are compulsory and there are significant corporate and management legal exposures in public, product and environmental safety.

Today, EG&G Sealol is a state-of-the-art manufacturing facility which combines the most advanced environmentally friendly manufacturing techniques and designs available. It has a highly motivated and environmentally conscious workforce and produces mechanical seals of the highest quality sold world-wide. Sealol is committed to remaining the world leader in Welded Metal Bellows seals and to continue to exceed industry expectations for product quality and reliability combined with continuous improvement on all environmental issues.

c) *Chep Ireland Ltd.*   *IS 310 and ISO 14001 Experience*

This company profile has been written with the assistance of Ms. Cathy Kelly and Ms. Joanne Aughey of Chep Ireland Ltd. It draws on information from company resources and documents.

The Company

Chep Ireland is a division of the worldwide Chep Pallet and Container Pool and is the largest supplier of pallets in Ireland. The company has been a quality supplier to over 60 "Blue Chip" companies in Ireland for the last 20 years. In addition Chep has an equipment hiring service that is part of an extensive European Depot network covering 80 depots across 10 countries.

The pallet was created to enable unit loads to be handled quickly and efficiently. It saved time and money. It revolutionised materials handling. But, as with many innovations, there were drawbacks. First the pallets had to be bought - a huge capital outlay for most businesses. Then there were the inevitable losses as well as depreciation costs. Every single pallet had to be tracked through the supply chain, recovered from delivery points and transported back to the owner. Administration was complicated, maintenance and repairs costly and pallet quality and safety significantly deteriorated over time. The result was mass confusion, with exasperated customers, high costs and very few companies able to recover their pallets.

The idea of hiring materials handling equipment from a common pool was originally conceived in Australia during the 1950's, when pooling was introduced to use the material handling equipment left behind by the US forces in the Pacific Islands. In 1974, GKN plc and Brambles Industries Ltd. joined forces in Europe to launch a European Pallet Pooling system. Chep Ireland which commenced in 1977 as a small operation of 4 people, has now become a substantial pool in it's own right.

Chep's distinctively marked blue pallets and containers are recognised and accepted in the USA, Canada, Australia, South Africa and Europe. In the UK and Ireland, the Chep pallet has become a trade standard, universally accepted for their good quality and durability. There are currently over 40 million Chep pallets in circulation in Ireland and Europe.

Operation of the Pallet Pool

In 1975 there were just 60,000 Chep pallets in the pool in the UK and Ireland. Today there are 14 million in circulation with over 80 million Chep pallet movements taking place each year. Chep Europe as a whole now has 32 million pallets.

Considering the quantity of pallets in transit and the level of co-operation required from thousands of locations and individuals, the pooling system itself could become enormously complicated and yet, in reality it is quite simple from the customer's viewpoint, as follows:

- Pallets are hired from the pool on a daily basis.
- The customer either collects from a Chep depot or the pallets can be delivered.
- The pallets are used to transport the goods and then left, under load, at the point of delivery.

At this point, there are three options:

either

- Empty Chep pallets are given in exchange for Chep pallets loaded with finished product.

or

- If empty pallets are not required, Chep offers a "one-way trip" where delivered pallets can be removed from the customer's hiring account, to be collected by Chep.

or

- The hire of the pallets can be transferred from one Chep customer to another, helping the continuation of the supply chain.
  This element of choice means that Chep is able to offer solutions to suit every customer's specific needs.

The Market

Chep's expertise is in the control of equipment through the supply chain, ensuring that thousands of delivery locations operate the Chep system smoothly and effectively. As well as standard and euro size pallets, Chep offers a comprehensive range of equipment for hire designed to suit the needs of the product being transported. The market covers the following sectors:

- Drinks
- Fresh produce
- Home improvements
- Horticulture
- Packaging
- Agriculture

In providing a service to customers Chep takes great care to listen actively to their customers and understand their business and distribution systems. The hire of any equipment includes a comprehensive customer service package which can offer a telephone help-line or personal visits to ensure that the customer is given adequate support to use the Pool in as cost-effective a manner as possible.

Site Activities

The activities carried on at the site in Jamestown Business Park, Finglas Dublin 11 are:

1. Occupation of the site as administrative headquarters in Ireland.
2. Hiring of materials handling equipment.
3. Management of the control of equipment through the supply chain.
4. Repair and maintenance of materials handling equipment.
5. Handling and storage of materials handling equipment.
6. Storage of raw materials used in the repair process.
7. Management of transport for issue/return of equipment.

The entire depot operations process is structured around recycling and reusing the pooled products of pallets and containers. Products are returned off hire into the depot where they are inspected and repaired where necessary and returned back into the pool for rehire.

Environmental Programme

1. Emissions and Controls:

The environmental policy sets out the duty of care which Chep must follow in terms of carrying on it's operations, particularly with regard to waste disposal. Informally, most processes are subject to best practice, as described below.

- **Water:**
Arises from painting process and pallet washing process. Controlled by approved disposal and by discharge via a sump.
- **Dust:**
Arises from normal activity. Controlled by effective housekeeping.
- **Noise:**
Arises from traffic, repair process and machinery. Controlled by focus on sources of noise.

2. Waste Minimisation:

Waste materials consist of timber, paper, shrink wrap and cardboard which are stored on site in a contracted waste bin. Waste timber is removed by a contractor for recycling into chipboard.

Further work is being carried out in tracing waste to source and identifying a suitable method of disposal/recycling.

Paper wastage occurs during office use in small quantities approximating to no more than one ream of A4 per working day. Action plans have been drawn up to reduce the paper wastage in the office area.

3. Energy Usage:

- **Electricity:**
Used to operate mechanised processes such as air compressor, paint booth and inspection plant.
- **Gas:**
Used to provide heat through central heating system and radiant gas panels.
- **Diesel:**
Used to power forklift trucks.

Chep's Environmental Commitments

Chep Ireland in the conduct of it's business commits itself to the protection of the environment and to the health and safety of it's employees, customers and the public. The company's policy is to continuously improve environmental management performance across it's operations. Good environmental management is seen by Chep Ireland as both socially responsible and effective business management.

Chep Ireland's environmental policy which includes health and safety, commits the General Manager and line management to ensure compliance with:

- National and EU regulatory requirements relating to Environmental Health and Safety Matters
- Company-generated standards and targets
- Environmental Management System Standards

It is the policy of the company to ensure that this environmental policy is understood, implemented and maintained at all levels in the organisation and is publicly available. Chep Ireland is committed to sustaining the natural environment compatible with the economic resources of the company. Adherence to the environmental policy and compliance with the procedures to implement this policy shall be mandatory on all Chep Ireland personnel.

In addition to compliance with appropriate environmental regulations the environmental objectives are:

- To reduce waste generation at source
- To reduce the use of energy at source
- To reuse and recycle to the maximum extent possible any energy or waste generated
- To effectively and safely treat and dispose of any non-recoverable wastes
- To minimise any detrimental environmental effects of products to include their handling, use and final disposal.

Copies of Objectives and Targets are also publicly available.

Environmental Management System Organisation

Chep Ireland's business mission is to be first choice quality provider of unit load materials handling equipment. In March 1994 the company achieved accreditation to ISO 9002. Recognising the changes in environmental policy throughout Europe, they then achieved IS 310 and ISO 14001 in November 1996.

Management Responsibilities

In working to implement the ISO Standards, Chep Ireland's organisation and management responsibilities were reviewed. All managers have Job Descriptions, together with budgets and personal objectives. As a result of this review, it was decided that more explicit environmentally orientated responsibilities would be designated in order to enable the company to proceed to develop it's formal Environmental Management System.

General Review and Environmental Effects Register

In compiling the environmental review, Chep Ireland addressed the following topics:

- current and future business plans
- organisation and responsibilities
- current configuration of site and processes
- raw materials consumption
- existing policies, programmes, activities and management system concerning the environment
- evaluation of the significant internal and external environmental issues.

This review was carried out by the Quality Action Team with expert input by an independent professional environmental risk assessor. The review covered legislative and regulatory requirements, significant environmental impacts both beneficial and adverse, existing procedures and practices on past site history in complying with regulations or procedures.

The review includes the following:

- a description of the organisation's activities
- an identification and evaluation (including risk analysis/prioritisation) of all the significant internal and

external environmental issues of relevance to the activities concerned

- a summary of the data on pollutant emissions, waste generation, raw material, energy and water consumption, noise and other significant environmental aspects, as appropriate.

The review will be evaluated every three years or sooner if circumstances demand.

In assessing the significance of identified effects, a scoring system was developed using risk assessment. This reduced the subjective element in reaching decisions. The conclusions drawn from the environmental review have been compiled in the Register of Regulations and the Environmental Effects Register together with the policies, objectives, targets and procedures necessary for maintaining operational control.

In evaluating the environmental effects, the company considered direct and indirect impacts arising from it's activities, products and services, past, present and planned, under normal, abnormal and emergency conditions. Among the effects considered were:

- Controlled or uncontrolled emissions to atmosphere
- Controlled and uncontrolled discharges to water
- Solid or liquid wastes
- Contaminated level
- Use of natural resources (energy, land, water)
- Noise, odour, dust.

The Environmental Manual

The contents of this manual reflect the Environmental Management System in operation within Chep Ireland. The Environmental Manual details the operation of the Environmental Management System on the Chep Ireland site at Finglas Dublin 11, structured to conform to I.S. 310 and ISO 14001.

The manual is supported by detailed Environmental Management Procedures (EP's), Specifications and Environmental Standard Operating Procedures (ESOP's). Any future changes will reflect the commitment of Chep Ireland to improve the Environmental Management System in place.

The Environmental Manual serves many purposes. Among these are the following:

1. The Environmental Manual serves as a source of reference for Environmental Policies and Procedures laid down by Chep Ireland in it's aim to achieve and maintain control of it's environmental impacts.
2. The Environmental Manual defines the responsibilities of personnel concerned with the operation and monitoring of the Environmental Management System.
3. The Environmental Manual provides interested parties with a basis for confidence in the company's commitment to a system of environmental management.
4. The Environmental Manual provides an opportunity for interested parties to appraise or audit the Environmental Management System of Chep Ireland. It allows the organisation to conduct it's own internal audits and so ensures the continued integrity of the system.
5. The Environmental Manual assists in the training and education of new staff in matters relating to the control of environmental impacts.
6. The Environmental Manual demonstrates Management's commitment to environmental issues to all staff.
7. The Environmental Manual is prepared and approved by the Management Representative and authorised by the General Manager.

Awareness and Training
Chep Ireland employs approximately 70 people at it's site at Jamestown Business Park, Finglas. The company has established and maintains procedures to ensure that all personnel are aware of their roles and responsibilities in carrying out work which can have a significant effect on the environment. Training needs are identified and appropriate training is provided. Records are maintained of training carried out.

Current and Future Business Plans
Chep Ireland is strategy led. In it's confidential document "Chep Ireland strategy 1994 -1998", the key aims of the business are:

• To grow Chep Ireland by 75% to £8 million total revenue by 1998.
• To develop, deliver and continuously improve a total quality

service offered to customers and retailers in order to meet present and future needs.

- To achieve and maintain the status of lowest cost quality suppliers to the markets served.

How these aims are to be met are described in detail in the document. An annual review ensures that the validity of the strategy and related programmes is current. All programmes, budgets and resource allocation decisions are made consistent with the strategy.

In the area of business development, one of the key objectives is to "research, identify and develop attractive new market opportunities in which Chep Ireland will have a distinct competitive advantage".

One such market opportunity to be researched is that of Returnable Secondary Packaging (RSP), whereby the outer packaging of consumer goods might be replaced with a returnable pool of plastic unit load equipment. Accordingly, Chep is extremely conscious of the synergy between pooling solutions and best environmental practice.

10.6   Pharmaceutical:

a) SmithKline Beecham, Integrated Pollution Control Experience
by Ian McAuliffe.

Background to SmithKline Beecham in Ireland

The SmithKline Beecham site in Currabinny, on the Southern shores of Cork Harbour, has been in operation since 1975. Originally it was part of the Chemical Manufacturing Division of Smith Kline and French which merged in 1989 with Beecham to form SmithKline Beecham Corporation. The site is a multipurpose Chemical Synthesis facility and makes a variety of ethical Pharmaceutical compounds which are then tabletted or made into injectibles in several of the SmithKline Beecham secondary plants.

SmithKline Beecham has a workforce of 190 including a high proportion of graduate engineers and scientific staff which reflects the emphasis on development work undertaken at the plant .The plant operates a four shift operation which runs for seven days per week for approximately forty eight weeks of the year.

Product Range

A range of ethical Pharmaceutical products are manufactured at the site :

- **Cimetidine** - This is the active ingredient in **Tagamet** which is an anti ulcer compound . Four key intermediate steps of this process are also manufactured on site.
- **Paroxetine** - This is the active ingredient of **Seroxat** - a compound prescribed for depression and three stages of the drug are manufactured on site.
- **Famciclovir** - This is the active ingredient in **Famvir** an Antiviral Compound and two key stages are manufactured.
- **Topotecan** - The active ingredient in **Hycamtin** - an anti cancer compound . Two stages of this compound are made on site.
- **Carvedilol** - This is an anti Hypertensive and four stages are manufactured.
- **Eprosartan** - An anti Hypertensive with a different mode of action to Carvedilol. Two stages of Eprosartan are manufactured on site.

Plant Details:

Process Plant

The processes are all Synthetic Organic in nature and reactions are batch type. Plant and equipment in the synthesis operation are as follows :

- Glass lined steel batch reactors.
- Solid / Liquid separation equipment comprise of basket type, inverting bag type Heinkel Centrifuges, Rosenmund Pressure Filters, Combined Filter Driers.
- Product Driers comprise of agitated stainless steel vessels which are capable of being heated, cooled, and which can take a high vacuum .

All operations on plant are computer controlled and are monitored from a large central control room.

Environmental Abatement Equipment

From the earliest days of operation, it has been SB Policy to treat the maximum amount of waste possible on the site.

The Environmental abatement equipment represents a considerable portion of the total investment on site - approximately 25 % of the total value. Environmental running costs are approximately 15 % of the total costs. The Environmental control plant is specifically installed and operated to deal with the following :

- Air Emissions.
- Water Emissions.
- Noise.
- Generation of liquid and solid wastes.

Air Emission Control

There are three incinerators on site which are designed and operated to destroy liquid and vaporous waste to greater than 99.99% removal efficiency. The incinerators are computer controlled and all have continuous monitors on the stack gas train which gives minute by minute information on the emission levels of Carbon Monoxide, Sulphur Dioxide, Total Organic Carbon and Hydrogen Chloride. In the event of the failure of Incineration plant, scrubbers for removal of gaseous emissions automatically come on line.

Water Emissions

Aqueous wastes from Chemical Processes as well as run off from storage areas and tank bunds are routed to the site Waste Water Treatment Plant. This is an Aerobic process and has been in operation since the plant was started up in 1974. The area has been upgraded recently . In excess of £5,000,000 has been spent on this area since 1989.The upgraded plant has the following features:

- A Chemical treatment Vessel to remove odours from incoming liquors.
- A solvent stripper to remove Organic solvents from streams before they enter the plant.
- Automatic pH adjustment of input streams.
- Denitrification Tanks - To remove Nitrate from the treated effluent.
- Aeration Tanks covered and vented into a peat filter to eliminate odours.
- Two large clarifiers - To clarify the treated effluent and return the settled sludge to the treatment plant.
- An Ammonia stripper - To remove Ammonia from the treated effluent.
- A Dissolved Air Flotation Unit to further reduce Suspended Solids from the treated effluent stream.

The plant is computer controlled and all information is fed back into the Environmental central control room.

Noise
Major potential sources of noise such as fans, cooling towers, blowers have acoustic hoods or noise attenuation devices fitted to them.

Generation of Liquid and Solid Waste
Fresh Solvents, recovered solvents, and Liquid wastes are stored in large capacity steel tanks which have conservation vents or are vented to the site Incinerator. These tanks have bunds, or a surrounding wall, which will take the tank contents if there is a large spillage.
Solids wastes are placed in sealed drums and stored in an area which is drained to the site Waste Water Plant if there is a spillage.

A number of rich solvent wastes are recovered in two Solvent Recovery Plants and are recycled back into the process.

Former Site Licenses
Prior to the issuing of the IPC Licence in December 1994, the site operated under three different Licences issued by the Cork County Council.

- The Site Air Pollution Licence issued under the terms of the 1987 Air Pollution Act.
- The Site Water Pollution Licence issued under the 1977 Water Pollution Act.
- The Site Waste Licence issued under the European Communities (Toxic and Dangerous Waste) Regulations 1982.

The Integrated Pollution Control License
In May 1994, sections of the EPA Act 1992 were brought into the Statute books by Statutory Instruments (SI) 82, 83, 84 and 85. The first date, 1st. September 1994, pertained to those pharmaceutical industries employing in excess of 200 people.

In the case of SmithKline Beecham, we were in the Summer of 1994, in the process of applying for Planning permission for a £25 million expansion programme. Accordingly, we decided to combine the planning application with the application for an IPC Licence. We applied under Schedule 5.6 (Manufacture of Pharmaceuticals) and Schedule 11.1 (Incineration of Hazardous Waste).

Application Process
The application process began in early May 1994 and ended with the lodging of the application in early July. In addition, an EIS (Environmental Impact Study) had to be completed and submitted with the IPC Application. The IPC Application documentation comprised of six substantial volumes containing extensive information on air emissions and control and abatement measures, water emissions control and abatement, noise, environmental management systems, waste minimisation. This information had to be supported with internal / external reports, maps, and drawings.

Compilation of such information in the time required (May to July) necessitated a team of five people working full time on the task. Several meetings were held with the EPA Inspectorate during the course of the

Application and these were most useful in getting the document into shape for final submission.

Consultation

In addition to the technical information needed in the application, the IPC guidelines included an emphasis on consultation. We decided to adopt the most comprehensive consultation process possible. Accordingly, we met with 16 external organisations, including Cork County Council, Cork Chamber of Commerce, Ringaskiddy Residents Association (Local Community Body) and Cork Environmental Alliance. In each case, detailed briefings were given to these organisations, including details on the IPC application, EIS and on the expansion programme. The amount of information requested by these organisations varied and in each case, we responded fully.

The IPC application process was insistent on transparency at all stages and submission to the EPA on the application were invited from interested parties. The application and EIS were lodged with the Agency on the 8th.July, 1994 and copies of these were also provided to the Cork Environmental Alliance at their request. All the documents provided were also made available in the Public File by the Agency.

Processing of the Application

The EPA commenced detailed examination of the IPC Application and EIS in early July 1994 and came back with requests for further information in the third week of August. As well as this, the Cork Environmental Alliance wrote to the EPA with detailed comments on the Licence Application / EIS.

There was regular contact between the EPA Inspector and the Company especially in the period coming up to the issuing of the proposed Licence which took place on the 28th, October 1994. The statutory period of 21 days for third party appeals and 28 days for appeal by the Applicant passed with no objections and SmithKline Beecham became the first company in the state to come under IPC with the formal issuing of the Licence on 6th, December 1994.

Layout of License

The Licence has two main sections :

- The front section comprises of fourteen sections
- The second section has six schedules.

The sections in the front part of the Licence incorporate the following :

- Environmental Management Programme which requires plans for the following :
  - ➢ Reduction of Wastes at Source.
  - ➢ Improved cleaning procedures.
  - ➢ Improvements in abatement systems.
  - ➢ Reduction in fugitive Emissions.
  - ➢ Savings in energy and material usage.
- Solvent Mass Balance for certain substances.
- Access to Information by the Public.
- Notification of Incidents.
- General Conditions for Emissions to Air, Water.
- General conditions for waste storage and disposal.
- Toxic and Dangerous Waste Disposal.
- Noise Emission Limits.
- Surface / Groundwater Emissions Monitoring.
- Reporting Schedule .

The six Schedules in the Second Part of the Licence comprise of the following :

1. Emissions to Atmosphere - Emission Limit Values.
   - Atmospheric Emissions - Abatement /Treatment Control.
   - Monitoring of Atmospheric Emissions.
2. Emissions to Waters - Emission Limit Values.
   - Effluent Treatment Control.
   - Monitoring of Emissions to Waters.
3. Toxic and Dangerous Waste Disposal - Off Site.
   - Other Wastes.
   - Analysis of wastes for disposal off site by Landfill.
   - Monitoring of Wastes before incineration on site.
4. Noise Emission Limits.
5. Surface Water Emissions Monitoring.
   - Ground Water Monitoring on Site.
6. Reporting Schedule.

Working with the IPC License

As previously detailed, the licence went into force in early December 1994 and this entailed a considerable change in the format of reporting of the monthly site environmental performance. As well as this, we had to start work on the reporting obligations on the following over a phased period of 19 months with the main part of the Programme to be completed within 12 months.

Report Required by IPC	Required (Number of months after IPC issue).
Environmental Management Programme	Three Months
Noise Sources Reduction Programme	Three Months
PER / Mass Balance	Three Months
Integrity of Bunded Structures	Three Months
Noise Sources Reduction Programme	Three Months
Screening of Treated Waste Water for a variety of Organic compounds	Three Months
Fugitive Emissions programme	Three Months
Public Access To Information	Three Months
Fugitive Emissions - Operational	Six Months
Noise Sources - Report	Six Months
Groundwater Investigation Programme	Six Months
Pipework Leak programme	Six Months
Study of Option of Sending Treated Waste Water Effluent to Public Sewer	Twelve Months
Implementation of Groundwater Report	Twelve Months
Pipework Leaks Programme Implemented	Twelve Months
Heat Recovery Study on Incinerator 1	Thirteen Months
Determination of Storm Water TOC Levels-Report	Nineteen Months

The required reports have all been submitted within the time required by the Licence. The reports which had to be furnished within three months, especially the Environmental Management Programme, imposed a considerable pressure on time and the Company enlisted the services of a Consultancy to compile this report.

Monthly Report

The report format had to be changed from that required by the Cork County Council to a format which would satisfy the IPC Licence. The major changes were in the Atmospheric emissions part of the report as additional information was required by the Agency on Incinerator Emissions as well as some atmospheric vents on site.

It was our experience that it was vital to draw up a detailed schedule of which months certain tests had to be done as some have to be done each month and others four, twice, and once per year etc.

The agency visited site on a regular basis to sample the Treated Effluent from the Biological Plant. As well as this, several samples were taken from Incinerator and Plant atmospheric Vents. There was also a Noise survey carried out early this year .

Audits, Environmental Management System, Waste

Audits

The Agency carried out a baseline Audit in December 1995. This comprised of a one day visit by an Agency Auditor who was accompanied by the EPA Inspector normally assigned to deal with SmithKline Beecham. Compliance with the terms of the Licence was examined in detail and no non compliances were noted. The EPA team placed a strong emphasis on items such as :

- Waste Minimisation.
- Document Control.
- Environmental Management Systems.
- Preventative Maintenance Systems.

They were supportive of those systems on site which were proactive and which incorporated proper planning and review techniques as they stressed that such systems serve to underpin the type of Environmental Management Systems desired by the Agency.

Environmental Management System

The amount of detail required in the Licence Application and in the Environmental Management Plan involved a considerable amount of time and expense. However, the large quantity of information available from these documents will be used as the foundation for an Environmental Management System on site which is part of our medium to long term Environmental Site Plans.

We commenced the installation of an Environmental Management System on site along the lines of IS 14001, which started in November 1995. This was carried out with the help and advice of SmithKline Beecham Corporate Environmental, who are very supportive of this development.

Waste Minimisation

As stated above, the EPA are encouraging of Waste Minimisation as a major part of the company's Environmental operations - especially waste reduction at source. There has been a Waste Minimisation Working Group on site since September 1994 which meets on a regular basis and carries out detailed reviews of :

- Waste generation per batch for each compound manufactured on site.
- The suitability of each stream for elimination and recovery .
- Each candidate stream is evaluated and laboratory or plant based work is carried out to progress the matter and evaluate the viability of the set target.

In 1996, the emphasis was on examination of plant decontaminations and recycling potential of paper, glass, cans and cardboard on site. Towards the end of that year, the process reviews started again (the second cycle of reviews) .

Conclusion

This Licence represents a significant progression of the strict Licences already in force and has a very strong bias in favour of prevention of Environmental effects at source. An Environmental Management System in particular serves to drive this preventative approach and provides a constant challenge to policy and operation. The high degree of access by members of the Public to all reports and communications between SmithKline Beecham and the EPA is, in our experience, a positive development. In overall terms, the IPC Licence application process, the IPC Licence itself, and the access to information inherent in the Licence were and continue to be, demanding but worthwhile.

b) Yamanouchi Ireland Co. Ltd. BS 7750 and ISO 14001 Experience
by Dr. Suzanne Geraty.

Introduction
Yamanouchi Ireland is part of the Yamanouchi group with headquarters in Japan. Yamanouchi Pharmaceutical Co., Ltd is Japan's third largest pharmaceutical company.

Yamanouchi Ireland Co., Ltd (YICL) is a bulk pharmaceutical manufacturing facility located on a large, very green field site in North County Dublin. The development of Yamanouchi Ireland Co., Ltd began in 1986, and after about two years construction and subsequent plant commissioning, the company commenced production in July 1988.

The company currently employs approximately 60 people (plus contractors as required) in the manufacture of famotidine, a treatment for stomach ulcers and over-acidity, nicardipine hydrochloride which is used to control cardiac hypertension and formoterol fumarate which is used to treat asthma. These products are sold, in bulk, for completion into dosage form by our licensees. Yamanouchi Ireland is also planning to commence manufacture of a fourth product in late 1997. This product (tamsulosin hydrochloride) is used in the treatment of benign prostrate hyperplasia (prostrate gland disorder).

YICL is a modern production facility which has incorporated best available technology into each operation on the site. All current manufacturing processes have been developed in Japan and the technology transferred to YICL. These processes have been registered with regulatory authorities in many countries.

Because of the type of products manufactured (bulk active pharmaceuticals) and our requirement to export to the United States, from the very outset we have been inspected and approved by the US FDA, whose quality management standards are among the most demanding to be found anywhere. We are also certified to ISO 9002 and are committed to the Responsible Care® Programme (internationally recognised programme for voluntary self regulation by companies in our sector).

YICL is also a member of the Clean Technology Centre (CTC) based in the Regional Technical College, Cork and Questor which is based in the School of Chemistry, Queens University, Belfast. A considerable amount of collaborative work is in progress between YICL and the above organisations.

YICL has always recognised the value of sound environmental management practices and quality assurance principles, from the commencement of operations, to environmental activities on the site.

Environmental Protection and Legislative Aspects

Even at the construction phase, the company's aim was to install the best possible environmental protection facilities. In broad terms our environmental protection facilities include a biological waste water treatment system, air scrubbers and a solvent waste incinerator with anti-pollution controls. Where possible, we have tried to recover materials used in processing operations (raw materials, solvents). Other recent site developments have included the installation of a firewater retention system and a meteorological station on the site. Initially we were required to hold three licences, each of which was managed by a different section in Dublin County Council:-

- Licence to discharge from waste water treatment plant to municipal sewer.
- Toxic and Dangerous Waste Permit to control storage and on-site incineration of waste. This includes incinerator emissions.
- Air Licence - process scrubbers and incinerator emissions were included.

However, with the introduction of Integrated Pollution Control Licensing (IPCL) in Ireland, in May 1994, the above three licenses have been replaced by one Integrated Pollution Control Licence which covers all the issues as listed. Issue and regulation of such licenses is the responsibility of the Environmental Protection Agency in Ireland.

Any policies and strategies we have at YICL in the area of environmental protection are primarily site-driven. Three core values would be:-

- Aim for continuous improvement in the area of environmental protection and management.
- Be open and honest with the public and try to explain our true environmental impact to interested parties.

- Aim for significantly more than minimal compliance with regulatory requirements, to implement best industrial practice.

The company has also developed a comprehensive policy for the protection of the environment. This policy, along with others, is displayed throughout the site to maximise awareness by all employees of the concepts espoused within it.

Yamanouchi has always aimed to have an open and transparent approach in dealing with the public. It's policy is to have environmental monitoring data available for inspection by the public in the security office at the main entrance. This policy was put in place long before the Freedom of the Environmental Information Act came into force.

Yamanouchi actively encourages groups to visit the plant and has established good communications with resident groups, environmental organisations, schools, colleges, the media and many other groups.

Each year, as part of the Environmental Management Programme, Yamanouchi invites the local community to visit the plant and to discuss issues, such as proposed expansions, company developments, environmental issues etc. This programme is augmented by regular requests for visits to the site from schools, colleges, local groups etc., which are facilitated on an on-going basis throughout the year. In any given year, approximately 200-400 individuals visit the plant on one of these types of visits.

Yamanouchi's (YICL) Approach to Environmental Management and Auditing

Introduction

Since day one, YICL strove to incorporate the concept of Good Environmental Management into all company activities. Efforts in this area were duly rewarded when, in 1989, the company won the "Irish Good Environmental Management Award" from the Department of the Environment and Eolas (National Science and Technology Agency). In 1990, the company went on to win the European Communities and the United Nations Award for Good Environmental Management.

In 1996 YICL were joint runners-up in the Better Environment Awards for Industry (Managing towards Sustainability; Commitment to the environment) sponsored by Forbairt.

Definitions and Reasons

Before discussing YICL's experience in the area of environmental management systems, it is worth outlining some of the basic concepts and definitions.

Management Systems and Environmental Auditing

According to recent EU definitions, management systems and audits have been described in the following way:-

management is a system which attempts to improve the performance.

A management system needs to be built as an aid to the formation of a menu of useful actions that management can relate to.

audits are instruments which attempt to verify performance.

An audit system would need to be built as a measurement tool for the auditor, it will have to focus on the requirements to the system which are not necessarily identical to management actions.

Another commonly accepted definition of environmental auditing was developed by the International Chamber of Commerce:-

"A management tool comprising a systematic, documented, periodic and objective evaluation of how well environmental organisation management and equipment are performing with the aim of safeguarding the environment by:

- Facilitating management control of environmental practices.
- Assessing compliance with company policies, which would include meeting regulatory requirements".

There is no doubt that the "Environmental Audit" is in vogue. Unlike other "crazes" it is unlikely to go away and future legislation will demand its continuation. There are several different reasons for companies adopting such an initiative including public pressure, green marketing, environmental impairment liability insurance, performance evaluation, scheme accreditation etc. The list of reasons and the process itself seem never-ending.

The Yamanouchi Experience - Quality Approach

Yamanouchi's approach to environmental management stems largely from our approach to quality management. I firmly believe that these two concepts are inseparable. In 1992, the company achieved accreditation to the International Standard ISO 9002. Although the plant already had approval from the FDA since 1989, (and were subsequently reinspected in 1994 and 1997) we still consider the implementation of ISO 9002 to be a very worthwhile exercise. It was our view that this quality management system allowed us implement an integrated management system which is internationally recognised by all facets of society. While quality management was by no means a new concept to the company, we felt that it gave us an opportunity to broaden our base in this regard.

Following on from the success of this programme, we considered its development into other areas of site activity including safety and environmental operations. Realistically, in an industry such as ours, it is a myth to regard QUALITY as being independent of safety or environmental protection. We made a decision therefore, to develop the integrated approach extending ISO 9002 into safety and environmental areas.

Generally, many companies now appreciate that quality/safety/environmental management are key determinants of their viability and there is neither a safe way alone nor solely a quality way, but only a right way to do things.

The application of business process management principles is a mechanism for developing one common management system approach and creating a vehicle which allows commitment to continuous improvement. I firmly believe that the way forward for companies is to focus on COMPLIANCE in an integrated way in all it's activities rather than to try to adopt different approaches for different issues.

Environmental Management Systems - Development at YICL

In 1992, Yamanouchi Ireland Co., Ltd decided to develop it's own Environmental Management System (EMS) and decided upon using the British Standard (BS 7750) which was published back in 1992.

Generally we were comfortable with using this standard (which was in draft form then) as this draft standard was generic and compatible with ISO 9000. However, before the company had developed it's implementation strategy for BS 7750, it was requested by the European Commission to participate in the European Union Pilot project on The Draft Eco Management and Audit Regulation (now known as EMAS). Yamanouchi was one of seventeen companies in Europe involved in this exercise and was in fact the only Irish representative.

- **Pilot Exercise**

In 1992, the European Union commenced a pilot study (as mentioned above) to investigate the implementation of the draft Eco Audit Regulation (subsequently renamed as the Eco Management and Audit Regulation).

Their objective was to gain practical experience with the scheme, and in particular to identify any problems, or indeed opportunities, it might present to participating companies.

Since our company had not begun to implement BS 7750, it was decided to undertake a comparison of the two systems in order to develop a template that would address both. It was concluded that the two systems were closely related and compatible. The results of the comparison were used to develop the company's implementation plan.

- **Implementation of an Environmental Management System**

Subsequently, we commenced implementation of an Environmental Management System which, it was hoped, would satisfy the requirements of BS 7750 and the EU regulation. A key element of both systems involved the identification, understanding and determination of the known and potential site environmental impacts.

In order to do this, we developed a site environmental profile by using an input/output model that could be applied in a genetic fashion at all levels of the organisation. This model applied, involved the use of a three tier approach for identification and analysis of the inputs and outputs mentioned above.

This was followed at a later stage with compilation of a Register of Significant Environmental Effects for the site.

The site environmental profile was in fact the cornerstone on which our register of significant environmental effects, required in both BS 7750 and the EU scheme was formulated.

From the results of these exercises it has been possible to identify the key environmental issues for the site. Subsequently, it has been possible to set pertinent environmental objects and targets.

Implementation of the system has also included the development of a legislative register, setting up a system for reviewing these documents and also identifying issues of legislative significance for the site.

Other elements of the environmental management system which have been developed either as a result of IPCL regulations or the requirements of BS 7750 include:-

- Environmental Manual
- Standard Operating Procedures
- Environmental Audit Programme
- Environmental Management Programme

The Registration Process
Yamanouchi Ireland began the process of registration to BS 7750 with an initial assessment (one day duration) on site by SGS Yarsley (accredited auditors under the scheme). This was subsequently followed by an in-depth desk top study (by SGS in the UK) of all the relevant documentation associated with the system.

The final registration audit took place in November 1995 and following a successful conclusion, YICL became the first company in the pharmaceutical sector in Ireland and the United Kingdom to be registered under the scheme. In March 1997, Yamanouchi Ireland were also officially registered to ISO 14001.

Issues central to an Environmental Management System
From our experiences in this area, we now feel competent to make some comments regarding what we see as some of the core elements of such a management system and the points discussed below represent the Yamanouchi perspective in this regard:

- routine setting of new environmental targets and objectives with subsequent evaluation of performance.

- a comprehensive documentation system.
- training/awareness programmes.
- waste minimisation programmes.
- energy management.

The adoption of an environmental management system approach has provided a framework whereby these, and other relevant activities, take place and are monitored and reported in a structured and a controlled manner.

Other Related Programmes
It is important to point out that as indicated in the introduction, YICL are also committed to the Responsible Care® Programme. The chemical industry is all too aware of it's challenges in current times in relation to the public's negative and somewhat suspicious perception of it.

The Responsible Care® Programme (originating in Canada during the 1980's) which was launched by the Federation of Irish Chemical Industries, FICI, (now known as Irish Pharmaceutical and Chemical Manufacturers Federation), IPCMF, in 1992, has been identified as a vehicle which can, to a large extent, address these issues.

To date three different codes of practice have been adopted by FICI (IPCMF):-
- Distribution
- Process Safety
- Protection of the Environment

Each code contains a set of guidelines for implementation of essential management practices, each element involving six stages of implementation. This programme was very much welcomed by our industry in Ireland as it addresses some of the "key" problem issues which have been identified, including the need for open communication with the public. The programme itself has a number of merits associated with it but, on a personal note, the one element it currently lacks is external verification, hence the need for schemes such as EMAS and BS 7750/I.S. 310/ISO 14001 etc. which (a) are voluntary and site specific, (b) provide a systemic approach to environmental management and (c) DEMAND EXTERNAL

VERIFICATION.

Conclusions

As a general comment, I think it should be recognised that environmental management is still in a transition phase in terms of it's broad understanding of the new challenges. Management needs time to adapt and take on board the outlook needed if environmental issues are to be properly addressed. I would hope in the years ahead that environmental management systems will be seen as an integral part of any aspect of an industrial operation such as finance, QA and manufacturing considerations.

It is certainly Yamanouchi Ireland's experience that integrated systems and integrated compliance is the only way forward for organisations - it has thankfully proved to be successful to date for YICL and we are committed to maintaining and improving, wherever possible, our performance to date.

10.7   Printing / Electronic Media:

a) *Printech International, BS 7750 and ISO 14001 Experience*
This company profile has been written with the assistance of Mr. Des O'Keeffe and Mr. Tom Murphy of Printech International. It draws on information from company brochures and previous articles written by the above.

The Company and it's Markets
Printech International Group are located in Cloverhill Industrial Estate, Clondakin, Dublin. They began operations in a terraced house in Amines Street, Dublin in 1978. Today, Printech are situated on a nine acre site with a 165,000 sq. ft. production facility. The workforce consists of 375 full-time and 200 part-time employees. The turnover for 1995 was £32million. The company is now one of the leading players in the supply of printed and electronic media and total fulfilment to the computer industry in Europe.

Printech started software-kitting (i.e. assembly) in 1989 on the Clondakin site and in 1993 opened a Kitting and Print-on-Demand plant in East Kilbride, Scotland. It also owns a Print-on-Demand facility near Rotterdam.

Printech have had a long history of achievement, being one of the first companies in Ireland to be accredited to I.S. 300 Quality Standard in 1988. In 1989, it became the first print and packaging company in Western Europe to acquire accreditation to ISO 9002. In August 1994 it was amongst the first in Europe to be awarded the Green Dove Award by SGS Yarsley. This was a forerunner to the achievement of BS 7750 in 1995 and certification to ISO 14001 in 1996. The company has long benefited from imaginative corporate decision making, and has succeeded in continuously improving it's market share, in the face of very stiff competition.

Why Printech embarked on an Environmental Management System
Environmental Concerns:
For a number of years preceding the introduction of a formal environmental management system there existed within the company a genuine concern for various impacts that the company were having on the environment.

Some typical examples of printing industry impacts would be:

- Energy and resource usage, (Electricity, gas and water)
- Raw material usage, (Paper, plates, inks, packaging, chemicals)
- General wastes (Landfill)
- Recyclable wastes (Paper, timber, aluminium, silver, plastics)
- Hazardous wastes (Chemical wastes, liquid effluent, air emissions)
- Nuisance (Noise, litter, dust, odours)
- Contracted activities (Transport, subcontracted printing work)
- Product end use and disposal.

A committee was formed which considered these environmental issues as they were identified, and then dealt with them, more or less on an ad hoc basis. This system had no formal structure, nor documented procedures, and was, in consequence, weak on control, and ineffective in dealing with these impacts.

Legal Obligations:
In the past, the method of management did not fully address legal obligations, such as compliance with effluent discharge license parameters, or local authority planning requirements. Since implementing an EMS the company has realised the benefits of being aware and ahead of planned legislation. Integrated Pollution Control licensing, for instance, will eventually oblige most industries to comply with stricter industry guidelines on pollution control, with the threat of heavy financial penalties resulting from non compliance with these requirements. Printech's EMS recognises and addresses the aspects of operations requiring such control, so compliance becomes more or less automatic.

Customer Pressure:
Printech's customer base comprises mostly of Multi-national, US based, computer hardware and software manufacturers. Such companies are renowned for being pretty strict with their suppliers in complying with standards of quality, reliability, and more recently environmental regulations. Indeed, these are very often the companies who drive the changes in manufacturing practice, which sooner or later becomes the way that we do business. Most of Printech's management systems have been developed as a result of pressure applied from these quarters. Several years ago Printech

recognised, in the signals coming from their customers, that environmental issues were getting more focus. Notably, there was a steady increase in the number of requests for detailed information on the environmental probity of their products and production methods. This obviously required them to reassure their customers that they were minimising the environmental impact of their activities, and the most obvious way they could do this effectively, was to implement a certifiable EMS.

Previous Approach:
In 1993 the environmental group participated in an Environmental Awareness Strategic Training Programme, organised by the Irish Productivity Centre. On behalf of Printech, they were awarded a Certificate of Accomplishment for their endeavours. More importantly though, this programme outlined the advantages of operating an environmental management system, based on a formal specification, like BS 7750:1992, for example. The group recognised that this approach offered a framework within which it could provide assurances to those concerned that the environmental management system would be operated effectively.

Why Printech chose BS 7750 Environmental Standard
Printech were aware that the Irish Environmental Standard, I.S. 310, was fairly advanced in development, but they decided that the BS 7750 was more appropriate to their needs. BS 7750 1992 was already available as the first certifiable national standard. Even if I.S. 310 had been available at the time they would still have opted for the BS 7750 specification.

Printech's quality system was based on the I.S. 300 quality standard which was almost identical to BS 5750 quality standard, later to be succeeded by the ISO 9000 quality standard. A preview of I.S. 310 showed them that, although apparently, quite a good system in itself, it was structured in a completely different way to BS 7750. Printech figured that the British Standard would more likely be closer to the eventual ISO 14001, and this has turned out to be the case.

Project Analysis

When the group reported back to headquarters, some intensive analysis of the situation took place. A report was prepared for the board of management outlining the following:

Negative aspects:

- No comparative role model existed on which to design the system.
- No definitive acceptance criteria were available to help verify the interpretation of the specification.
- Development of the system would require full time staffing for at least one year, plus large part time participation.
- Some considerable capital investment was also envisaged.
- Overall estimated cost was reckoned to be in the region of 100K
- The system would also require ongoing maintenance expenditure

Positive aspects:

- Cost savings, increased profitability.
- Energy savings, waste reduction and better waste segregation, increased efficiency.
- Improved products, competitiveness, market share.
- Better public image, relationship with the local community.
- Employee motivation, better working environment.
- Conforming with legal requirements, avoiding penalties.

Project strategy:

Having had discussions with various parties, the environmental system manager proposed the following approach:

- That a working group, or committee, comprising of key members of staff should be set up. The development and implementation of any management system requires the participation and co-operation of people in key positions in the company. Printech choose its facilities manager to the lead the team, as this person would have hands-on-knowledge of those aspects of the plant which impact most on the environment.
- That a full time environmental officer should be appointed, at least for the duration of the project, and probably beyond.

- That sufficient funding and resources be made available to see the project through. At the outset Printech had no idea how much work it was taking on, or what it was all going to cost. There were the cost of consultancy fees which are fairly predictable, and they knew there were certain things about the plant which needed to be put right. But the amount of time and effort given by the committee and others, which certainly carried a substantial cost, is very hard to evaluate. These costs will vary greatly from one company to another. It is therefore crucial that sufficient resources are provided to ensure that agreed action items are fulfilled, so that momentum is not lost.

- That an unequivocal commitment from top management be published, pledging support for the development of the system. The initial impetus for this venture in Printech came from the production director, who took an active interest in the campaign throughout. This support meant the EMS project was being properly represented at board level, and this was evidenced by approvals which flowed during crucial phases of the scheme. This commitment was communicated regularly, through in-house publications, special presentations and ceremonies, specially devised to give the environmental campaign a high profile throughout the company.

Environmental Committee Structure
The following is taken from Printech's environmental manual and describes the environmental committee structure.

Steering Committee
Firstly, the ground rules by which the committee would proceed were agreed, namely, terms of reference outlining responsibilities were drafted, goals were set and reporting mechanisms established. The general group, or steering committee, would direct the development of the system, formulate a plan of action and monitor the progress of the project. The general areas of activity were identified, and sub committees were formed with responsibility for each. These groups were made up, in the main, of steering committee members whose particular skills or expertise would help them accomplish their assigned tasks. They would plan and organise according as they saw fit, and report on their progress to the steering committee.

Sub Committee 1

This group comprised of the facilities manager, the quality assurance manager, the analyst programmer, and the newly appointed environmental engineer. This group would interpret the requirements of the BS 7750 standard, and address these requirements through the development of a documented system. They would ensure that the system was compatible with other management systems already in place, notably the quality assurance and health and safety systems.

Sub Committee 2

This group comprised of the environmental engineer (again), the production manager, and the purchasing officer. Their task was to carry out the preliminary environmental review, using some professional help, and compile the registers of legislation and environmental effects, which would form part of the documented system.

Sub Committee 3

This group comprised of the health and safety officer, the person with responsibility for new products, and various volunteers, whose job was to co-ordinate public relations and to hype up the environmental theme and awareness amongst the staff. They were also responsible for general communications and the development of a training programme.

The Documented System

In the introduction to BS 7750: 1994 specification, there is a schematic diagram of the stages in the implementation of an environmental management system. It sets out in a clear, logical sequence of actions which, if followed, will allow the elements of the system to fall nicely into place.

It is obvious, for instance, that you would carry out a thorough review of your current activities before you could establish a register of environmental effects, and what your objectives and targets should address, in order of significance, any adverse effects which are identified in the register. A programme is then put in place which describes how you intend to fulfil these goals, and the operational control verifies these activities, and so on.

Environmental Manual

Printech's environmental manual is derived specifically from section four of BS 7750 specification, and so it should be. The point here though is, that Printech have written it clause by clause, line by line, as per the eleven elements, sub elements, and sub elements of this section. This approach makes sense for a couple of very good reasons. Firstly, it ensures that the company have addressed, or at least attempted to address, every element of the specification, which they are required to. Secondly, when the system is being audited, it makes reference to manuals and documentation very simple. The same approach was used when designing the quality system.

Referencing

Within each section of the manual Printech describe in detail, how it intends to address that element of the specification. In many cases, in order to achieve this, it is necessary to develop one or more written procedures with supporting documentation. So, at the end of each section of the manual the appropriate procedures are referenced.

Similarly at the end of each procedure the associated section of the manual has been referenced, plus any documents related to that procedure. The documents themselves are also registered in such a way as to allow them to be related directly to the procedure. For example, if procedure number five has two special documents attached, let's say a Document Change Order and a log, then the order form could be numbered EMS 05-01 and the log numbered EMS 05-02.

This method of numbering enables each document to be traced right back to the relevant element of the standard. So, if someone is wondering why they might have to fill out a form, or how it functions, they can just check the reference number, say EMS 05-01.

This tells them that the document is part of the environmental management system (EMS) and is the first document referred to in procedure No. 5. If they then check their procedures manual, which everyone using the document has access to, they can familiarise themselves with the procedure and learn why it is performed. They will also be referred to the relevant section of the manual, and if they are really interested, can read the specific element of the specification, to understand why the procedure was written in the first place. This method of referencing and numbering is invaluable for audits. Auditors are very fond of asking the question "Why are you doing this? ", and with such a simple system as this the question nearly answers itself.

Annexes

Printech's manuals and documentation are completely reviewed on an annual basis, or as required, together with the rest of the system, but by and large they are not expected to have to change very often, at least as long as the company intends to operate to the BS 7750 specification. There are elements of the system, however, which must be allowed to evolve and change without the formalities associated with making changes to the documented system. An example would be the legislative register, which must be updated as new laws are enacted, or the register of effects which may change as a result of some objective being achieved, or some new process being installed. To allow these changes to take place with ease, a special set of "Annexes" to the system have been set up. Each annex is structured according to it's own particular requirements, and may contain reference documents, such as pieces of legislation, databases, or files, and this structure, and how it is used, is described within a procedure. To date the company has six annexes. Together with the two already mentioned there are, Emergency Response Plan, Site Inspections, The Audit Programme and the Management Programme.

Records

Any procedure which has associated documentation will have hard copies of live documents filed under the procedure number, and the entire documented system is computerised, for the purposes of efficiency and convenience.

The Benefits of BS Certification to Printech

As with the cost, the benefits associated with such a scheme as this are hard to fully evaluate. Printech knows for instance, that the fact that they operate an environmental management system has tipped the balance in their favour on several occasions, winning them contracts, and their sales people believe BS 7750 certification to be a valuable marketing tool, but it is difficult to put a figure on it.

The company is also portrayed as having a responsible attitude generally, and it demonstrates Printech's management capabilities favourably.

Printech now finds it much easier to respond to customer / public queries or concerns regarding environmental issues.

There is peace of mind in knowing that the company is in compliance with current and proposed legislation.

Site management is easier. Improved economies, energy savings, waste minimisation, improved working environment are some of the benefits that have been realised. In 1994 Printech won the best factory category in the South Dublin County Council / Gunne Estate Agents Tidy Districts and Environmental Awards scheme.

Major Initiatives

- Energy Efficiency: through campaign messages to encourage conservation, by shortening machine cycle times, and installation of automatic lighting and dust separation systems. Dust separation allowed waste heat to be returned to the factory and was one of a number of measures giving rise to a 6.2% (against a target of 5%) in energy use between March 1994-95.
- Technology: state-of-the-art direct to plate lasexposer eliminates the use of photographic films and hazardous chemicals associated with developing films. The process itself has no emissions and a silver recovery unit works with the lasexposer, reducing the silver content of waste to undetectable levels.
- Recycling: the majority of waste paper is sent away for recycling after being segregated into stock types and quality. The remainder comprises of highly varnished printed materials and card/plastic mixes which are compacted for landfill.
- Re-use: cardboard boxes and white paper are made from recycled waste paper which is unbleached and does not contain pernicious constituents; shrink-wrap used on manuals is also recycled.
- Printing plates: these are recycled for metal scrap and the company is investigating the possibility of re-using plates a number of times before disposal; alcohol used in cleaning plates is recirculated many times before being sent away for recycling.

- Paper: as chlorine is traditionally used to bleach pulp for papermaking, the process has an adverse effect on the environment at the pulp stage, though it is believed that chlorine compounds, such as chlorine dioxide, do not have such effects. Printech's policy is to use either ECF or TCF paper. The former involves compounds of chlorine which are generally regarded as safe in the bleaching process, whilst the latter is totally chlorine free.
- Supplies: Printech's total paper supplies are ultimately sourced from managed forests in Scandinavia.
- Inks: all inks are oil-based, non-toxic, and do not contain any heavy metals. The company is currently investigating the use of vegetable oil based inks such as soya oil, which are environmentally friendly since the main raw material is obtained from regenerative sources.
- Adhesives and varnish: adhesives used in the binding process are completely non-toxic (when solid, these can be eaten). Varnishes are water soluble and do not contain any VOC's.
- Disposal: any manual can be re-pulped and recycled as paper. Incineration creates no hazardous emissions, while manuals can be acceptably landfilled, being 98% biodegradable. This would also make landfill more acceptable 'for the end user' as all waste manuals on site would be re-cycled.

Where to Now

Membership of the BS 7750 / EMAS Users Group (UK) has allowed Printech's environmental manager to represent Printech's and Ireland's interests at the group meetings since their inauguration in January 1995. This affords the opportunity to Printech to influence future developments of environmental management systems, as the meetings are regularly attended by senior representatives of bodies such as UKAS, BSI, EARA etc. who have direct input into these developments. It is also a useful venue for comparing documented systems, and for assessing the performances of accreditation agencies.

A registration to ISO 14001 international standard has given Printech an opportunity to rebuild their system on generic lines. On the other hand an upgrade to EMAS would demand continuous improvement and greater communication with the public. Either approach will maintain Printech's position at the forefront with it's competitors.

Some of Printech's immediate priorities concern it with dealing with the training of employees in the handling of chemicals and carrying out investigations into VOC's from inks, and printing processes. In co-operation with it's vendors, sub-contractor's and customers they will set tighter controls on all aspects of their activities which have an environmental impact.

Plans are already being developed to implement an environmental management system at Printech's plant in Scotland.

The company's overall objective is to maintain and enhance it's position through continuous improvement, as one of the most environmentally responsive print and packaging companies in Europe.

Telecommunications:

a) Nortel Ltd., IS 310 and ISO 14001 Experience
This company profile has been written with the assistance of Ms. Sandra Morgan, Safety, Health and Environmental Specialist, Nortel. It draws on information from company documents and an article previously written by the above.

The Company
Northern Telecom (Ireland) Ltd. (Nortel) is located in a 17,600 m² design and production facility at the Mervue Industrial Estate located to the north-east of Galway city. This facility was established in 1973 to manufacture telephone systems for the Irish and European markets. There are 700 employed by Nortel in Galway at present and it is a 24 hour and 7 days a week operation.

Nortel is an integrated business unit dedicated to the end-to-end business of the Meridian 1 PABX product. The 3 key business functions are: R&D, manufacture and order fulfilment, with the emphasis on high quality, superior service and low cost. Nortel capitalises on leading edge technology expertise in front end materials planning and logistics to support sales growth in the European marketplace.

The Meridian/PABX (private automatic branch exchange) product range is comprised of several PCBA's (printed circuit board assemblies) arranged in a cube assembly. These cubes can then be stocked up to four tiers high to form a PABX.

The manufacturing process involves the population of printed circuit boards with electronic and mechanical components, using SMT (Surface Mount Technology). During the SMT process solder and flux are printed onto the printed circuit board using a screen stencil. The electronic parts are then placed on the Printed Circuit Board (PCB) automatically by the SMT machine. The populated boards are then passed through a carefully controlled heating process which allows the solder to melt and flow creating the necessary electrical connection. Due to the advanced nature of the manufacturing process at Nortel no CFC cleaning agents are required (except those used as refrigerants).

Printed circuit boards are also populated using a through hole process. With this technique the Alegs of the electronic components pass through the PCB. Fluxing agent is then sprayed to the base of the board. The populated board then passes through a wave of molten solder which creates the necessary electrical connection. Again due to the advanced nature of the soldering process, no CFC cleaning agents are used in the process. There are two SMT lines in operation at Nortel and two wave solder machines.

The populated printed circuit boards are referred to as a pack. After assembly the packs undergo stringent testing. On completion the packs are loaded with the required software. The packs are then assembled into the Meridian 1 PABX Private telephone exchange system. Approximately 6,500 PABX systems were manufactured in 1995. These units are supplied to the customer complete with telephones which are supplied by Nortel' Cwmcarn plant in Wales.

Environmental Status at Nortel

General

As there is a growing awareness of and concern about the impact of industry on the environment individual companies are beginning to examine their environmental impact. Nortel have implemented an Environmental Management System at its Galway facility as part of its heightened environmental awareness campaign. Furthermore, it is a Northern Telecom corporate objective to have certified Environmental Management Systems in all of its manufacturing sites by 1998.

Past and Present Performance

Nortel as a corporate body is committed to achieving the highest standards of environmental excellence. Nortel's research facilities in Canada and the United Kingdom have been at the forefront of life cycle assessment and design for the environment within the telecommunications sector.

This awareness of environmental consideration led directly to the elimination of CFC's from all Nortel's facilities world-wide. CFC free printed circuit board assembly was introduced to the Mervue facility in 1992. Nortel also operates a take back programme where scrap material and redundant equipment is returned to Nortel's recycling facilities (Foots Cray, Kent, UK - within Europe).

Management Structure

Presently, responsibility for environmental issues and environmental management lies with a number of personnel. The senior management (Leadership Team) has overall responsibility for environmental issues among all other issues for the site, including production and personnel. The Human Resources Director is the Senior Management representative with day to day responsibility for environmental issues.

Employee Awareness and Training

There is an employee induction scheme in operation at Nortel. In this process new employees are introduced to Nortel and it's operating systems, including the developing environmental management system. A copy of the content of the Training/Induction Scheme is available through the SHE Specialist or the Training Manager.

Continuous assessment of environmental awareness is reviewed by the SHE Team which meets at least once a month or more frequently as determined by their activities. The SHE team consists of staff from a cross-section of activities within the company, including Quality, Production, Human resources, Site Services, Material, Occupational Health, Engineering, Logistics and Product Design. The Safety, Health and Environmental Specialist is designated as the team leader. The team reports to the Human Resource Director and the Managing Director. The team has received formal training for it's activities.

Information Management

Nortel are aware that increasing numbers of people are interested in the amount of information which is publicly available concerning a company's environmental performance. In addition, the 1990 EU directive on freedom of access to environmental information (and our own national regulation implementing this) requires member states to ensure that certain information held by controlling authorities and government departments is available to the public upon request (accepting the need for commercial confidentiality).

Greater public access to information relating to a company's legal environmental control limits and it's performance in meeting these, results in increasing public scrutiny. The Habitat website along with the annual environmental report are important factors in Nortel's dissemination of information to interested parties. Nortel respond to requests for information through the SHE specialist.

Nortel's corporate environmental division has developed a computer package to monitor the environmental performance of each of it's sites. This system, known as PERI (Public Environmental Reporting Index) accumulates data on a quarterly basis on each sites waste, emissions, resource utilisation, recycling programmes, permits, licenses, past land use, remediation (none ever required on site), waste audits, targets and incentives. The corporate division also provides resources on design for the environment and recycling options.

Employee and community awareness is a major part of Nortel's corporate environmental programme. Environmental issues are highlighted within the site by the prominent display of environmental information on dedicated environmental notice boards. Employees are encouraged to develop waste reduction strategies by participating in suggestion schemes. On a community basis Nortel Galway has sponsored the Down to Earth theatre group to visit local schools and act out various environmental issues. Nortel Galway has also sponsored tree planting programmes. There is a Nortel corporate Internet website called Habitat. The corporate Environmental Ethics and Quality (EEQ) produce a monthly news bulletin which is e-mailed to all NT sites, Human Resources (HR) produce a bi-weekly site Newsletter which addresses environmental issues among other items. The site is shut down for a communications session quarterly, last October ('96) the session was on 'Environment in Nortel'.

Approaching an Environmental Management System
Introduction
Nortel conducted a General Review during which all aspects of the organisation were considered with the aim of identifying strengths, weaknesses, risks and opportunities on the basis of evaluating current environmental performance and establishing an environmental management system.

General Issues
Most manufacturing activities have an environmental impact, and

they are almost always negative ones. Environmental assessment of any activity or product must therefore measure as many of these impacts as possible in an objective way. The judgement of the comparative importance of different impacts, however, tends to be subjective. There is little general agreement, for example, on the relative importance of pollution to water or air. How does one judge two processes, one of which produces minimal greenhouse gases in the atmosphere, but a high chemical oxygen demand (COD) against the other which produces little COD, but a lot of greenhouse gases. There is no agreed methodology.

Specific Issues

Environmental Consultants with expertise in environmental impact assessment and environmental management were retained to assist in the development and implementation of the environmental management system. An environmental core group was set up which comprised both of Nortel and Consultancy personnel, to achieve this. This cross-functional team were managed by Nortel's Environmental Specialist.

Using the environmental impact assessment framework and techniques (such as interviews, direct inspection, etc.), environmental issues were identified and prioritised in terms of impact on the local environment. The following significant issues were recognised and prioritised namely:

- Waste management
- Resource utilisation
- Air emissions
- Water usage and discharges

Other impacts include:

- Noise
- Off-site impacts

At this point the strengths and weaknesses of the environmental performance of the site were outlined in relation to the priority areas. Proposed actions (short-term and long-term) for improvement of environmental performance and environmental protection were presented in the Register of the Organisation Objectives and Targets.

Priority 1 - Waste Management
The principal wastes produced by Nortel are plastic, cardboard, paper and old Printed Circuit Boards. Since September 1996 Nortel have been sorting all solid waste produced on site through an on-site Recycling Centre. The various wastes streams cardboard, plastics of different grades, paper, printed circuit boards (PCB's) and aluminium are segregated and sent where possible to an appropriate recycling contractor. This programme is aimed at reducing the amount of material sent to landfill and increasing the volumes recycled. All non recyclable waste material is compacted prior to landfilling at Galway County Council landfill site at Carrowbrowne, Co. Galway.

Priority 2 - Resource Utilisation
The raw materials used at Nortel are electronic components, packing materials and consumables. There are five diesel tanks on site. In addition, there are two Nitrogen storage tanks containing liquid Nitrogen. Gas used for cooking in the restaurant is stored in gas cylinders. There is also an area designated as a storage area for process chemicals.

There are three sources of energy used on site. They are electricity, diesel oil and bottled gas. Electricity is madwort and provides all motive power. Bottled gas is used in the kitchen and fed from bottles. Diesel boilers are also used on site for control heating.

Both demand and consumption contribute to the cost of supplying electricity. The Electricity Supply Board (ESB) generation and supply system must have adequate capacity to provide for the highest National Demand that could occur at any time. The highest National Demand is approaching 3,000,000 kW. Electricity consumption must be provided for by generating stations using fuel sources across the country. The term Aload refers to the electrical load a customer places on the ESB supply network at any instant and is commonly measured in kilowatts (kWh). The terms Aload and Ademand are interchangeable. For billing purposes Ademand refers to the average load over a 15-minute period. Electricity consumption is measured in kilowatt-hours (kWh). Nortel's electrical demand is composed of the sum of many individual demands. If plotted, the height of the peak on the profile corresponds to the daily Amaximum demand. For billing purposes, the ESB measures the average demand in each 15-minute period between 08:00 and 21:00, Monday to Friday. The highest demand measured in each two-month billing period is the Amaximum demand@. The higher the Amaximum demand the higher the demand and energy charges.

Nortel is utilising the ESB's identified peaks to determine their use of backup generators. The sites Site Services Group have an Energy Management Team to focus on reduction initiatives during 1997.

Priority 3 - Air Environment

Air emissions from Nortel's activities arise from Boiler stacks, organic solvents from SMT and wave solder lines, Lead and Tin from SMT and wave solder lines. Off-site impacts include hauliers and employee vehicle emissions. Emissions from major component and electricity generation. All of the above emissions contribute to the atmospheric environmental concerns.

Atmospheric emissions are produced from a number of sources on site. Notwithstanding this, no air pollution licence was required under the Air Pollution Act 1987 (as amended) or regulations made thereunder. At present, Galway Corporation have legislative control over air emissions. The conditions are very general and state, for example, that all operations on site must be carried out in such a manner as to ensure that no odour or duct nuisance occurs beyond the site boundary. To date there have been no odour or dust nuisance complaints received, therefore odour or dust are not considered to be an issue.

Halon gases are used in fire suppression systems and refrigeration.

Priority 4 - Water Usage and Discharge

The main water issue concerns are:

- waste water from the stencil screen wash
- waste water from the kitchen

Surface water run-off drains to a storm water collection system which outfalls into Lough Atalia. All foul water is discharged to a municipal sewer which eventually outfalls into Galway Bay adjacent to the Dock in Galway. However there is a municipal waste water treatment plant proposed for Galway city which when constructed would treat all foul water arising in the city catchment. Ongoing debate over the siting of the Treatment plant on Mutton Island in Galway Bay is delaying the construction.

The waste water effluent arising from the screen wash is licensed by Galway Corporation. A once off analysis of the waste water for lead gave lead concentration of 3.7 mg/L. The sample was not analysed for tin which is also a component of the solder paste. No discharge limits have been specified by Galway Corporation in their discharge permit. However, the EPA has published guidelines recommending 0.5 mg/L for lead and 2 mg/L for tin in waste water discharges. Nortel is in the process of purchasing an 'enclosed' screen wash unit from the UK. This unit reuses all water emissions.

Nortel have installed a grease trap on the kitchen effluent line. This now reduces the fat, oils and grease concentrations to the effluent stream. The licence emission limit for fats and greases is now being met.

Noise
Recent BATNEEC guidance notes for noise in relation to scheduled activities state that when limits are established for noise emissions attention will be focused on location of the activity and the zoning of the surrounding area. Emissions levels will also take into account the proximity to noise sensitive locations. Noise limits will be applied for each individual situation.

Off Site Impacts
As Nortel receives many components from local and international suppliers which are incorporated into their products there is an off site impact on the environment. This impact is difficult to quantify since there are so many suppliers. However, Nortel have implemented a scheme of assessing suppliers, initially a cross-section of both $ value supplies, hazardous material and existing local suppliers with significant impacts. Nortel also collect some environmental information about their suppliers - their products, materials, processes, policies and their Material Safety Data Sheets (MSDS's).

The Fruits of Certification to International Standards
In line with the corporation's objective for all manufacturing sites to implement an Environmental Management System (EMS) by 1998, Galway's system was certified to both the Irish Standard I.S. 310 and the international ISO/EN 14001 Standard in December 1996. In adhering to this standard, Nortel has identified all the impacts of it's operations, both direct and indirect; recorded their existing controls in protecting the environment and is implementing a strategy for improving it's environmental performance. This strategy encompasses partnering with external groups to educate and raise awareness amongst both customers, suppliers and the local community.

To achieve implementation of the EMS and it's certification, Nortel's Managing Director and the management team were assisted by the Safety Health & Environmental, specialist. A key message of Nortel Galway's environmental policy is to integrate environmental considerations into every aspect of the business. This is demonstrated by a business plan which includes environmental objectives and a budget specifically designated for their achievement.

Energy and waste reduction targets have been set by the corporation relating to the minimisation of energy resource consumption, raw material resource consumption, and, through technology, the reduction or elimination of water, air and soil emissions or discharges. Progress in meeting these objectives is collated and recorded on a quarterly basis and reported to shareholders through the company's Annual Report. Additionally, the company publicises it's environmental performance and initiatives on the Internet.

Each employee is encouraged to participate in Nortel Galway's environmental initiatives. As Nortel is a 'clean' industry, efforts to date have focused on environmental improvements and waste minimisation. Such activities have included an internal drive on paper which resulted in donations to local community charities or environmental based initiatives along with tree planting within the Galway city area.

Activities which highlight Nortel's commitment to environmental management have included CFC elimination in 1990, with Nortel being one of the first manufacturing companies in Europe to report total elimination of CFC's from the manufacturing process. (This also brought a cost benefit of US$9,200 to the company at that time).

Energy Efficiency

In 1990, the company installed a computerised energy management system. This controls high energy using equipment as well as controlling the working environment (the system has boilers, air-handling units and chiller units connected to it). Each section of the production area has a detector fitted and the equipment is run on the lowest possible amount of energy. The return on the company's investment was paid back within 2 years. Energy efficiency will continue to be a key driver in 1997 and will add value to both the operational and cost efficiency of the plant.

Nortel Galway has won the Chief Financial Officers Award for Achievement related to the Environment, and a Bank of Ireland Local Heroes award for environmental initiatives.

The company is at the initial stages of formalising a system for dealing with the 'design for the environment' issues that will be impacting largely on the way the electronics industry will be conducting business in the future. Legislation expected to be introduced in it's European market, i.e. Germany, will require the Galway operation to have clear management tools for considering the environmental aspects of it's future products and their end-of-life uses.

Manufacturing processes are being researched to eliminate hazardous materials. For instance, a screenwash is being re-engineered to eliminate solvents and lead-free solder has been developed. It is proposed that Galway undertake lead-free manufacturing trials during 1997.

Recycling of Waste and Packaging

Waste products from the manufacturing process are recycled locally and the site now accommodates an in-house recycling centre which is managed by Nortel Site Services and Connaught Waste Recycling. This is in direct response to the difficulties the company had in identifying local/national waste recycling contractors to deal with it's waste streams.

Supplier packaging is recycled for use in product packaging to customers, and the company, through it's packaging engineer and it's European Packaging Council are planning initiatives with customers regarding pending EU packaging legislation.

The company donates computer equipment to local schools, old office furniture is donated to a hospice and also offered for sale along with old lighting to employees. All scrap steel is recycled through Galway Metal.

During 1996, a budget allocation was specifically set aside by Nortel to educate and promote within the local community the importance of preserving the environment. Activities involved sponsoring the Irish Environmental Theatre Company, *Down To Earth*, to conduct both shows and workshops in local schools. *Down to Earth* also conducted two shows at Galway Town Hall during the Galway Arts Festival; attended the Nortel Christmas children's party and educated the employees themselves with a sketch during the company's October communications session.

The Future
Nortel has undertaken a tremendous amount of work and has implemented it's EMS with enthusiasm. They believe that implementing an EMS is only the beginning and that the realisation that managing your environmental impacts is good for your customers, the community, your employees - and therefore ultimately for your business - brings about the true integration of environment into the day-to-day running of the company.

As an world-wide organisation Nortel are continuing to focus on product 'Design for the Environment' in order to design future products and processes with environmental criteria as the key consideration. Nortel Galway are very active in pursuing these design goals.

In the short to medium term Nortel's environmental team in Galway will focus on:

- integrating their environmental, health, safety and quality management systems;
- progress 'design for the environment' criteria into product and process changes;

- reduce energy consumption; and
- assessment and participation of their supply chain.

Appendix 1

Third and Fourth Schedules to the Waste Management Act, 1996

THIRD SCHEDULE
Waste Disposal Activities
1. Deposit on, in or under land.
2. Land treatment, including biodegradation of liquid or sludge discards in soils.
3. Deep injection of the soil, including injection of pumpable discards into wells, salt domes or naturally occurring repositories.
4. Surface impoundment, including placement of liquid or sludge discards into pits, ponds or lagoons.
5. Specially engineered landfill, including placement into lined discrete cells which are capped and isolated from one another and the environment.
6. Biological treatment not referred to elsewhere in this Schedule which results in final compounds or mixtures which are disposed of by means of any activity referred to in this Schedule.
7. Physico-chemical treatment not referred to elsewhere in this Schedule which results in final compounds or mixtures which are disposed of by means of any activity referred to in this Schedule.
8. Incineration on land or at sea.
9. Permanent storage, including emplacement of containers in a mine.
10.Release of waste into a water body (including a seabed insertion).
11.Blending or mixture prior to submission to any activity referred to in this Schedule.
12.Repackaging prior to submission to any activity referred to in this Schedule.
13.Storage prior to submission to any activity referred to in this Schedule, other than temporary storage, pending collection, on the premises where the waste concerned is produced.

Successful Environmental Management

FOURTH SCHEDULE

Waste Activities

1. Solvent reclamation or regeneration.

2. Recycling or reclamation of organic substances which are not used as solvents.

3. Recycling or reclamation of metals and metal compounds.

4. Recycling or reclamation of other inorganic materials.

5. Regeneration of acids or bases.

6. Recovery of components used for pollution abatement.

7. Recovery of components from catalysts.

8. Oil re-refining or other re-uses of oil.

9. Use of any waste principally as a fuel or other means to generate energy.

10. Spreading of any waste on land with a consequential benefit for an agricultural activity or ecological system, including com-posting and other biological transformation processes.

11. Use of waste obtained from any activity referred to in a preceding paragraph of this Schedule.

12. Exchange of waste for submission to any activity referred to in a preceding paragraph of this Schedule.

13. Storage of waste intended for submission to any activity referred to in a preceding paragraph of this Schedule, other than temporary storage, pending collection, on the premises where such waste is produced.

FIRST SCHEDULE TO THE EPA ACT, 1992

1. **Minerals and Other Materials**

1.1 The extraction, production and processing of raw asbestos.

1.2 The extraction of aluminium oxide from an ore.

1.3 The extraction and processing (including size reduction, grading and heating) of minerals within the meaning of the Minerals Development Acts, 1940 to 1979, and storage of related mineral waste.

1.4 The extraction of peat in the course of business which involves an area exceeding 50 hectares.

2. **Energy**

2.1 The production of energy in combustion plant the rated thermal input of which is equal to or greater than 50 MW other than any such plant which makes direct use of the products of combustion in a manufacturing process.

2.2 The burning of any fuel in a boiler or furnace with a nominal heat output exceeding 50 MW.

3. **Metals**

3.1 The initial melting or production of iron and steel.

3.2 The processing of iron and steel in forges, drawing plants and rolling mills where the production area exceeds 500 square metres.

3.3 The production, recovery, processing or use of ferrous metals in foundries having melting installations with a total capacity exceeding 5 tonnes.

3.4 The production, recovery or processing of non-ferrous metals, their compounds or other alloys including antimony, arsenic, beryllium, chromium, lead, magnesium, manganese, phosphorus, selenium, cadmium or mercury, by thermal, chemical or electrolytic means in installations with a batch capacity exceeding 0.5 tonnes.

3.5   The reaction of aluminium or it's alloys with chlorine or it's compounds.

3.6   The roasting, sintering or calcining of metallic ores in plants with a capacity exceeding 1,000 tonnes per year.

3.7   Swaging by explosives where the production area exceeds 100 square metres.

3.8   The pressing, drawing and stamping of large castings where the production area exceeds 500 square metres.

3.9   Boilermaking and the manufacture of reservoirs, tanks and other sheet metal containers where the production area exceeds 500 square metres.

4.   Mineral Fibres and Glass

4.1   The processing of asbestos and the manufacture and processing of asbestos-based products.

4.2   The manufacture of glass fibre or mineral fibre.

4.3   The production of glass (ordinary and special) in plants with a capacity exceeding 5,000 tonnes per year.

4.4   The production of industrial diamonds.

5.   Chemicals

5.1   The manufacture of chemicals in an integrated chemical installation.

5.2   The manufacture of olefins and their derivatives or of monomers and polymers, including styrene and vinyl chloride.

5.3   The manufacture, by way of chemical reaction processes, of organic or organo-metallic chemical products other than those specified at 5.2.

5.4   The manufacture of inorganic chemicals.

5.5   The manufacture of artificial fertilisers.

5.6   The manufacture of pesticides, pharmaceuticals or veterinary products and their intermediates.

5.7   The manufacture of paints, varnishes, resins, inks, dyes, pigments or elastomers where the production capacity exceeds 1,000 litres per week.

5.8   The formulation of pesticides.

5.9   The chemical manufacture of glues, bonding agents and adhesives.

5.10   The manufacture of vitamins involving the use of heavy metals.

5.11   The storage, in quantities exceeding the values shown, of any one or more of the following chemicals (others than as part of any other activity)-methyl acrylate (20 tonnes); acrylonitrile (20 tonnes); toluene di-isocyanate (20 tonnes); anhydrous ammonia (100 tonnes); anhydrous hydrogen fluoride (1 tonne).

6.   **Intensive Agriculture**

6.1   The rearing of poultry in installations, whether within the same complex or within 100 metres of that complex, where the capacity exceeds 100,000 units have the following equivalents-

1 broiler   = 1 unit

1 layer, turkey or other fowl   = 2 units.

6.2   The rearing of pigs in installations, whether within the same complex or within 100 metres of that complex, where the capacity exceeds 1,000 units on gley soils or 3,000 units on other soils and where units have the following equivalents-

1 pig   = 1 unit

1 sow   = 10 units.

7.   **Food and Drink**

7.1   The manufacture of vegetable and animal oils and fats where the capacity for processing raw materials exceeds 40 tonnes per day.

7.2   The manufacture of dairy products where the processing capacity exceeds 50 million gallons of milk equivalent per year.

7.3 Commercial brewing and distilling, and malting in installations where the production capacity exceeds 100,000 tonnes per year.

7.4 The slaughter of animals in installations where the daily capacity exceeds 1,500 units and where units have the following equivalents-

1 sheep = 1 unit,

1 pig = 2 units,

1 head of cattle = 5 units.

7.5 The manufacture of fish-meal and fish-oil.

7.6 The manufacture of sugar.

7.7 The rendering of animal by-products.

8. **Wood, Paper, Textiles and Leather**

8.1 The manufacture of paper pulp, paper or board (including fibre-board, particle board and plywood) in installations with a production capacity equal to or exceeding 25,000 tonnes of product per year.

8.2 The manufacture of bleached pulp.

8.3 The treatment or protection of wood, involving the use of preservatives, with a capacity exceeding 10 tonnes per day.

8.4 The manufacture of synthetic fibres.

8.5 The dyeing, treatment or finishing (including moth-proofing and fireproofing) of fibres or textiles (including carpet) where the capacity exceeds 1 tonne per day of fibre, yarn or textile material.

8.6 The fell-mongering of hides and tanning of leather in installations where the capacity exceeds 100 skins per day.

9. **Fossil Fuels**

9.1   The extraction, other than offshore extraction, of petroleum, natural gas, coal or bituminous shale.

9.2   The handling or storage of crude petroleum.

9.3   The refining of petroleum or gas.

9.4   The pyrolysis, carbonisation, gasification, liquefaction, dry distillation, partial oxidation or heat treatment of coal, lignite, oil or bituminous shale, other carbonaceous materials or mixtures of any of these in installations with a processing capacity exceeding 500 tonnes per day.

10.   Cement

10.1   The production of cement.

11.   Waste

11.1   The incineration of hazardous waste.

11.2   The incineration of hospital waste.

11.3   The incineration of waste other than that mentioned in 11.1 and 11.2 in plants with a capacity exceeding 1 tonne per hour.

11.4   The use of heat for the manufacture of fuel from waste.

12.   Surface Coatings

12.1   Operations involving coating with organo-tin compounds

12.2   The manufacture or use of coating materials in processes with a capacity to make or use at least 10 tonnes per year of organic solvents, and powder coating manufacture with a capacity to produce at least 50 tonnes per year.

12.3   Electroplating operations.

13.   Other Activities

13.1   The testing of engines, turbines or reactors where the floor area exceeds 500 square metres

13.2   The manufacture of integrated circuits and printed circuit boards.

13.3   The production of lime in a kiln.

13.4   The manufacture of coarse ceramics including refractory bricks, stoneware pipes, facing and floor bricks and roof tiles.

References & Acknowledgements

BS 7750: Specification for Environmental Management Systems. British Standards Institution (BSI) 1992.
CEFIC (European Chemical Industry Council), Information Booklets.
Chemical Industries Association (CIA) - UK, Information Booklets.
Chemical Manufacturers Association (CMA) - US, Information Booklets.
Department of Environment List of Legislation, Regulations and Directives - ENFO.
Dobris Report.
Environmental Technology Best Practice Programme (UK).
EPA Guide to Waste Licensing.
EPA Summary of its Powers, Structures & Functions (LC3).
EMAS 1993: Council Regulation (EEC) No 1836/93 of 29 June 1993.
HILARY 1994. The Eco-Management and Audit Scheme: A Practical Guide. Stanley Thornes (Publishers) Ltd (UK).
Introduction to Waste Management - Distance Learning Work Unit of Sligo Regional Technical College.
IPC) Licensing - Guide to the Implementation and Enforcement in Ireland.
I.S. 310 : 1994 Environmental Management Systems - Guiding Principles and Requirements. National Standards Authority of Ireland (NSAI).
ISO 14001 Environmental Management Systems - Specification and Guidance for Use.
ISO 14004 Environmental Management Systems - General Guidelines on Principles, Systems and Supporting Techniques 1996.
Responsible Care® Management Systems - Guidelines for certification to ISO 9001 - Health, Safety and Environmental. Management Systems (and BS 7750 - Environmental Management Systems) in the chemical industry.
Waste Management Act, 1996
Waste Management (Farm Plastic) Regulations, 1997
Waste Management (Packaging) Regulations, 1997
Waste Management (Licensing) Regulations, 1997
Waste Management (Planning) Regulations, 1997

Internet Resources:
The following Internet Home Pages were used for environmental information and Environmental Reporting /Disclosure:
• Envirolink

- European Environmental Agency
- Gaia Consulting
- IBM
- Intel
- International Institute for Sustainable Development
- MGMT Alliances Consultants
- Nortel Habitat
- Rachel's Hazardous Waste News -Gopher
- Responsible Care® - CMA
- Stoller Consultants
- UNEP International Environmental Technology Centre
- US Environmental Protection Agency Home Page

INDEX

Accident/Spillage Prevention, 38
Aer Rianta, 207
Acid Rain, 31
Agri-Environmental Plan, 27
Air, 153

    air emission reduction and monitoring programme, 155
    effects of pollution, 153
    industrial air pollution control, 153
    licensing, 155
    TA Lüft standard, 154
Air Pollution Act, 1987, 54, 55, 77, 154, 182
Alternative Energy Requirement (AER) Initiative, 36
Best Available Technology Not Entailing Excessive Cost (BATNEEC), 55
"Blue Flag" for beaches, 25
Bruss G., GmbH, 273
BS 7750, 95

    annexes, 96
    specification,96
BSE Crisis, 26
Business Charter on Sustainable Development, 42
Business Opportunity, 39
Chambers of Commerce of Ireland, 28
Charter of European Cities & Towns Towards Sustainability, 23
Chemicals, 160

    classification and labelling, 160
    NFPA 30 and factory mutual guidelines, 139
    risk reduction, 161
    storage, 139
Chep Ireland, 289
Chlorofluorocarbons (CFC's), 32
Colleges and Universities, 28
Communication, 39, 197
Company Image, 38
Company Profiles, 209
Consultancies, 28
Continuous Improvement Strategy, 37

Copenhagen Agreements, 39
Corine Programme,33
Cost Reduction, 18
Customer Requests, 38
Directive for Civil Liability for Damage caused by Waste, 1991,19
Disaster Management and Business Contingency Planning, 130
Dobris Assessment, 20
DuPont (UK) Ltd., 257
Eco-Label Standard, 25
Eco-management and Audit Scheme (EMAS), 97
          annex I-III, 99
          articles, 98
          article 3, 97
          guide to implementing EMAS, 99
          Council Regulation (EEC) no 1836/93 of 29 June 1993, 97
          Council Regulation No. 3037/90, 100
          difference between EMAS and ISO 14001,40
          NACE classifications, 100
          National Accreditation Board, 101
EMAS Regulation & IPC Licensing Initiative 90
Eco-Tourism, 25
Education and Training, 193
          awareness training 193
          environmental education, 195
Employee Involvement, 43
Energy, 167
          control and reduction of energy consumption, 167
          EC Save Programme, 1992,167
          effects of energy usage, 167
          energy conservation programme, 168
ENFO, 22, 28
Environment
          carrying capacity, 20
          Europe, 18
          European developments, 19
          in context,17
          information on, 28
          Ireland, 21
          recent Irish developments, 22

sustainable developments, 23
Environmental Auditing, 199
    audit process, 205
    introduction, 199
    objectives of, 200
    use of external consultants,203
    what is an environmental audit,199
    why undertake, 201
Environmental Bulletin periodical, 29
Environmental Control (Local Authorities), 49
Environmental Effects Register, 178
    analysis of effects, 179
    compiling the register, 179
    determining the significance of emissions/discharges, 179
Environmental Impact Assessment (EIA), 173
    carrying out an EIA, 174
    necessity of, 173
Environmental Impact Statement (EIS), 62, 67, 80, 82, 84
Environmental Management System (EMS), 37, 44
    benefits of, 37
    considering, 37
    links with other management systems, 39
    the initial steps, 44
Environmental Management System (EMS) Standards, 92
    choice of EMS standard or EU regulation, 92
    the ISO 14000 series, 101
Environmental Policy, 42
    establishment, 42
    preparation of, 42
Environmental Protection Agency (EPA), 28, 50
    advisory committee, 51
    divisions, 50
    directors, 50
    EPA Act. 1992, 22, 53, 54, 55, 56, 58, 61
    Licensing and Control, 53
    mission statement, 50
    powers and functions, 51
    strengthening management and regulation,52
    the regulatory situation, 47

Environmental Management Ireland (EMI) magazine, 29
Environmental Manager/Co-ordinator, 44
Environmental Programme, 45
Environmental Review, 177
        key areas, 177
Environmental Risk Management, 129
        civil law, 131
        civil liabilities, 131
        common law, 131
        control of contractors, 142
        co-ordinated approach, 130
        cost of risk, 129
        energy conservation, 138
        environmental purchasing policy, 134
        insurance, 135
        legal situation, 131
        loss control initiatives, 136
        loss control prevention, 129
        maintenance of records, 142
        recycling, 142
        remediation, 134
        risk environment, 133
        risk transfer, 129
        spill control, 143
        standards, 132
        statute law, 131
        training and education, 137
Environmental Technology Best Practice Programme (UK), 137
        six step solvent management framework, 140
EU/EC Directives, 22, 47
EU/EC Legislation, 22, 47
European Developments, 19
European Environment Agency (EEA), 18
European Environmental Information and Observation Network
(EIONET), 18
External Contractors, 173
        examples of services commissioned, 173
External Safety, 172
        emergency plan, 172

external safety obligations, 172
risk reduction and emergency planning, 172
Farming,
factory, 26
intensive, 26
organic, 28
Fire Water Retention, 139
EPA (draft) guidance notes, 139
Freedom of Information on the Environment, 24
Friends of the Earth, 29
Globalisation, 17
Global Warming, 32
Greenpeace, 29
Green Tourism, 25
Guidelines for Pollution Prevention, 143
cleaning, 144
deliveries, 143
de-watering, 145
emergencies, 145
site drainage, 143
storage, 144
training, 145
waste storage and disposal, 144
Henkel Ireland,136
Hydrochlorofluorocarbons (HCFC's), 32
IBM PC Company, 233
Information and Communication, 197
internal communications, 198
external communications, 198
Insurance, 39
Integrated Pollution Control (IPC) Licensing, 54
application for, 56
completing the application form, 59
getting started, 58
"guide to the implementation and enforcement of IPC
licensing" publication, 58
implementing an IPC licence, 64
implementation of, 56
lodging and processing the application, 61

monitoring and enforcement, 66
principal categories, 55
"proposed determination", 63
review of an IPC licence, 65
the IPC concept, 54
the scope of, 54
Integrated Pollution Prevention and Control (IPPC) Directive, 47
Intel Ireland, 243
International Institute for Sustainable Development, 29
Internet, 29
Irish Energy Centre, 129
building energy management system (BEMS), 130
energy audit grant scheme, 129
I.S. 310, 94
Environmental Standards Consultative Committee (ESCC), 94
National standards Authority of Ireland (NSAI), 94
ISO 9000 Quality Standard,39
ISO 14001, 102
basic guide to implementing, 112
content of, 105
environmental policy, 107
general requirements, 107
synopsis, 107
ISO 14004, 106, 183
Lethal Dose
LC_{50}, 34
LD_{50}, 34
Least Damaging Alternative, 35
Legislation, 38
Life Cycle Analysis (LCA), 36
Local Agenda 21, 23
Local Authority, 49, 53
Local Government (Water Pollution) Acts, 1977 and 1990, 49
Maastericht Treaty, 19
Management of Environmental Performance, 147
Management System Verification (MSV) elements, 118
Market Strategy, 37
Montreal Protocol, 33
National Sustainable Development Strategy, 21

Nitrous Oxide (NOx), 33
Noise, 158
      noise measurement and noise control, 158
      nuisance, 158
      reduction programme, 159
Nortel Ireland, 331
Occupational Exposure Limits (OEL's), 34
Occupational Health & Safety, 170
      causes of occupational health risks, 171
      information and procedures, 171
      occupational health risks, 171
      risk reduction, 171
Organisation, 147
      description of, 147
      identification of responsibility and authority, 148
      organisational systems, 147
Ozone Depletion, 32
      ozone depletion substances (ODS), 32
Ozone Layer, 32
Planning, 148
      analysis of current situation, 149
      ongoing evaluation of planning, 150
      location considerations, 148
      technical specifications of the building regulations, 150
" Polluter Pays Principle ", 28, 133
Pollution Prevention, 30
      guidelines for, 143
Pollution Regulation, 30
      acceptable level, 30
      control level, 30
Precautionary Principle or Principle of Precautionary Action, 35
Printech International, 319
Products & Packaging, 169
      environmentally friendly products and packaging, 169
      environmentally friendly programme, 170
Project specification, 44
Public Authority, 48
Record Retention, 38
Register of Environmental Regulations, 180

compiling the register, 180
environmental legislation, 180
"Green Paper" on environmental liability, 180
list of legislation, 181
Renewable Energy, 36
Rural Environmental Protection Scheme (REPS), 27
Responsible Care® Management Systems, 114
in Ireland, 115
Irish Pharmaceutical Chemical Manufacturers Federation
(IPCMF), 115
CEFIC (European Chemical Industry Council), 115
codes of management practices, 116
the CIA approach, 121
the CMA approach, 115
the role of the CEFIC, 125
Responsible Care® Management Systems - Guidelines for certification
to ISO 9001,123
REPAK scheme, 23
Review of Fifth Environmental Action programme (5EAP), 20, 180
Risk Assessment, 35
SEAC Student Environmental Action Coalition (USA), 29
Sealol, EG&G, 281
Sierra Club, 29
Single European Act, 1987, 19
Site Condition, 38
SmithKline Beecham, 299
Soil, 156
pollution control, 156
protection and monitoring programme, 157
sources of soil pollution, 156
Soil and Ground Water Sampling, 141
Solvent Management, 140
State Laboratory and the Environmental Research Unit, 29
Stockholm Environmental Institute, 29
Successful Health and Safety Management HS(G)65(1991), 123
Sustainability, 17
sustained development, 17
Sustainable Farming, 26
Symantec Ltd., 221

TC 207's Development of other Main Standards, 101
The ISO 14000 Series, 101
    benefits of, 103
    comparison of the ISO 14000 series and ISO 9000 series, 103
    ISO 14013, 114
    ISO 14020, 114
    ISO 14031, 113
    ISO 14040/41/42/43, 114
    ISO 14060, 114,
    listing of standards, 102
    significance of the new standard, 102
    workings of technical committee (TC) 101
Threshold Limit Values (TLV), 31, 34
Toxicology, 33
Treaty of Rome, 19
Volatile Organic Compounds (VOCs), 33
Waste, 161
    classification of, 162
    control and minimisation, 164
    council directive on packaging and packaging waste 94/92/EC, 166
    disposal of, 161
    hazardous waste, 166
    non-hazardous waste,164
Waste Management Act, 1996, 66
    examples of waste minimisation, management, avoidance, 69
Waste Management (Farm Plastic) Regulations, 1997, 88
Waste Management (Packaging) Regulations, 1997, 83
Waste Management Regulations, 1997,73
Waste Management Licensing, 76
Waste Management Plan, 73
Waste Management Planning, 76
Water, 150
    conservation of water programme, 151
    ground water control, 150
    tap water control, 151
    waste water discharges, 152
    waste water discharge licence, 152
Yamanouchi Irl. Co. Ltd., 309

Zero Discharge, 35
Project Specification, 44